# *His California Story*

## In Christian Perspective

# His California Story

In Christian Perspective

*by*

*Lesha Myers, M.Ed.*

Exodus 20:15

ISBN 978-0-9794506-0-0

Unless otherwise noted, all Bible verses are from the King James Version.

www.Cameron-Publishing.com

This book is lovingly dedicated to:

All of the wonderful California history students
it has been my pleasure to teach
over the past 15 years

and

their parents who have inspired me
with their faithfulness.

Thank you for blessing me.

Preface

# About This Book

A note to my readers, from Mrs. Myers

Since this is a history book, let's begin with the basics. Can you define history? Is it a

a. class to take a short nap in?
b. bunch of meaningless facts about dead people?
c. record of what happened in the past?
d. record of how God has dealt with people and nations in the past?

If you chose d., you are correct. History is a written record of how God has interacted with man. The Bible is a history book. The lesson begins in Genesis 1:1, where God records how the world was made, and continues through the Revelation, where He tells us how it will end. God is in control of all things. This means that everything in history is a providential event. It also means that nothing happens that God does not allow. God is not the author of sin, but He can use our sins to bring about His purpose.

Are you ready for the next question? Why do we study history?

a. Because it is a required school subject.
b. Because it is interesting to see how other people lived.
c. To learn from the mistakes of people who lived before us.
d. To teach us about God.

The correct answer is d. again. We study history to learn about God and how He has revealed Himself to people who lived before us. Since God does not change, He is the same today as He was in the pages of history. We learn how He judged cultures when they disobeyed Him and how He blessed them when they obeyed.

If history is a written record of God's dealing with people who lived before us, and if its purpose is to teach us about God, why aren't our history books written to meet these goals?

They used to be. If you read a history book written 100 years ago, it will reveal the hand of God. Today, however, most educators have turned their backs on God. They do not know Him and do not recognize how He has worked in the past. Most history books are not written by Christians and do not record a Christian worldview.

What is a worldview? It is the way we look at or view the world. It is what determines how we act. It is our standard and philosophy of life. It is why we do what we do. There are basically four worldviews.

The first is called *statism*. In this worldview the state, or government, acts as god. Man exists to serve the state or collective good. The state decides what is right and what is wrong. We see evidence of statism in our society today when the law can say that it is right to kill an unborn child.

The second is called *humanism*. In this worldview man acts as his or her own god. Every person decides for himself what is right and what is wrong. We see evidence of humanism in our society when people are accused of "being judgmental" for not accepting the sin they see in another's life.

The third worldview is called *animism*. An animist believes that god created the world and then inhabited it. Therefore god exists in every part of creation: rocks, trees, animals, and humans. Everything has a soul and a divine spark. What is right is what happens in nature. What is wrong is what changes nature. We see evidence of animism in today's society in some environmental activities that prevent changes because they would disturb nature.

The fourth, and only correct, worldview is *biblical*. It says that God is God and has revealed Himself in His Word and Son, as well as in the creation, in our conscience, and in history. God determines what is right and what is wrong. Man obeys Him. Unfortunately, we see very little of the biblical worldview in today's society. Once, almost everyone saw life in terms of a biblical worldview. Today, however, it is held in low esteem.

Every history book is written from a worldview. Let's look at an example to help us understand how this is so. Let's say that we will be reading about how Christian missionaries took the gospel to a primitive tribe of natives in another land. While telling the natives about Christ, the missionaries also helped them improve their standard of living. Missionaries taught them how to grow food, make clothing, keep clean, and stay healthy. They also taught the natives how to live according to the Bible. How would this example be recorded by authors writing from each of the four worldviews?

The statists would condemn the Christian missionaries for teaching God's laws. God does not determine what is right or wrong, they would say, so the Bible should not be taught.

The humanists would also criticize the Christian missionaries. They would accuse the Christians of being narrow-minded and accepting only one view of how to live. What is right for the Christians may not be right for the natives, they would argue.

The animists would agree that the Christians were wrong, but they would have their own reasons. They would object to the teaching that there is only one way to God (through Jesus Christ). They also would object to the changes the missionaries introduce to allow the natives to have a better life. They would argue that these changes would upset the "balance of nature" so that the natives would no longer live "in harmony with their environment."

The author writing from a Biblical worldview would applaud the Christian missionaries since these men would be carrying out God's command to go and make disciples of all nations. The author would approve the missionaries' efforts to help the natives take dominion over their land and govern themselves according to God's word. This view would be the only correct interpretation of the missionaries' actions.

The book you are about to read, *His California Story*, is written from a biblical worldview. It discusses California history from a biblical perspective. You will read what happened in California's past, as well as why it happened. You will read about how God blessed people when they obeyed Him and how He judged them when they disobeyed.

You may think that I am reading my worldview back into history and interpreting events in the way that I want. Rest assured that I am not. I am simply recording the thoughts of the people who lived here at the time. My sources, or where I get my information, are listed at the end of this book in the bibliography. If you want to pursue your study of California history, these books would be a good place to begin.

I hope you enjoy your study of California history as you discover the way God has worked in the formation and upholding of our state. I pray that God will reveal Himself to you as you learn about His California story.

# Psalm 78: 1-8

Give ear, O my people, to my law;
incline your ears to the words of my mouth.
I will open my mouth in a parable:
I will utter dark sayings of old:
Which we have heard and known,
and our fathers have told us.
We will not hide them from their children,
showing to the generation to come the praises of the LORD,
and his strength,
and his wonderful works that he hath done.
For he established a testimony in Jacob,
and appointed a law in Israel,
which he commanded our fathers,
that they should make them known to their children:
That the generation to come might know them,
even the children which should be born;
who should arise and declare them to their children:
That they might set their hope in God,
and not forget the works of God,
but keep his commandments:
And might not be as their fathers,
a stubborn and rebellious generation;
a generation that set not their heart aright,
and whose spirit was not steadfast with God.

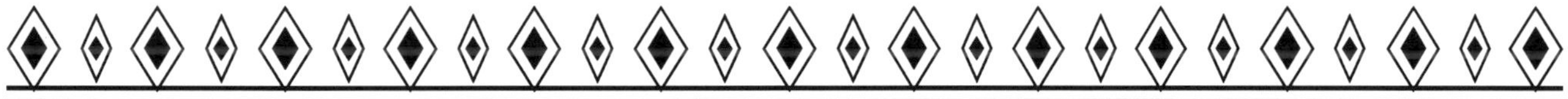

# Table of Contents

Unit 1

# The California Indians

After this I beheld, and, lo, a great multitude, which no man could number, of all nations, and kindreds, and people, and tongues, stood before the throne, and before the Lamb, clothed with white robes, and palms in their hands; And cried with a loud voice, saying, Salvation to our God which sitteth upon the throne, and unto the Lamb.

~~ Revelation 7:9-10

Most of the ceremonies the California Indians performed were designed to win the favor of spirits they believed lived in the land—the spirit of the acorn trees, of the salmon, or of the deer. Songs, dances, and chants were visual prayers. The Indians hoped the spirits would answer these prayers and give them abundant food and success.

# In the Beginning

TO BEGIN OUR STUDY OF HIS CALIFORNIA story, we need to travel back to Noah's flood, a time that many California Indian legends record. Because the world was so wicked, God sent a great flood. In His mercy, He saved a righteous man named Noah and his family.

God shut Noah, his family, and at least two of every kind of animal up in a huge boat, an ark. Then He made it rain for forty days and forty nights. The water covered every mountain on the earth. At the end of a year, the ark finally landed on the mountains called Ararat. Later, God told the people to multiply and fill the earth, but they rebelled. So, God confused their languages and they could no longer talk to one another. You can read about this in Genesis, chapters 6, 7, and 8. Families traveled all over the earth. Some came to California and became the people we call the California Indians.

You have probably studied the Native Americans who made their home in North America, the people that Columbus misnamed *Indians*. You might think of movies, books, and television shows. Maybe you picture a man on a horse, clothed in a stunning headdress and holding a staff made of feathers. Possibly you remember friendly animals perched on an Indian's shoulder listening to him or her sing. You might think of teepees, totem poles, birch bark canoes, or fierce battles between tribes and settlers.

You must put all of this out of your mind because none of it applies to the people who lived in California.

These people did not form tribes like the Indians of the East, or the Navajo, Sioux, or Apache. Instead they lived in family groups away from their neighbors. Language also separated these natives. Sometimes languages changed so much that people living only ten miles apart could not understand each other.

Because so many families lived in California and because their way of life differed, it is hard to study the California Indians. What we might say about one group may not be true for another. Still, there were similarities. To help us, we will study one group of people, the Pomo. This will give us a general introduction to the people who lived in California before the Spanish arrived.

To make this study easier, you will read a story about a young boy named Chikokawe. Although this story is fictional, it is based on a true picture of the Pomo way of life. But before we begin, there are a few things you need to know.

Tules (pronounced TOO-lees) are long, slender plants that grow in wet areas near marshes and streams. When dried, they could be woven into mats. The Pomo used tules to make baskets and sleeping mats. They also arranged several layers of tule mats over bent poles to make huts.

*Many Indian legends are similar to Biblical accounts. Compare this one to Noah's flood found in Genesis 6-8.*

## How Falcon Man Was Saved From the Flood

### A Miwok Legend

The Coyote man and the Falcon man had a big fight. Then the Coyote man gathered up all of the people and took them away with him across the ocean, leaving the Falcon man all alone. The Coyote man made the rain come and cover the world with water. The water grew deeper and deeper and covered all the hills and all the mountains until nothing was left but water.

The Falcon man could find no place to rest. He had nothing to stand on. He had to fly and fly and fly until he was all tired out. After awhile, he could fly no longer and fell on the water. He was floating around almost dead when his wing caught on a little stick. This stick stuck up from the top of the roundhouse of the Grebe [a diving bird similar to the loon] who came up to see what was the matter. He found the Falcon man, who was a relative of his, nearly drowned. He pulled him down into his roundhouse and saved him.

Then Coyote man let the water down and brought the people back.

# The Pomo Beliefs

BEFORE WE BEGIN OUR STORY, WE NEED to understand Pomo beliefs because they were very different from those of Christians. Christians believe in the One True God, the Creator of heaven and earth. We believe that God loved us so much that He sent His Son Jesus Christ to die for our sins. We believe He also left us His Holy Spirit who gives us the power to obey and please Him.

## Spirits

Pomo beliefs were complicated. They believed Coyote created the world and people. However, they did not worship Coyote or consider him a god. Instead they believed in multiple spirits who lived in nature like the spirit of the acorn trees, the spirit of the river, or the spirit of the salmon. When the spirits were pleased, they would provide much food.

## Taboos

The people tried to keep the spirits happy by obeying taboos. Taboos are forbidden actions. For example, Pomo men could not speak to their mothers-in-law, they could not eat meat when a relative got sick, and they could not leave their homes for four days each month. Pomo women could not gather acorns without singing certain songs. They believed that if they broke a taboo, the spirits would punish them.

## Power & Poison

Pomo beliefs also included *power* and *poison*. Power was not muscular strength or might. It was spiritual energy. The Pomo believed that by performing certain ceremonies they could gain a force that would protect them from spirits and others who might try to harm them.

Finally, to the Pomo, poison was not something that entered the bloodstream and caused sickness like rattlesnake venom. It was sorcery, like a curse. By using chants or certain objects considered magical or powerful, they believed poison could cause sickness and even death.

## The Effect

Power, poison, and taboos shaped Pomo life. They lived in fear. Many things could harm them—their neighbors, the spirits that lived in the land, or even enemies who lived in the same village. They were slaves to their false beliefs.

How blessed Christians are to know that we do not have to earn God's favor by our works. There is nothing we can do to earn our salvation; it is a gift paid for by the blood of Jesus Christ. How thankful we are that God does not hold us in bondage. God gives us His law to follow for our own good, but His commandments are not burdensome. When we follow Him, our yoke is easy and our burden is light. (See Matthew 11:30.)

## Something to Think About

Think about the Pomo beliefs as you read the story about life in the village. Think about how they shaped the Pomo lives. Think about how different your life is, and finally, think about the ways Jesus Christ sets you free.

*Compare this legend to Genesis 1-3.*

## The Creation and Fall of Man

### A Maidu Legend

The world-maker told the devil that he would make a man. He took two smooth, yellow sticks and put them on the bed beside him at evening. Early the next morning, a man and a woman lay on the bed. The devil was very angry that he could not make a man.

After this, the world-maker set the man he had created on the earth to gather food. At this time, all of the animals were tame. The man reached and took whatever he wanted. The soil was very good also. All things grew in plenty. The world-maker told the man to take whatever he wanted, but he also gave him one rule. The man must bring his food home to cook it. He could not make a fire in the woods.

So when the man went out to catch game, the devil told him to cook in the woods. And he did. Therefore, when all of the animals, fish, grasshoppers, birds, and insects saw the smoke in the woods, they became wild as they are today. The ground was changed so that food was harder to find. The world-maker changed the air so that it was no longer warm all the year.

Before this time there was no sickness or death. After the man ate in the woods, many died. The world-maker told the man and woman that if they were good, at death they would go to the spirit-land by the right-hand path. If they were bad, they would go by the left-hand path to darkness.

Chapter 2

# Life in the Village

Chikokawe is a Pomo word meaning *quail.* It is pronounced Chick-oh-KA-way.

Chikokawe awoke with a start. At first he did not recognize where he was. He stared at the people walking down the main aisle of the hut, their heads hidden in the smoke that floated at their shoulders. Children shouted, infants were being fed, and beds were being put away. Then he remembered—he was in the winter hut of his Pomo village. Last spring, after the rains stopped, the Head Man had burned their old flea-and-vermin-infested hut, and his family had moved to their summer place near the river. In the autumn, they had moved again to the hills. Now it was almost time for the rains to begin. A chill in the air had warned the family that it was time to return to their winter village and join the other members of their band.

This picture was drawn by a man who lived with the Pomo in 1871 and 1872. The Pomo village in our story would have contained many tule-covered huts that looked like these overgrown haystacks. Up to 50 people could have lived in one, including grandparents, parents, sisters and brothers, and the families of the grandmother's sisters and mother's sisters.

## The Winter Village

A few days ago, the men built a new winter hut. They bent a framework of poles into an oblong shape and fastened bundles of tules onto it. A narrow slot at the top served as a smoke hole. Chikokawe's extended family lived here. Separate sleeping cubicles were arranged along the main aisle so that each family could have its own fire. Provisions for the winter littered the spaces between.

Chikokawe's village would have been located in Deep Valley, near where the Russian River runs through present-day Ukiah.

For the past several weeks, Chikokawe's extended family had lived by themselves in the hills. There had been much to do. Acorns, buckeyes, berries, and other food had to be gathered for the long winter months ahead. The acorn harvest was good this year. Chikokawe remembered other years when the spirits were angry and acorns had been hard to find. His people had to cut down trees to remove acorns from holes where woodpeckers had hidden them. Even so, there had been much hunger that winter.

Thinking of food, Chikokawe realized he was hungry. Reluctantly, he pulled his bare body out of his bed of woven tules. He shivered in the crisp morning air. "Winter will come soon," he thought to himself. "I hope Mother makes me a rabbit-skin blanket." Until then, Chikokawe would smear mud on his body to keep warm.

Edging past the many baskets of seeds, roots, powdered dried salmon, and acorns, Chikokawe slipped quietly out of his hut. The village was waking up. Some of the boys, as punishment for disrupting the community, carried wood to the sweathouse. This was the men's gathering place. Sometimes they even slept there. Women were not allowed inside unless they were very old.

As the firetender piled wood on the fire, the sweathouse became hotter and hotter. The men fanned the heat away from themselves and joked, "Eh, you old woman. How do you like to eat fire?" When they could stand the heat no longer, they dashed out the low door, ran to the stream, and plunged into its icy water. Chikokawe joined them.

Refreshed from their bath, they returned to their homes for the morning meal. Chikokawe watched his mother work with Little Brother wrapped in the carrying basket on her back. All that could be seen of her little one was a tiny head and two shiny black eyes that peered over the top of the basket. Every few days, Mother took Little Brother out of his basket, bathed him, and re-wrapped him. When he wasn't being fed, he rode on his mother's back so that her hands would be free to work.

> The names of Chikokawe's sister and friend are also Pomo words. Kula is a fruit similar to a pumpkin, and Misalla means snake. The Pomo never shared their real names. They believed a poison man who knew their real name could harm them. Instead they received nicknames. Kula may have been born when the kula ripened, and Misalla's mother may have seen a snake near the time he was born.

## A Closer Look

*To help you understand this story, there are a few things you need to understand about how the California Indians' way of life differed from yours.*

### Education

The first big difference was education. California Indian children did not attend school because there were no schools. Parents taught their children what they needed to know: how to collect food, build homes, and make clothing. Boys learned a profession like fishing, hunting, gambling, money-making, arrow or spear making, or how to become shamans, poison men, or chiefs. Important information, especially religious history and taboos, was passed orally from grandparents to grandchildren.

Science is the study of the order God has created. The Indians did not see order in their world. Instead, they saw unpredictable spirits who might do anything. The Indians believed that just beyond their or their neighbor's territory, the world ended. They did not see the world as God's creation. Since the Indians had a false view of God, they also had a false view of science.

The only history the Indians learned was the beliefs, traditions, and taboos passed orally from one generation to the next. When a man died, his name could never be spoken aloud again. Nothing he owned was passed on to his sons or left to remind the living of his deeds. He was forgotten as each generation passed.

The California Indians had no literature, and most had no art. They knew little math, and they did not develop a calendar. Since their taboos forbade change, no alphabet or form of writing was ever developed.

Little Brother, one of the few babies in the village, was born the past summer while his family lived near the river. It was hard to have a large family with so many mouths to feed. But babies were not real people until they were three days old, so some families left them in the woods to die before the third day. Most families in the village were small.

### Acorns for Food

One of the women handed Chikokawe a bowl of acorn mush. Taking the basket in his left hand, he passed it to his right while saying prayers to remove any poison. Of course, Chikokawe did not have to fear poisoning from his own family. However, the Pomo life contained many dangers. People, spirits, rocks, waters, trees, and animals all contained power to do harm. Boys were taught to be careful. Using his two fingers to scoop out the acorn mush, Chikokawe emptied the basket.

Kula, Chikokawe's sister, chanted as she pounded acorns nearby. Acorns, the most common food of the village, took hours to prepare. First, she spread the dried and roasted acorns on a stone and cracked their shells. When she had collected enough of the inner meat she pounded it into fine flour. But the flour tasted very bitter. Later Kula would take the acorn flour down to the river, put it in a leaf-covered hole in the sand, and pour water over it again and again. This removed the bitterness.

Preparing acorns was a lot of work, especially since they were served at almost every meal. The sound of acorns being pounded, with the women's acorn songs and chants, could almost always be heard.

Kula rose from her seat and stretched. She brushed the sand off her shredded tule skirt and adjusted the necklaces she wore as ornaments. Walking towards Chikokawe, she said accusingly, "We could have used your help yesterday storing the acorns in their granaries. Mother and I looked all over for you when it was time to leave. Where were you?"

Chikokawe answered in a haughty voice, "The Head Man needed me."

It was a lie and Kula knew it. Chikokawe was nearly ready to begin his profession of money-making. Then he would not have to work with or obey the women. He had hidden himself yesterday until the women had left. Then he joined some of the other boys who had done the same thing.

Acorns were collected in the fall and then stored in granaries for winter use.

They played their favorite arrow-throwing game. Each boy tried to throw his arrow so that after bouncing off a dirt mound, it continued. The winner's arrow traveled the farthest. Chikokawe lost twice and received two cracks over his elbow from each player. His swollen arm still hurt, but he could not show weakness, especially in front of women. Still, he had hoped to sneak away again today.

There was so much work to do to prepare for the winter. When the rains finally came, it would be better. He would spend days playing games. In the evening he would enjoy the warmth of the sweathouse, and Grandfather would teach him the ways of his people.

Almost every village in California contained a sweathouse. When sweathouses were located near water, they helped the people keep clean. When the heat became unbearable, the men jumped into the cold stream. This was supposed to keep the people healthy.

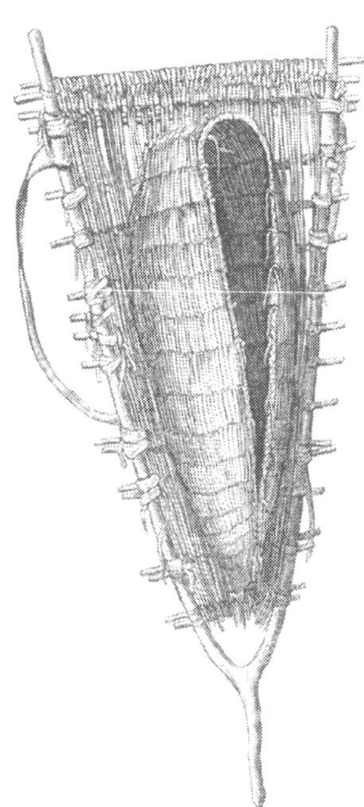

Indian women made baskets for decoration and for household use. Chikokawe's mother would have carried Little Brother in a basket like the third from the top.

He had many things to learn—how people were created, what spirits lived in the woods, how to avoid being poisoned, and the taboos he had to follow to become a money-maker.

Chikokawe finished his acorn mush, and his mother called out, "Chikokawe, please stay near the hut. You will be needed to help collect acorns today!" With a proud smirk that seemed to say, "I told you so!" Kula returned to her work. Chikokawe sighed. It didn't look like he would be able to slip away after all.

Soon Chikokawe, Kula, and Mother, still carrying Little Brother, slung their cone-shaped baskets over their backs and attached them to their foreheads with a sling. They didn't weigh much now that they were empty, but on the way home the trio would have to bend forward to support some of the baskets' weight on their backs. Chikokawe was upset. "It's women's work to carry burdens," he grumbled to himself. "Soon, I won't have to work so hard."

"There are many acorns this year," mother said with gratefulness. "Soon, when the Head Men and Chief decide, we will have a Big Time to thank the spirits for a bountiful acorn harvest." Chikokawe brightened. A Big Time was great fun. The men danced the acorn dance in the roundhouse. The women prepared food for all, and children played games.

With these happy thoughts, the work went faster. By evening, the baskets had been filled many times. The trio stored the acorns in granaries off the ground so that squirrels could not steal them. Chikokawe wearily trudged back to the village with the last basket.

## Village Activity

Suddenly Chikokawe's weariness left him, and he roared with delight. His *awihinawa*, or very best friend, was back in the village! "Hello! Hello!" Chikokawe shouted, slapping Misalla on the shoulder. "When did you move back? Where did you live this summer? Did you kill your first deer?"

His friend danced with excitement. "We just got back! Wait until you see how many fish we caught!" Several seasons ago the two boys had pledged their eternal friendship to each other. There had been a ceremony uniting their families as well. An *awihinawa* was a very special friend, the only one outside of your family that you can trust in every situation.

"Come!" Chikokawe cried. "Let's go see if there are any berries left on the hill!" From their perch on the hillside, Chikokawe and Misalla could see people busy at the day's work. Women made baskets with their willows, obsidian knives, and bone awl needles. Some were made just for beauty. They would be sold, given as presents, or placed on the body of a dead person who was being cremated. These were decorated with feathers, beads, and beautiful patterns. One woman's husband had killed 100 woodpeckers so that she could use their red scalps to decorate her basket.

Chikokawe and Misalla could see men busy at their professions. Some were making spears and arrowheads. They chipped obsidian to put a sharp edge on the points. Fishermen made and repaired their nets. Moneymakers broke sea shells into rough circles and polished them on the rocks. They drilled small holes in them and strung them into necklaces. In another part of the village, men cut rabbit skins into strips to weave them into blankets. Women cleaned skins and made clothes. Other men, in the distance, chopped wood for the winter, while many napped under the shade of the trees.

Soon the sun's journey brought it low in the sky. The smoke from many evening cook fires drifted above the village. The boys saw the Chief taking his evening walk and instructing the people. "My people, you must be good to one another. Have no hard feeling and use no harsh language," he said. "Support and uphold one another. Be good to your relatives, and take care of your children. Be good to the unfortunate and treat others well."

## War and Peace

Some modern writers tell us that the California Indians were peaceful people. It is true that they did not have large and fearsome wars like some of the eastern American Indian tribes. But they did not live in peace. This should not surprise us. Peace without God is not possible, and the California Indians did not know the Lord and Savior Jesus Christ.

The Pomo had enemies inside and outside their villages. Conflicts with neighboring villages were frequent. These could be started when people trespassed on Pomo land or by poisoning (sorcery), thefts, or kidnapping. Some battles were short, while others were long and violent. Women and children on food-gathering expeditions were often attacked. They could be cruelly treated before they were killed.

Enemies also lived within Pomo villages. Several families lived in one village, each with its own hut and Head Man. Families could fight with other families. Feuds started over perceived wrongs and could last a very long time. The Pomo lived in fear that they might be poisoned or killed. Murder was not punished by prison or capital punishment as in our time. Instead it could be forgiven with money. People only had to pay money to the victim's family, and the deed would be forgotten.

The people only felt safe in their dealings with their own family, or in the case of men, with their *awihinawa.* Marriages between families helped strengthen friendly ties, but true peace was not possible.

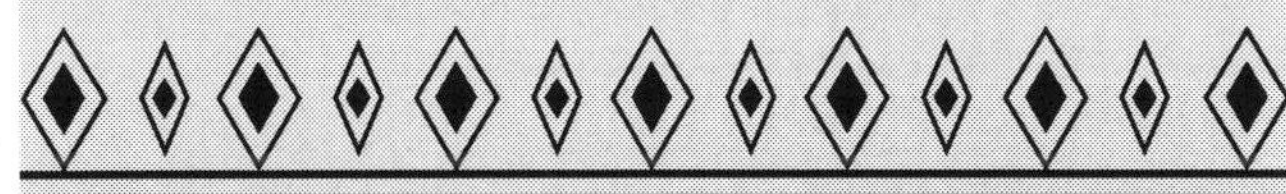

## California Indian Women

The life of a California Indian woman was not easy. Although the Pomo treated their women fairly well, women were little more than slaves in other areas. Very often they were purchased. In some bands men could have more than one wife, while in others only the chief could have multiple wives. A man who had more than one wife had more food provided for him since women gathered all of the food.

Divorce was easy in some villages—the husband simply left. In others, divorce was harder because the marriage joined extended families. Then feuds could start if a man divorced his wife.

If a woman was beaten by her husband, she had no place to turn. Her life was often filled with hard work and drudgery. Women performed most of the day-to-day work in the village except for the professions. They carried all of the burdens, even very heavy loads.

On the other hand, women also took the opportunity to treat men cruelly. When a man became old and feeble, he often was required to work for the women. He was given the hardest tasks in revenge for the women's life of suffering.

The Bible gives clear commands for marriage: the wife is to respect her husband and be a helper for him, while the husband is to love and cherish his wife. The Indians' lives would have been happier if they had followed these commands.

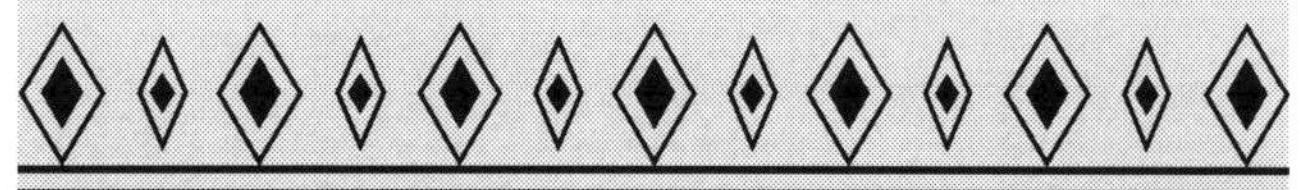

Some tightly-woven baskets could hold water for cooking. Heated rocks were placed in a basket that contained water and food. The heat from the rocks boiled the water and cooked the food.

The Chief stopped and talked to a group of Head Men, or leaders of families. The Chief made all of the decisions for the village, but first he had to make sure that everyone would agree with them. The Chief casually talked to everyone to see how they were feeling and then announced the decision the group had made. No problem was ever talked about openly or directly.

The men entered the sweathouse. After his dinner of ground grasshoppers and roasted seeds, Chikokawe and his grandfather, along with Misalla and his grandfather, would join them. They would learn the beliefs of their people. They would also receive some of their grandfather's power. Each grandfather taught his favorite grandson. They had more time as they grew older and could not participate in other activities that required strength.

The boys ambled down the hill, kicking up dust as they went. Chikokawe felt a warm happiness spreading through his insides. He and Misalla would have the whole winter to be together.

# A Visit To an Indian Village

**From Mrs. Myers' Photo Album**

*I like to travel, and whenever I have the opportunity, I visit historical sites in California. I'll share pictures of several of these as we study California's history together.*

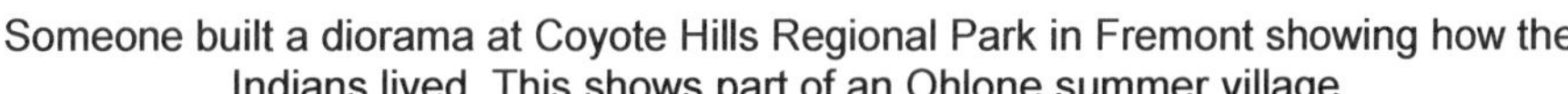

Someone built a diorama at Coyote Hills Regional Park in Fremont showing how the Indians lived. This shows part of an Ohlone summer village.

An acorn granary at Pt. Reyes.

A partially constructed family hut at Pt. Reyes shows the bent poles and tule mats used.

On a rainy day, my daughter and I got to visit the Miwok village in Yosemite. That's my daughter, my favorite traveling companion, in the poncho. At first I wasn't too happy about trampling around the wet grounds, but then I realized this would have been real life in a winter camp. See those dark spots near the entrance to the roundhouse? Those are puddles, and the Miwok would have had to walk through or around one to enter any dwelling.

The sweathouse (above left) was dug into the ground and smaller than I expected. The entrance was left incomplete so visitors could look inside. You can see the wooden supports for the long tunnel-like entrance.

The roundhouse (above right) is constructed from bark. Since tules did not grow near Yosemite, the people would have built their huts from bark as well. As Christians, we did not enter this roundhouse. In a very simplified way, the roundhouse is similar to the Christians' church. People still perform dances and ceremonies addressed to the spirits. We didn't think this honored God.

I hope you have a chance to visit a re-created Indian village. But if you do, remember our discussion of the different worldviews. The people at the village probably will think differently than you. Perhaps you will have a chance to witness to them. If so, remember to be kind and inviting. Our message is one of love and forgiveness.

Chapter 3

# Medicine and Sickness

The next day, after the evening meal, Chikokawe sat near the fire in his family's hut, talking with the other children. Mothers were getting the younger children ready for bed. Suddenly, Deerhunter stumbled into the hut and dropped to the floor. For a moment all was still; then women and children began to shriek and scream. The women, terrified, scratched their faces and chests until the blood streamed down. "Don't take Deerhunter's spirit away to the land of the dead!" they wailed, throwing shell money into the air. They hoped the spirits would be distracted by the money so they wouldn't harm Deerhunter.

The Head Man quickly took charge, "Call the shaman and guard the entrance to the hut!" he commanded. "Don't let anyone enter until he arrives!" Then he began to chant and entreat as he examined Deerhunter.

The shaman arrived quickly. Deerhunter lay in the middle of the hut. Long strings of shell money, baskets, and blankets hung from a pole placed near his head, payment for the shaman's services. Sometimes when a person was old and considered a burden, very little money was placed on the pole, or, the person was left in the woods to die. But Deerhunter's family loved him, and the pole contained much wealth.

In 1816, a group of Russians visited California and drew this picture of a Pomo shaman (SHAH-mn) in ceremonial dress.

The shaman tried to find out where Deerhunter had been that day so that he could learn which spirit caused this sickness. He made a costume representing various spirits Deerhunter may have met. Perhaps he had broken a taboo or offended one by forgetting to offer the proper prayers. Deerhunter shuddered in terror as the shaman rushed toward him wearing this costume. He relaxed a little as the shaman removed the costume piece by piece, and the shaman watched closely to see which part caused the most terror. That way he would know which spirit caused the illness.

Once he knew which spirit he was dealing with, the shaman began the cure. He opened his sacred bundle while singing, "I am opening, I am opening, I am opening, I am opening." The bundle contained a coyote's paw, obsidian knives, rabbit bladders filled with pebbles, four feather headdresses, a human bone, various herbs, and other medicines. These objects were so powerful that if even the shadow of the bag fell on a child, he or she would die.

The shaman sighed and silently complained, "Another case, and I will have to obey the taboos of our people. I will have to go without meat or grease for at least eight days. I will only be able to drink water before sunrise and after sunset. Because of all the sickness in our village, it has been six moons since I have been able to eat the foods I like."

The Head Woman of the family had other thoughts. As she watched the shaman, she could see the beads of sweat forming on his forehead as he concentrated on his songs, chants, and prayers. One mistake on his part would mean instant death for Deerhunter. "I hope this is not a long, expensive illness," she thought in frustration. "If it's not one thing, it's another! Now, all meat must be removed from the house, and we must be sure to follow all the taboos. We are never free of them."

Chikokawe hoped that Deerhunter would not die. He remembered when Elder Relative had died. His body had remained in the hut for four days to allow his spirit time to leave. Then he was taken outside and cremated. Many gifts and all of Elder Relative's possessions were burned with him. Nothing was passed on to his family. All of the relatives cried and wailed in grief for a year. Elder Relative's name could never again be spoken out loud, or his spirit might come back to trouble the village.

When the shaman had finished his last song, the men brought out pipes and tobacco. Each man drew six mouthfuls of smoke. Then the shaman left. He would return tomorrow night and again for four days when, it was hoped, Deerhunter would be well again.

## Poison!

As soon as the shaman was gone, the Head Man took command again. "Search the hut!" he ordered. "Look for anything that might have been used to poison Deerhunter." Every Pomo Indian was very careful. If an enemy got some hair, nail clippings, or even a piece of clothing, he could use these to cause illness. The guards stationed outside watched for any movement.

There were many other ways to make an illness worse. An enemy could shoot an arrow of poison oak onto the roof of the hut. He could also kill a rabbit and place it near the hut so that the taboo against fresh meat would be broken. Everyone must be very careful for the next four days. The entire family would be in danger.

## Coyote Creates Sickness

"Grandfather," asked Chikokawe after the men had completed their search and things had quieted down, "Why do people become sick?" Grandfather leaned forward on his elbow as he prepared to explain the people's beliefs in a special ceremonial language. He knew that a person who told religious history while sitting upright would become hunchbacked.

"After Coyote created all of the people, he went to one of the villages, married a woman, and settled down. Other people were very rich, but Coyote was poor. He thought about what could be done and decided that he would make some of the people sick so that he could heal them. Soon the Chief's wife grew sick. No one knew what to do. Finally, Coyote offered to cure her in exchange for four strings of beads.

To prepare for deer hunting, men spent four days being "fixed." They followed strict taboos and could eat no meat or fat for four days to gain power. No one could touch them during this time. During the hunt they disguised themselves as a deer and tried to act as a deer would so they could get very close.

He made a shaman's costume and entered the Chief's house singing and shaking his rattle. The woman was lying on the floor. At her head a large pole contained the four strings of beads. Coyote sat by the bed and sang chants for a long time. He returned every morning and evening for four days. Then he took her down to the river and sprinkled water on her four times. After this she was well. That is how Coyote created sickness. Now it is time for sleep. Tomorrow will be busy." As Chikokawe fell asleep, Grandfather transferred some of his own power to his grandson by rubbing his back.

### Family Feuds

The next day as Chikokawe and his Grandfather sat in the hills keeping watch over the family hut, Chikokawe asked, "Why are we so careful about being poisoned? Didn't the shaman determine which spirit caused Deerhunter's illness?"

"Yes, that is true," replied Grandfather. "But our family, like all families, has many enemies. We are involved in several feuds. Feuds are wars between families. They can begin by something as simple as an insult. Some of our feuds started long ago.

"Sometimes our enemies wait until one of us is sick, like Deerhunter. Then they add poison to the illness. This is very dangerous because the sickness can spread to the family. So you must be very careful. You must always watch and observe the taboos."

Chikokawe thought to himself as he shivered in the cool evening air, "I hope Deerhunter is cured soon. I am hungry for meat."

## Shamans

The shaman was the most important person in the village. People both respected and feared him. Providing a link between the physical and spiritual worlds, he acted as both a doctor and a religious leader. The Pomo believed he had the power to kill or to cure.

Shamans helped sick people in three ways. First, they knew a lot about the medicinal plants that grew near their villages. Many herbs and plants restored health, and the shamans knew which ones to use.

Second, shamans used trickery. In the "sucking cure," they appeared to suck an object out of the body. After an elaborate ceremony, the shaman produced a stone or object and claimed it caused the illness. In the "singing cure" the shaman sang, shook a rattle made of cocoons, and smoked tobacco. The tobacco was supposed to have healing powers. Sometimes this trickery did help people—they believed they would get better, so they did.

Third, shamans used sorcery. Years ago, people called shamans *witchdoctors* because they called upon the powers of darkness to do their work. They summoned the spirits that the Indians believed lived in the land to help them. Christians call these spirits *demons.*

We can add shamans to the thinking that caused the California Indians to live in fear, along with power, poison, and obeying the taboos. They did not know the One True God and the healing and freedom that only He can bring.

## Progress

Progress was not possible in the California Indians' culture. They could not hope to better their living conditions. They could not, for example, invent a labor-saving mill to grind acorns. Indian women were taught exactly how to gather, store, and pound acorns. They sang required songs and chants at each step. If a woman were to change any part of the process, she thought she would offend the spirits and be punished. If anything bad happened in the village, she would be blamed. Until the California Indians learned that their taboos were false, their society did not change. Afterwards, they could learn about the exciting world God created.

## The World of Nature

When we study about the California Indians, we sometimes hear that the people lived in harmony with their surroundings and took only what they needed from the land. If they killed a deer for food, we hear they used the hide for clothes, the bones for tools, and the sinews for cord. We are told that they never wasted anything.

We are also told that we should be more like the Indians. They lived simply, so we should live simply. They never polluted the land, so we should not pollute the land. They exercised good stewardship over the land, so we should also. However, these statements are not entirely true.

The Indians lived simply because they had to. They had no other choice. Their beliefs did not allow them to take dominion over the land and prosper. They could not use what God created to make their lives better.

*Continued on page 18*

# Something to Think About

YOU HAVE LEARNED A LOT ABOUT THE Pomo way of life. You have compared the Indians' culture with its worship of nature to a Christian culture with its worship of the One True God. So, how should you view the California Indians?

People throughout California's history have wrestled with this very important question. Two answers people thought of are very wrong. Let's look at those and then consider the Christian response.

### Two False Views

First, people looked at the California Indians as happy and innocent. They would have been fine if only the Spaniards had never arrived, these people say. Even if we did not have evidence from the historical record, which we do, we would know this view was untrue. God created everyone with a sin nature, and no society without Him is pure or peaceful.

In the second false view, the Indians were considered less than human. They needed to be killed or enslaved, people said. This is such an evil thought. The California Indians, along with everyone else, were created *imago dei,* which means in the image of God. Because they bear God's image and have a soul that will live forever, they have great value and should be greatly respected.

### The Christian View

Christians need to view the California Indians honestly and with love. For hundreds of years, these people lived in California, lost and without hope. Following their ancestors' example, they turned their backs on God, and the culture fell deep into sin. As we have seen, it was impossible for the culture to change because the people were held in bondage by their ungodly beliefs. All areas of their lives and every thought were influenced by their false religion.

Sadly, our own culture is not blameless either. We don't have to think very hard to come up with a long list of the things we do that are contrary to what God tells us in the Bible. From our movies to our laws to our personal responsibilities, there is much that needs to be redeemed.

The Lord offers hope and salvation. When each of us hears and obeys the gospel, our culture can honor God, but we as Christians must become involved in shaping our culture.

## The Blessed Gospel

We must share the Good News, the Christian gospel, with those the Lord brings our way. We must live lives that please God. We must redeem our culture. We must do this in love and respect people's right to choose for themselves whom they will follow.

Our gracious Lord did not leave the California Indians in darkness. In later years, He sent His ministers to share the Good News of Christ's death and resurrection with His California Indian children. He freed the Indians from their taboos. He rescued all who were willing from death and destruction. Today, California Indians are among the multitude which surrounds the throne of grace in heaven. Will you join them?

The California Indians could not live in sturdy homes because their beliefs did not permit them to cut down trees. A Northern California Indian from the Wintu band explained,

> "We don't chop down the trees. We use only dead wood. But the white people plow up the ground, pull up the trees, kill everything. The tree says, 'Don't. I am sore. Don't hurt me.' But they chop it down and cut it up. The spirit of the land hates them. The rock says, 'Don't. You are hurting me...'"

Christians believe God created resources, like trees, for their use. God wants us to use resources to make ours and others' lives better and to advance His kingdom. He wants us to wisely use and care for what He provides.

The California Indians did not live in harmony with nature; rather for most, nature determined how they could live. They made their clothes and homes from whatever the land supplied. They did not plant, plow, or water any crops. When the weather was good, food was plentiful. When the weather was bad, food was very scarce, and people went hungry.

In many villages, old people and babies could be murdered or left to die. If a woman gave birth to twins, one was usually killed because it was supposed that two mouths to feed would be too great a burden. If a woman's husband abandoned her, she was allowed to kill her children because they had no supporter.

The California Indians learned much from the Spaniards and Americans. They learned how to prevent disease by keeping their homes clean, how to grow enough food so they wouldn't starve, and how to make clothes so they would be comfortable and healthy. Most important, the Spaniards and Americans taught the people the Biblical truth that all human life is precious in the sight of God.

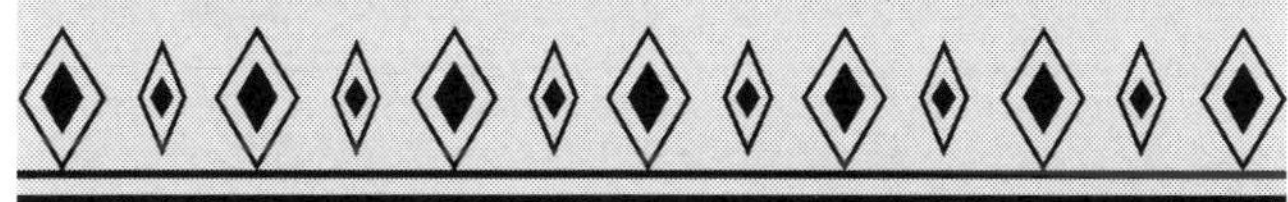

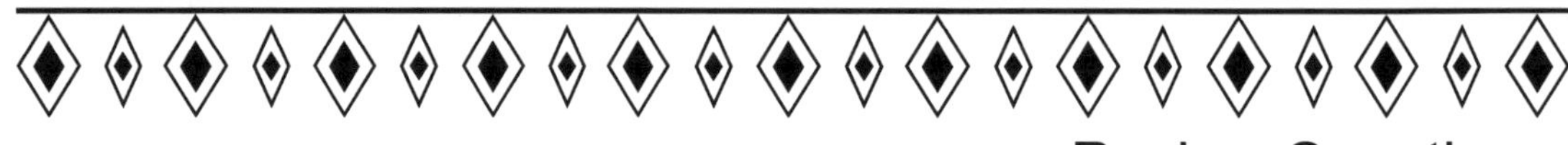

Review Questions

# Unit 1 Roundup

## Chapter 1

1. Describe the two Biblical events that caused the people we call the California Indians to travel to California.

2. What impressions or ideas about American Indians did you have that were not true for the California Indians?

3. Define these words:

   Power

   Poison

   Taboos

4. Write a paragraph describing Pomo beliefs. Make sure you use the words *spirits*, *power*, *poison*, and *taboos*.

5. **Thought Question:** If the California Indians descended from righteous Noah, why didn't they know about the One True God? Why did they believe in spirits, power, poison, and taboos?

## Chapter 2

1. The Pomo village contained the following buildings and structures. Describe each one and tell what it was used for.

   Family hut

   Roundhouse

   Sweathouse

   Acorn granary

2. What is a *professional*? Describe some of the Pomo professions.

3. How were acorns prepared for eating? Describe each step.

4. What is an *awihinawa*?

5. What activities might take place in the Pomo village?

6. **Thought Question:** Why did the Pomo have to move their homes three times each year?

## Chapter 3

1. Describe these words:

   Shaman

   Feud

2. How did the Pomo think sickness was created?

3. What are three ways a shaman treated sickness?

4. Why were the Pomo so careful and protective when one of their family became ill? (Hint: Think about what their enemies could do.)

5. **Thought Question:** Why do we have sickness in our world?

## Things to Ponder

This unit discusses several thoughts about the Pomo that are half-truths—something that is partly true, but mostly false. For each of the following half-truths, write a complete paragraph describing the full truth. Turn the half-truth into a topic statement, for example:

- "The Pomo were not peaceful people."
- "Compared to some of the eastern American Indian tribes, the Pomo could be considered peaceful, but they still had wars."
- "In a way the Pomo were peaceful, but in many ways they were not."

Once you decide on a topic sentence, be sure to back it up with facts and examples.

Here are the half-truths:

1. The Pomo were peaceful people.

2. They lived in harmony with their environment or surroundings.

3. The Pomo beliefs allowed them to live happy and prosperous lives.

4. The California Indians respected all life.

Unit 2

# The Explorers

## The Mariners' Psalm

Those who go down to the sea in ships,
Who do business on great waters,
They see the works of the LORD,
And His wonders in the deep.
For He commands and raises the stormy wind,
Which lifts up the waves of the sea.
They mount up to the heavens,
They go down again to the depths;
Their soul melts because of trouble.
They reel to and fro, and stagger like a drunken man,
And are at their wits' end.
Then they cry out to the LORD in their trouble,
And He brings them out of their distresses.
He calms the storm,
So that its waves are still.
Then they are glad because they are quiet;
So He guides them to their desired haven.
Oh, that men would give thanks to the LORD for His goodness,
And for His wonderful works to the children of men!

~~ Psalm 107: 23-31

# Long Ago, Far Away

FOR THOUSANDS OF YEARS THE LAND called California lay hidden, undiscovered by the rest of the world. Sea shells and fossils found on mountains show that the state was under water at one time, perhaps after the flood. Later, perhaps before the ice age that followed the flood, the land enjoyed a tropical climate. Scientists have found the remains of gigantic pre-historic animals, such as mammoths and saber-toothed tigers, in the La Brea Tar Pits and places in Southern California. The California Indians may have come to California after the climate began to change.

Although there is evidence that people other than the California Indians visited, the land remained undisturbed for thousands of years. Why?

If you want to visit another land, you get in your car and drive. If the place is far away, you fly. You can reach the other side of the world in less than 24 hours. If you get hungry along the way, you stop at a restaurant. If you are tired, you check in to a motel.

The explorers did not have any of these conveniences. They had to travel in small ships, carry all their food, and go wherever the ocean currents or wind drove them.

Let's study why it was so hard to reach California and the courage required to make the voyage. Let's learn about the men who risked their lives to journey to this land and who opened the way for Spanish colonization. Let's begin with Christopher Columbus and study the chain of explorers who came to California.

It took courage for the early explorers to sail away from the sight of land. Some sailors believed that if they sailed too far away, they would fall off the edge of the earth. This picture shows Columbus' three ships: the *Pinta*, *Santa Maria,* and *Niña*, the first ships to sail across the Atlantic Ocean.

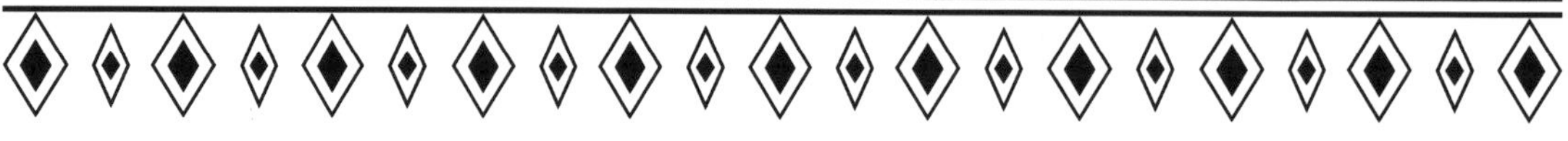

Chapter 4

# Columbus and Cortés

The tall, blue-eyed captain peered anxiously over the throbbing bow of his ship, trying to catch a glimpse of land. He brushed the salt-caked red hair from his eyes. Nothing! Only the endless waves reflecting back the shimmer of the moon on the empty sea. It was late, past ten o'clock, but the captain could not sleep. Restlessly, he paced up and down the deck.

Wait! A light that looked like a little wax candle rising and falling appeared on the horizon. He called his servant, who also saw it. Could it be land? After a few minutes it was gone, and the *Santa Maria* continued on its lonely course.

Christopher Columbus reflected on the events of the past few months. After years of asking and begging, Queen Isabella and King Ferdinand of Spain had finally agreed to finance his expedition to the rich lands of the Indies. Like most educated people of his day, Columbus believed that the world was round. By sailing west over the unexplored Atlantic Ocean, he hoped to reach the lands in the East.

Columbus was driven by two goals. First, he wanted to find a shorter route to China so that Spain could trade for spices, silk, tea, and pearls. Second, he also wanted to bring the Gospel of Christ, Christianity, to a lost world. Sound, capable men and boys from Spanish families along with criminals from Spain's prisons made up his crew. After nearly a month of sailing on an unexplored sea, they became restless.

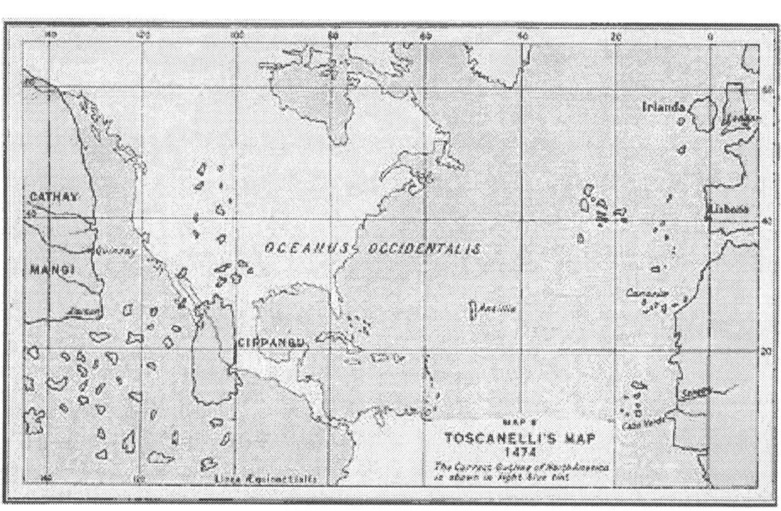


In 1275, Marco Polo wrote a book about his visit to Cathay (China), which he said was just beyond the islands of Cipangu (Japan). Two hundred years later, a scientist and scholar named Toscanelli drew a map of the world showing Japan only about 3,500 miles from Spain. (The distance is really about 12,000 miles.) Columbus used Toscanelli's map to plan his voyage. The map to the right shows Toscanelli's work drawn over North and South America. It is easy to understand why Columbus believed he had arrived in the Indies, as the smaller islands were called, since they were in the same area Toscanelli placed Cipangu. Columbus died never knowing that he actually discovered two new continents.

“This Genoese foreigner knows nothing,” they murmured among themselves. “Every minute Spain grows farther away and nothing lies ahead. Let’s throw the foreigner overboard and be done with him!”

The usually pleasant Columbus grew stern. “We must not turn back,” he said. “We have come to find the Indies, and we will continue with the help of Our Lord!”

Finally, at two o’clock in the morning, the lookout on the *Pinta* shouted, “Land! Land!” The next morning Columbus went ashore on the Bahamas Island the natives called Guanahani. He thanked the Lord for His mercy and called the island San Salvador, meaning Holy Savior.

Christopher Columbus is the first link in the chain of explorers who brought the Spaniards to California. Many others followed. About 30 years later, Magellan’s crew sailed around the entire world and Balboa traveled across Panama to find the Pacific Ocean as the explorers traveled closer to California.

Columbus was not a Spaniard. He was from Genoa, a region of Italy, and was called a *Genoese*.

When Columbus landed on the island he named San Salvador, he wrote about the natives, “So that they may feel great friendship for us, and because I knew that they were a people who would be better delivered and converted to our Holy Faith by love than by force, I gave to some of them red caps and glass bells which they put round their necks, and many other things of little value, in which they took much pleasure, and they remained so friendly to us that it was wonderful.”

# Hernán Cortés

Conqueror of Mexico

The next man in the chain of explorers who made it possible to reach California was an adventuresome and headstrong young man named Hernán Cortés. He sailed to the West Indies from Spain when he was nineteen years old. At Hispañola, now called Haiti, he received land and became a farmer. Seven years later, he took part in the conquest of Cuba and became a wealthy and respected man. In 1519, when Cortés was 33 years old, the Spaniards discovered gold in Mexico and planned a conquest. They chose Cortés to be the commander because of his abilities and wealth. He used his entire fortune to equip the conquest. Cortés landed at what is now Vera Cruz (True Cross) in Mexico with about 500 soldiers.

About 200 years before the arrival of Cortés, the cruel Aztecs conquered most of the Indian tribes living in Mexico. Their culture, although highly civilized, grieved the Lord. They practiced human sacrifice. Tens of thousands of men, women, and children were brutally murdered as offerings to the Aztec gods each year. The Aztecs forced conquered tribes to pay tribute (taxes) plus give their sons and daughters to be used as victims.

Cortés believed he was chosen by God to end this wickedness. Like Jonah at Nineveh, Cortés tried to persuade the Aztecs to repent of their sins. He told the Aztecs that their bloody human sacrifices provoked God's wrath. He told them about the living God and urged them to put their trust in Him. Unlike the Ninevites, the Aztecs would not repent. In fact, Montezuma, the Aztec leader, said that more sacrificial offerings would be needed to wash away the insult caused by Cortés' words.

At first, the Aztecs cautiously welcomed Cortés and

## Cortés' Words to the Aztecs

Cortés tried to teach the Aztecs about God. This is what he told Montezuma and his men:

"I made them understand by the interpreters how deceived they were in putting their hope in idols made of unclean things by their own hands. I told them that they should know there was but one God, the Universal Lord of all, Who had created the heavens and earth and all things, and them and us, Who was without beginning and immortal; that they should adore Him and believe in Him and not in any creature or thing."

his men into Mexico City, the Aztec capitol. Later when Montezuma was accidentally killed by his own people, Cortés' men had to flee for their lives. Some of the men did not escape and were murdered on the Aztecs' altars. Cortés returned with the help of other Indian tribes and finally conquered the city. It took two years. After the conquest of Mexico City, Spanish missionaries taught the Indians about Catholicism. Many were converted to the Catholic faith.

The travels of Hernán Cortés.

Although not all of Cortés' deeds were admirable, he was a great explorer. He set out to investigate the sea above the newly conquered land from a port he had established on the western coast of Mexico at Zacatula. After much hardship, these ships discovered Baja California which they thought was an island.

Baja California has always been a very hostile land. It rains very little, and there are no rivers except where it joins what is now the United States. The land is very mountainous and desert-like. When water can be found, the land is very fertile, but water is very scarce. Further, in Cortés' day, Baja California was very difficult to reach. It could take a month to travel from Mexico. Many storms would spring up in the gulf quickly and unexpectedly.

Cortés built a settlement at La Paz on the tip of the peninsula. From the beginning, it faced many problems. The land could not be farmed, and the settlement could not support itself. Supplies were difficult to send across the stormy gulf. Many men died of starvation.

During all of these problems the land was called California for the first time, a name taken from a popular novel which described a rich, mythical country. Cortés hoped that by calling the desolate land California, the settlers would be encouraged to stay. It was too hostile however, and the settlement was abandoned.

## How California Got Its Name

A novel written in the sixteenth century describes a rich land named California. The land was inhabited by strong and courageous black women who lived the life of Amazons. (Amazons are a mythical race of female warriors.) Their weapons were made of gold, which was the only metal produced in this land. The queen of this land, Calafia, joined the infidels, as the Muslims were called, to attack Constantinople. Her forces were defeated, and she was captured and enslaved for a year. At the end of that time, she asked to become a Christian and to marry a prince of the land. This is a portion of the novel:

Know ye that on the right hand of the Indies there is an island called California, very near the Terrestrial Paradise and inhabited by black women without a single man among them and living in the manner of Amazons. They are robust in body, strong and passionate in heart, and of great valor [very brave]. Their island is one of the most rugged in the world with bold rocks and crags. Their arms are all of gold, as is the harness of the wild beasts...they ride.

From *Las Sergas de Esplandian*
by Garci Rodrigues Ordonez de Montalvo

Chapter 5

# The Chain Comes to California

## Juan Rodríguez Cabrillo

First Spaniard to California

Cabrillo is pronounced Ca-BREE-yo.

The search for riches brought the chain of explorers to California. In 1542 the viceroy, or ruler of New Spain (Mexico today), ordered Juan Rodríguez Cabrillo to try to locate the Strait of Anian. The Strait of Anian was a shortcut that was supposed to exist through the continent of North America. Cabrillo could not find it because it did not exist, but he did discover California.

Cabrillo sailed from Mexico with two poorly built ships. While it only took Columbus about a month to travel across the Atlantic Ocean, it took Cabrillo three months to reach what is now California. He had to sail against the winds and currents. When he landed at San Diego Bay, the Spaniards became the first recorded Europeans to walk on California soil. Indians attacked Cabrillo's men while they were exploring San Diego, but the men did not fight back. Instead they treated the Indians kindly.

Cabrillo explored the coast of California until storms forced him to the island of San Miguel. There, while trying to defend his men from an Indian attack, he fell and broke his arm near the shoulder. In spite of his injury, by the following week he had resumed the journey and reached Fort Ross where violent storms forced him to turn back. On the return trip, he found Drake's Bay and perhaps Monterey Bay. He missed San Francisco Bay, however, even though the ship's log showed that there was no fog the day they sailed by the Golden Gate.

The expedition returned to San Miguel Island for the three winter months. Sadly, Juan Rodríguez Cabrillo died from an infection in his broken arm. Brave and courageous to the very end, he made his men promise they would continue the journey.

# The Cabrillo-Ferrelo Expedition

1542-1543

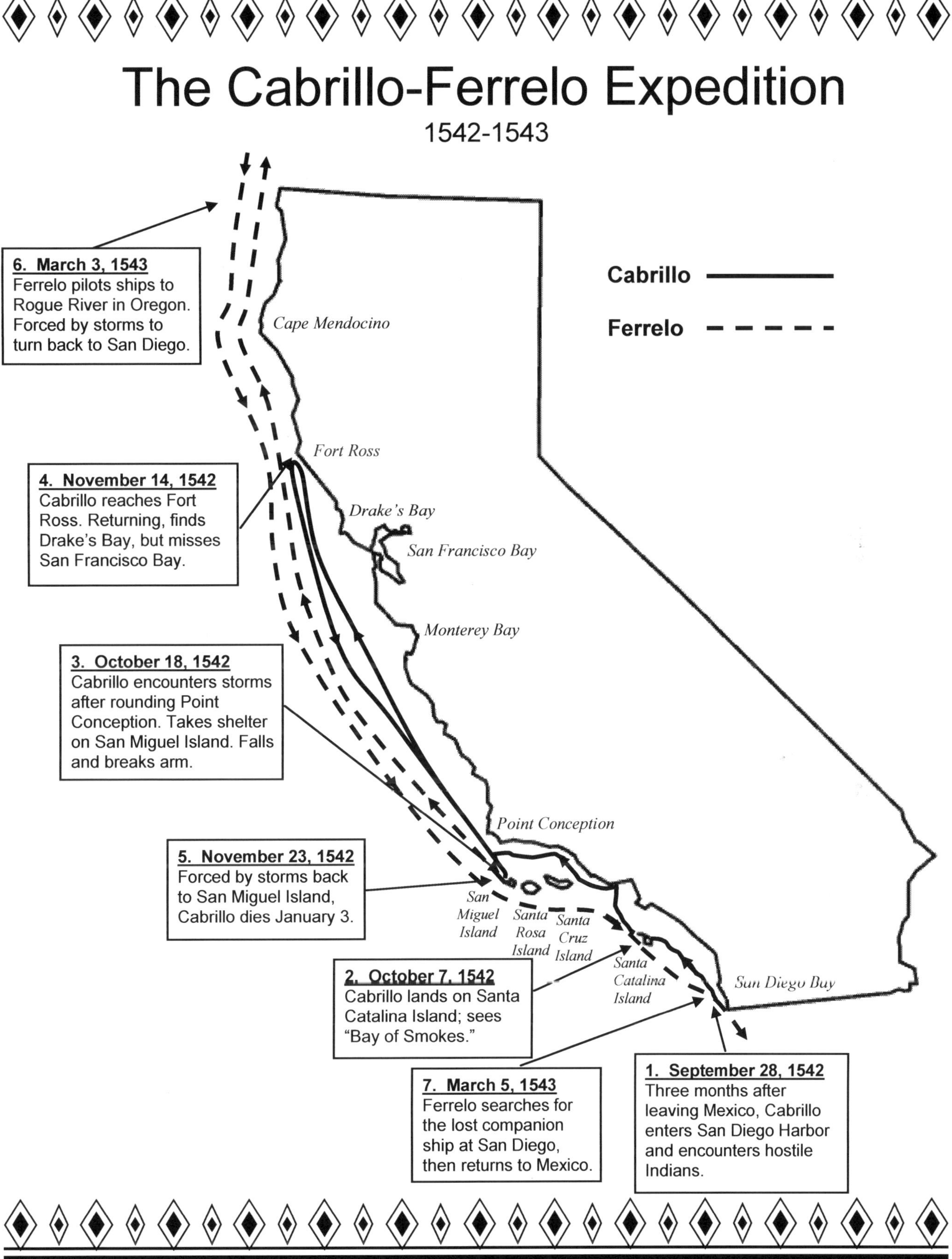

## Why was it so hard to reach California?

Why did it take so long for the Europeans to find California and even longer to colonize it? Two reasons, both involving the ocean.

### Wind and Currents

From Spain's perspective, California was located at the farthest end of the earth. To reach it, Spaniards had to sail through the middle of the Atlantic Ocean, around the very stormy and treacherous Cape Horn at the tip of South America, and then up into the Pacific Ocean.

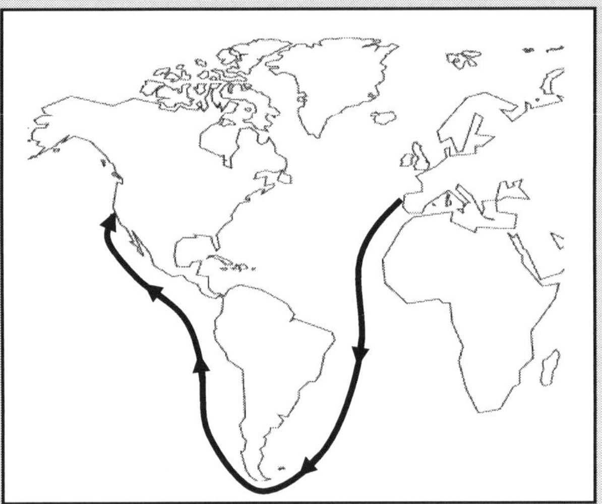

*Pacific,* which means *peaceful*, was not a good description of this ocean. Fierce storms could spring up quickly. Then, when the sailors came to the *Doldrums* near the Equator, there was no wind at all. Sometimes the men waited weeks before they could move on. Once past South America, ships had to fight against winds and currents to reach California. They did not have maps to tell them of dangers and many

*Continued on page 30*

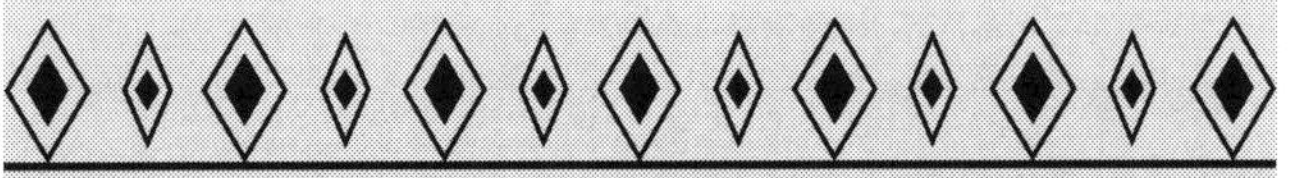

After Cabrillo died, Bartolomé Ferrelo took command and sailed north. He did not approach the coast until he was past Fort Ross, so he did not see San Francisco Bay or Monterey Bay. He is believed to have sailed beyond the northern border of California before he was forced by storms to turn back. Off the coast of what is now Oregon, the two ships of the expedition lost sight of each other, and Ferrelo was unable to find the smaller ship. After three weeks, the ships were reunited at Baja California.

Supplies were too low to resume the voyage, so after nine-and-one-half months the Cabrillo-Ferrelo expedition returned to New Spain without having found the Strait of Anian. But they had learned much about the coast of California that would be helpful to future expeditions.

## The Bay of Smokes

While Cabrillo was sailing near what is now Los Angeles, he recorded a most interesting fact: the entire basin was filled with smoke from Indian campfires, and he could not see the landscape.

The Los Angeles Basin has a unique feature called a *thermal inversion*. This means that the temperature of the air reverses itself or inverts. Warm air, including the smoke from the campfires, rises until it reaches the inversion. Since it cannot rise any farther, it spreads and fills the entire valley. Cabrillo called it "The Bay of Smokes."

Today the people living near Los Angeles suffer from air pollution. However, this is not just a problem for the 21st century. Pollution troubled the people living in the area at the time Cabrillo sailed along California's coast and probably for many years before.

# Francis Drake

## The English Privateer

Sir Francis Drake

In the last half of the sixteenth century, Spain, under Philip II, was the greatest power on the earth, but England was beginning to challenge it. Religious strife between England and Spain grew as Protestantism thrived through the efforts of reformers such as Martin Luther and John Calvin. Spain was a Catholic nation while England was Protestant.

At this time, Spain controlled all of the trade in the Pacific Ocean. England resented Spain's claim to own the seas, and English ships made voyages to the Americas to smuggle goods, capture Spanish treasures, and plunder towns. One of the most famous English captains was Francis Drake.

In 1577, Queen Elizabeth gave Drake something called a *letter of marque.* This letter gave Drake permission to attack Spanish ships and seize their cargo. Called a *privateer,* Drake could keep part of what he captured, and the rest went to England. If caught, Drake and his men would be treated as prisoners of war rather than pirates—the difference between life and death. Most nations, including the United States, could grant private captains letters of marque until about the mid-1800s.

lost their ships and their lives. If all went well, the trip could take months, if not years.

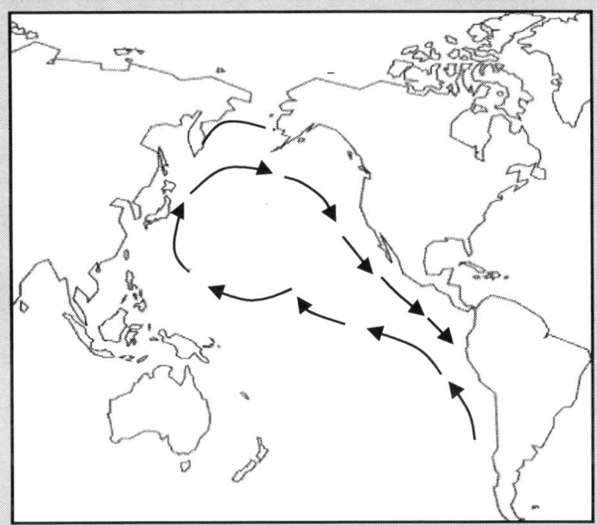

Sailors found it easier to move with the winds and currents towards Asia. Besides, treasure—gold, silks, and spices—could all be found in the rich Asian lands. To return to Mexico and ultimately Spain, the men would ride the wind and currents up the coast of China, across to Alaska, and down the coast of the California. Although a longer distance, it took less time to work with the ocean rather than against it.

### Scurvy

The second reason why the trip was so difficult involved food. When the sailors ran out of fresh food, they sickened. Their gums bled, their teeth fell out, and blue bruises covered their bodies. Infections, like the one Cabrillo got when he broke his arm, would not heal. Sailors' legs swelled, and every movement became painful. Many died.

This disease is called scurvy, and it is caused when people do not eat food containing vitamin C. When the sailors could eat fresh food, they healed almost immediately. Unfortunately, fresh food was not available in the middle of the ocean. Years later, the British would discover that sauerkraut and limes could keep sailors healthy on long voyages.

## What is the Strait of Anián?

Almost all of the explorers spent some time searching for what the English called the Northwest Passage and the Spanish called the Strait of Anián. A *strait* is a narrow body of water, like a channel or passage, that connects two larger bodies of water. The explorers hoped to find a narrow channel that connected the Pacific and Atlantic Oceans.

If this shortcut could be found, ships would not have to travel all the way around South America to reach Asia. Travel would be faster and less dangerous. Many people claimed to have seen this strait and even to have sailed through it. Spain was very anxious to find it. None of the explorers found it because it does not exist.

Even so, many maps of the time showed the Strait of Anián, such as this map drawn in 1687. Although hard to see, the map-maker (called a cartographer) has drawn a thin line showing the strait, through what should be Canada. Note also that at this time, the cartographer though that Baja California was an island:

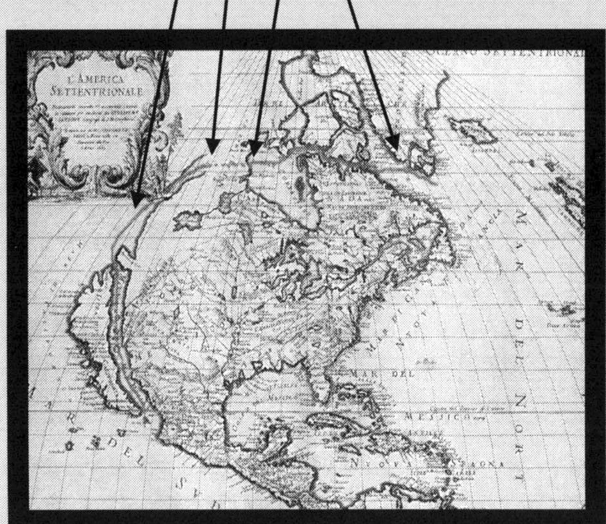


With an easier way to reach California, surely this rich land would have been colonized and populated. Since it was so hard to reach, it remained a neglected treasure for many years.

Queen Elizabeth gave Drake five ships and insisted that Drake's own ship, the *Golden Hind*, be royally decorated. He carried musicians, rich furniture, silver goblets, gorgeous uniforms, and many attendants. He also carried a chaplain since Drake probably was a Christian. Drake's father was a Puritan minister who had carefully instructed his twelve children in the faith. Drake's ship was the only one to reach the Pacific Ocean. Four ships were lost on the trip. One sank and, although Drake did not know it, the other three returned to England.

Once in the Pacific Ocean, Drake used his letters of marque and attacked Spanish towns and ships according to Queen Elizabeth's orders. Soon his ship was so full of treasure that there was hardly room for all of it. Drake was also a man of honor. When the captain of a ship taken at Panama was wounded, Drake cared for him. Additionally, Drake, who did not know that his other ships had returned to England, gave the captain a letter ordering any other English ship to leave the Spaniard alone.

When Drake was ready to return to England, he could not go back the way he had come, since Spanish ships would be watching for him. Instead, he sailed up the coast of California looking for the Strait of Anian, the sea route that supposedly existed across the North American continent. He did not find it, but he did stop probably at what is now called Drake's Bay, about 30 miles north of San Francisco. He needed to repair his ship, and he stayed for a month and a half in June and July of 1579. Drake called the land Nova Albion, or New England.

The Indians were very friendly and treated Drake and his men well. At their first visit, some of the Indians made speeches, and they exchanged presents. Then something happened which horrified the Englishmen. The women started to shriek and tear their faces and chests with their nails until the blood streamed down. They threw themselves on the ground or against hard stones. Drake and his men begged them to stop, but the women would not.

Finally, the Englishmen turned to prayers, asking God to open the eyes of the blinded Indians so that they would learn about Him. Then they started singing the Psalms. The "bloody sacrifice," as Drake's men called it, was stopped by the power of God. The Indians were fascinated with the singing of the Psalms.

This was the first Protestant religious service in what would become the United States. It was held at Drake's Bay, almost 30 years before the first settlement was built at Jamestown on the Atlantic coast.

At the end of July, Drake sailed on to the Philippines and eventually to England, becoming the first Englishman to sail around the world. A grateful Queen Elizabeth knighted him.

Sir Francis Drake's plans to return to California as governor of a trading company were never fulfilled. He continued to serve Queen Elizabeth. In 1588, he led some of the English ships that defeated the great Spanish Armada. The Armada was the largest group of sailing ships ever assembled in the world. Their defeat was a great blow to Spain but increased England's power.

## The Manila Galleons

As time passed and Mexico became more settled, a profitable trade developed with the East. Spanish treasure ships called Manila Galleons, sailed from Mexico, or New Spain as it was then called. These bulky and hard-to-steer ships followed the wind and the currents on a four-month journey to Asia.

Stopping at the Spice Islands or the Philippines, they loaded up with exotic treasures—gold, silks, spices, sugar cane, porcelain, ivory, dyewoods—from the rich Asian lands.

Since King Philip of Spain would only allow two Manila Galleons to make the long trip each year, the ships were huge. They might carry 1,000 passengers. Conditions were miserable. To make room for cargo, passengers stayed in damp and cramped quarters. Many suffered and died from scurvy. Other ships sunk or completely disappeared.

To return to Mexico and ultimately to Spain, the men sailed north from the Philippines and followed the wind and currents up the coast of China, across to Alaska, back to somewhere between Cape Mendocino and Point Conception in California. By the time they reached the California coast, the ship's supplies had run out and it might need attention, so they frequently landed in California to repair and refuel.

The trade lasted for about 250 years until Mexico gained its independence from Spain. It made many people wealthy.

Francis Drake captures the Spanish treasure ship, the *Cacafuego*

Since Drake was the first Englishman to raid Spanish ships in the Pacific, he caught the captains unprepared to defend themselves. His greatest prize was the *Cacafuego*. This ship carried so much treasure that it took Drake's men four days to unload it. It contained fruit, sugar, and other provisions, plus 80 pounds of gold, thirteen chests of silver coins, 26 tons of unrefined silver, and a quantity of jewels, silver plate, and precious stones—perhaps worth about two million dollars. Of this, Drake kept about $625,000 for himself, the crew received about $500,000, and the rest went to the English government.

## Pirate or Hero?

Was Sir Francis Drake a pirate and scoundrel as the Spaniards claimed, or a hero and savior as the English believed? The answer depended on whether you were English or Spanish. Spaniards thought Drake was little more than a common thief who robbed them of what was rightfully theirs. Englishmen thought Drake helped England to maintain its freedom.

King Philip II of Spain continued to pursue his father King Charles V's plan to conquer the world and impose Catholicism on all of his subjects. There was more religious freedom in England at the time (although true Christians, including Drake's father, were still persecuted for their faith), and the thought of becoming subjects of the Catholic Pope was very distasteful to Englishmen. Since most of Spain's wealth, and hence the money to finance acts of war, came from the New World, the English believed that to stay free they must cut off the source of these riches. They believed the actions of Sir Francis Drake helped them to remain free of Spain's control.

## Prayer Book Cross

In 1894 Ernest Coxhead created Prayer Book Cross, which remembers or commemorates the first use of the Anglican Book of Common Prayer in a Protestant religious service at Drake's Bay in the United States.

Prayer Book Cross still stands in on a hill in Golden Gate National Park. It is very difficult to get to since there is no parking nearby, but it can be seen when driving along John F. Kennedy Drive or Park Presidio Bypass Drive just before reaching Cross Over Drive.

## Sebastian Rodrígues Cermenho

The man who wrecked his galleon

Drake's actions in the New World caused the Spaniards to panic. When war broke out between Spain and England, many privateers with letters of marque followed Drake's example and captured Spanish ships as an act of war. Spain had to protect the treasure ships, the valuable Manila Galleons. The viceroy, the governor of New Spain, planned to build a settlement in California where the galleons could anchor for supplies, repairs, and refreshment. Other ships would protect the galleons by sailing with them to New Spain.

First Spain needed to determine where to build the settlement. The king decided to allow a man named Cermenho to explore the coast at his own expense using a Manila Galleon. In return, he could ship his own goods on the galleon and make a lot of money.

Cermenho left the Philippines in July 1595 and in November sighted the coast of California slightly north of Eureka. His ship had been damaged in a storm, so he took shelter in Drake's Bay. Then disaster struck. In November 1595, the galleon was blown toward shore and wrecked. Abandoning the damaged ship and the treasure, Cermenho and his crew of 70 crammed into a small launch and sailed down the coast looking for harbors. They missed the San Francisco Bay but otherwise produced a very good description and map of the coast and all of its harbors.

As the voyage progressed, the crew ran out of food and drink. The men almost died. Cermenho tells what happened next:

> "We went on shore and found many wild onions and prickly-pear trees, and likewise God willed that we should find a dead fish among the rocks, with two mortal wounds, and it was so large that the seventy of us sustained ourselves on it for more than a week, and if it had not been so large we would have perished there of hunger."

There was still no water until "God was pleased," Cermenho recorded, to send a wind which caused them to enter a bay that had a stream of good water. This is an example of the sailors' deep faith. On these sea voyages they relied on God to care for them.

When Cermenho's weary and sick crew finally reached New Spain, the viceroy was more upset about the lost galleon than he was impressed with Cermenho's map. After this, the valuable galleons would no longer be used for exploration.

# Sebastian Vizcaíno

The Last Spanish Explorer

Viscaíno is pronounced Veez-ka-EE-no

Seven years after Cermenho wrecked his Manila galleon, in 1602, the new king of Spain, Philip III, decided to try once again to find a place to build a settlement in California. He wanted to protect the Manila galleons as well as provide fresh food for scurvy-stricken sailors returning from the Philippines. Sebastian Vizcaíno was selected to find a location.

Vizcaíno's crew of 200 included his own son as well as expert map makers. The expedition carried provisions for eleven months. They left Acapulco in May and finally reached San Diego in November, after seven months of battling the severe, contrary winds. Landing at San Diego, they rested for ten days to allow the sick to recover and then explored the coast as far north as Monterey Bay.

Vizcaíno described Monterey Bay in glowing terms. He said that it was very large and sheltered from winds. It contained water, wood, and large pine trees to make ship masts. Furthermore the natives were very gentle. Vizcaíno said he thought they "could be brought within the fold of the Holy Gospel." He drew detailed maps of the area.

Soon all of the fresh food was gone, and more than 45 men were sick with scurvy. Vizcaíno decided that one of the ships, the *San Tomás*, should return to New Spain with the sickest men and the reports of the trip so far. Of the 34 men on board the *San Tomás*, 25 died before the ship reached port.

The other two ships sailed north and became separated in a storm. Neither ship sighted San Francisco Bay. Reaching Cape Mendocino, Vizcaíno decided to turn back. By this time, the men were very sick and provisions were rotten, so the ships returned to New Spain. They reached Mazatlan in February where Vizcaíno, one of the few healthy men left on board, walked 39 miles inland through mountains looking for food and help for his crew. Returning with fresh food, he helped his men to get well. The crew reached to Acapulco in March. Sebastian Vizcaíno commanded the last major sea voyage to California. No other explorers would visit for the next 167 years.

# Spanish Expansion

THE SPANISH STOPPED EXPLORING THE COAST OF CALIFORNIA IN 1602. With a new queen, England lost interest in the area. Spain's power declined, and the royal treasure did not have money for expensive expeditions. California was forgotten.

Meanwhile, back in New Spain, the Spaniards pushed north after Cortés conquered Mexico City. Working to convert the Indians to Catholicism and teach them trades, the Spaniards built many missions along the frontier.

The route along the coast toward Arizona and California was of special interest to the Spaniards. If this area could be colonized, supplies could be moved overland to the Baja Peninsula and into California so that colonies could be planted there. The biggest obstacle to this plan was the hostile Indians in the area, particularly the Apaches. The Indians destroyed many missions and towns and killed many people, delaying the colonization of California.

After Cortés reached Baja California, interest in this country remained high, especially when pearls were discovered. However, sixteen attempts to form colonies in this hostile land all ended in failure. Finally, the Spanish king asked the Jesuits to establish missions for the Indians of Baja California. The Jesuits were one of three missionary branches of the Catholic Church active in New Spain. (The other two were the Dominicans and the Franciscans.) In 70 years the Jesuits set up a total of fourteen missions along the Baja peninsula.

At these missions Indians were not only taught the Catholic faith but also how to grow their own food, raise cattle and sheep, build stone dwellings, irrigate their crops, weave, and many other useful trades.

White settlers were not permitted in Baja California. The Jesuits argued that the conversion and civilization of the Indians was the main goal. They felt that settlers would only interfere with this goal. Pearl-fishers continued to visit the area in the south but were not allowed to settle.

From their starting point in Mexico City, the Spaniards expanded into Baja California, California, and much of the southwestern United States.

# What about the bay?

How come all those explorers missed San Francisco Bay?

The Golden Gate, as the entrance to San Francisco Bay is called, blends in with the Oakland-Berkeley Hills in the background, hiding one of the most remarkable harbors in the world.

It seems remarkable that every exploration of the California coast missed its most valuable feature: the San Francisco Bay. How come every explorer and every captain of Manila galleons who traveled down the coast for 250 missed the bay's entrance? Historians have offered three possible explanations for this oversight.

## Fog

The first explanation is that the entrance to the bay, now called the Golden Gate, was hidden by fog. Fog is a problem in this area, especially during the summer. Fog may have hidden the bay on some occasions, but not all. Accounts in the ships' logs of some expeditions, especially Cabrillo's and Drake's, indicate that conditions were clear on the days they sailed past the entrance to the harbor.

## Earthquake

Another explanation is that the bay was not there. According to this theory, at one time the Golden Gate was a chain of mountains. A beautiful valley containing a freshwater lake existed in place of the bay. In an earthquake, the valley floor sank and the mountain chain broke. Sea water rushed in and created San Francisco Bay. This theory finds support from Indian legends, especially from the Coastanoan tribe that lived in the area around San Francisco. The Coastanoans told early settlers that their grandparents walked across the Golden Gate to Monterey. If true, the earthquake must have occurred sometime between 1602 (Vizcaíno) and 1769 (when the Spaniards discovered the bay).

## Limited Visibility

The most likely explanation for the bay's being missed was suggested by a Harvard historian named Samuel Eliot Morison. In a small ship about the size of the explorers', Mr. Morison retraced several of their voyages. While trying to determine the location of Drake's Bay, he sailed along the Golden Gate in the same way that the explorers would have. He reported that one can almost sail up to the opening before seeing it. The Berkeley-Oakland hills in the distance make it look like one continuous range of hills. According to this explanation, it is perfectly reasonable that the bay was missed by most explorers with the possible exception of Cermenho. Since he sailed down the coast in a small launch, he probably stayed very close to the land. His purpose was to map the coast, so he would have examined it closely. Yet San Francisco Bay did not appear on his map.

## God's Providence

One observation is clear no matter which explanation is correct: God, in His Providence, did not want San Francisco Bay to be discovered before the Spanish expedition of 1769. If the bay had been discovered when Spain was at the height of its power, during the voyage of Cabrillo for example, California could have been settled sooner. If Drake had discovered it, the area might have been colonized by the English. In either of these situations, California might never have joined the United States. Instead, California may have become a separate country. God in His providence did not allow this to happen. History shows that it was His will for California to become a part of the United States.

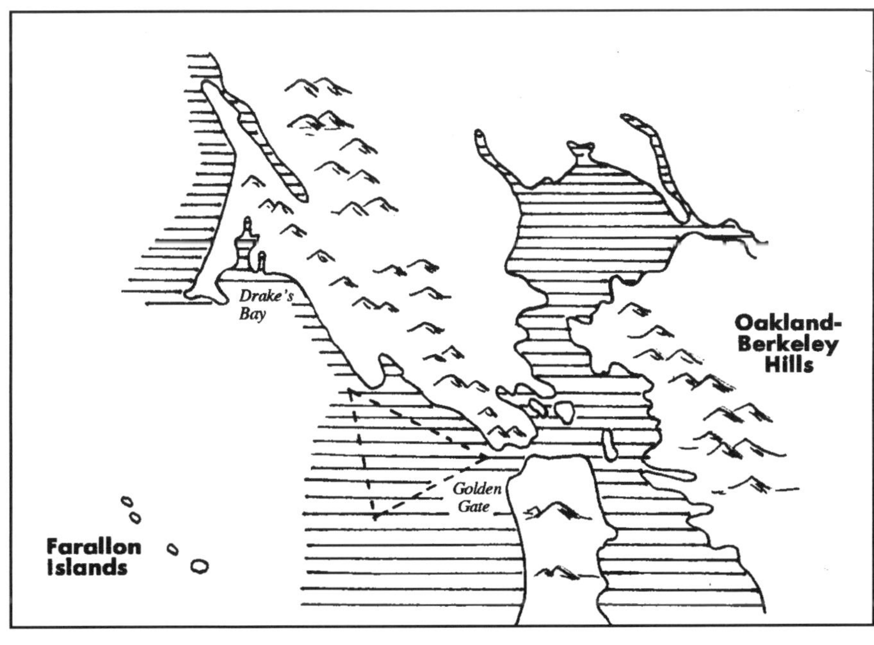


Unless a ship sails in the area marked by the triangle, it is very difficult to see the entrance to San Francisco Bay. The mountains in the background (Oakland-Berkeley Hills) hide its opening.

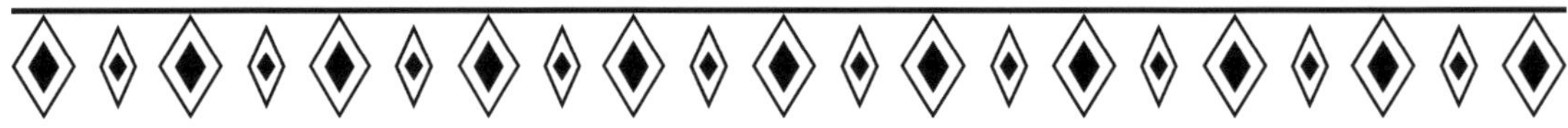

Review Questions

# Unit 2 Roundup

## Chapter 4

1. Why did Columbus believe he had arrived in the Indies?

2. What problems did Cortés' settlement in Baja California face

3. **Thought Question:** What do you think might have happened if Columbus and Cortés had never lived?

## Chapter 5

1. Identify each of the following explorers and tell what he did:

| | |
|---|---|
| Cabrillo | Cermenho |
| Drake | Vizcaíno |

2. Explain why it was so hard to reach California. Use the words *wind*, *currents*, and *scurvy*.

3. Why was the valley around Los Angeles called the Bay of Smokes?

4. What is the Strait of Anián, also called the Northwest Passage?

5. What is a *letter of marque*? What is the difference between a *pirate* and a *privateer*?

6. What is a Manila Galleon?

7. Why did the people of San Francisco build Prayer Book Cross?

8. Who are the Jesuits and what did they do?

9. **Thought Question:** Think about how your life might be different if the Spanish or English had built a prosperous colony in California in the 1600s. Write a paragraph describing your thoughts.

## Things to Ponder

This unit introduces the concept of God's providence, that is, the way He plans and provides for His people. Think about the way God cares for you. Think about the way He provides for you. After you have written down two or three thoughts, discuss them with an adult.

Unit 3

# Spanish Colonization

Go forth from you country
And from your relatives
And from your father's house,
To the land which I will show you.

~~ Genesis 12:1

# The Cross & the Sword

IN THE 300 YEARS AFTER COLUMBUS visited the West Indies, Spain slowly built many colonies in the New World. They developed a colonizing system they called the Cross and the Sword.

## The Colonizing System

The cross stood for the *missions* that the Spanish built along the frontier, the land just beyond the Spanish settlements. Spanish priests, called padres, lived at these missions and tried to teach the Indians about Catholicism. If needed, they also taught useful skills, such as how to farm and make clothing.

The sword symbolized the *presidios* or military forts that the Spanish built near the missions. These forts protected the padres as well as the Indians who lived at the missions, who were called Mission Indians.

*Pueblos* or towns followed. When most of the Indians living at the mission had become Catholics and Spanish citizens, it turned into a *pueblo*, and mission churches became regular churches. New priests replaced the original padres or missionaries, who moved on and built new missions. The cross and the sword system was repeated, and the borders of the Spanish frontier crept farther north.

In 1765, it was time for the frontier to reach California.

## The Cross and the Sword in California

Charles III was king of Spain, and he needed money. All of the countries of the world had just fought the Seven Years War (also called the French and Indian War). Spain fought against the British and lost the riches of Florida. To refill the Spanish treasury, King Charles III sent a man to New Spain to look for new ways to make money.

Although the Spaniards did not know about California's wealth, its gold and other natural resources, they learned that the Russians had build a fur-trading colony in Alaska. Perhaps the Russians would move down to California. Spain did not want to lose any more of its territory, so it decided to act. The cross and the sword would travel to California.

Let's follow the Spaniards to California and learn about the missions and presidios they built near California's harbors. Let's learn about the men and women who made their homes in this rough land. Let's follow the events that allowed Spaniards to flow into California as well as those that later abruptly halted these journeys.

Chapter 6

# The Sacred Expedition

## Two Great Men

The Cross and Sword Leaders in California

Gaspar de Portolá, California's first governor and leader of the Sacred Expedition

In 1769 Spain began to colonize California with the cross and the sword. It mounted an expedition history books call the "Sacred Expedition."

Soldiers and missionaries traveled on the Sacred Expedition. Junípero Serra led the missionaries, the "cross" part of the journey. Gaspar de Portolá, California's first governor, represented the "sword" and led the soldiers.

### Two by Land and Three by Sea

The Spaniards sent five separate groups to California—two by land and three by sea. All three ships carried food, clothing, guns, and supplies. One of the other ships carried military men and a future governor of California, Pedro Fages (pronounced FAH-hays). Fages commanded the "leather jackets," a special group of soldiers. Stationed at the presidios, these men wore leather vests or jackets made out of eight or more layers of deerskin, thick enough to stop arrows.

Junípero Serra, California's best-known Franciscan missionary.

Captain Rivera, another future governor of California, led the first land expedition. His group marked a trail from Lower or Baja California to Upper California that the second land group could follow. They carried more supplies, including all of the mules, cattle, chickens, and sheep that would be needed for the settlements.

Governor Portolá led the second land expedition, and Father Serra traveled with him. Their group carried more supplies but fewer animals. They were accompanied by Indians from the Baja California missions who would help to build the new settlement in California. All of the travelers experienced great hardships.

## The Arrival

In July 1769, a weary group of men finally assembled on a hill overlooking San Diego Bay as the sea and land groups met. The *San Carlos* had been the first ship to leave New Spain, but it arrived last and in terrible shape. During the voyage the ship's water containers leaked, and new water obtained along the coast made the men sick. The men also suffered from scurvy. Shortly after the ship docked at San Diego, the entire crew died except for one sailor and the cook. The *San Antonio* fared better. At first the crew seemed healthy, but eight men died. Unfortunately, the third ship, the *San José*, sank and everyone died.

Of the two land parties, Captain Rivera's reached San Diego in fair condition, although not without losses of men and animals. The men suffered from hunger and thirst as they braved the deserts and unknown land. Governor Portolá's land party managed the best because they followed Captain Rivera's trail markings.

Once in San Diego, Governor Portolá looked over the situation. It was desperate. Almost half of the men had died, and most of the remaining were very sick. He needed supplies. If they did not arrive soon, more men would die, and the colony would have to be abandoned. Assembling as many healthy sailors as possible, he sent them and the *San Antonio* back to New Spain with an urgent request for more men and supplies.

Meanwhile, Governor Portolá had a job to do. His orders required him to select sites for a mission and presidio at both San Diego and Monterey, California's best known harbors. Leaving the sick men in the care of Father Serra, he collected the healthiest and trekked north.

## The Two Stories

At this point, the story of the Sacred Expedition splits into two parts: Portolá's march to Monterey, and Serra's efforts to begin San Diego Mission. First we will follow Portolá on his six-month journey; then we will return to Serra, who founded San Diego Mission. Both Father Serra and Governor Portolá reported to their superiors in New Spain, and their letters still exist. We can learn much about the Spaniards' trials and adventures by reading portions of their correspondence. The following letters, while fictional, were written using many of Governor Portolá and Father Serra's own words. Additional information has been added from other historical sources. The letters describe the first six months of Spanish colonization.

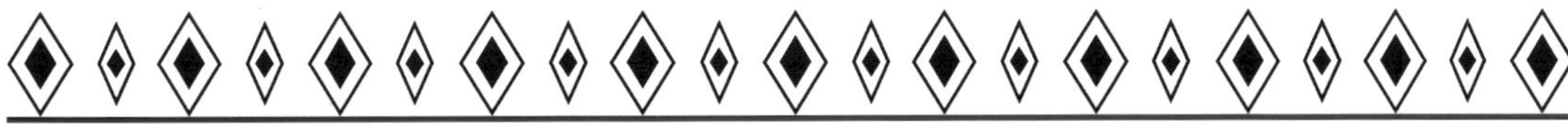

# The Sacred Expedition

## Portolá's March Through the Interior of California

The palo alto in about 1875.

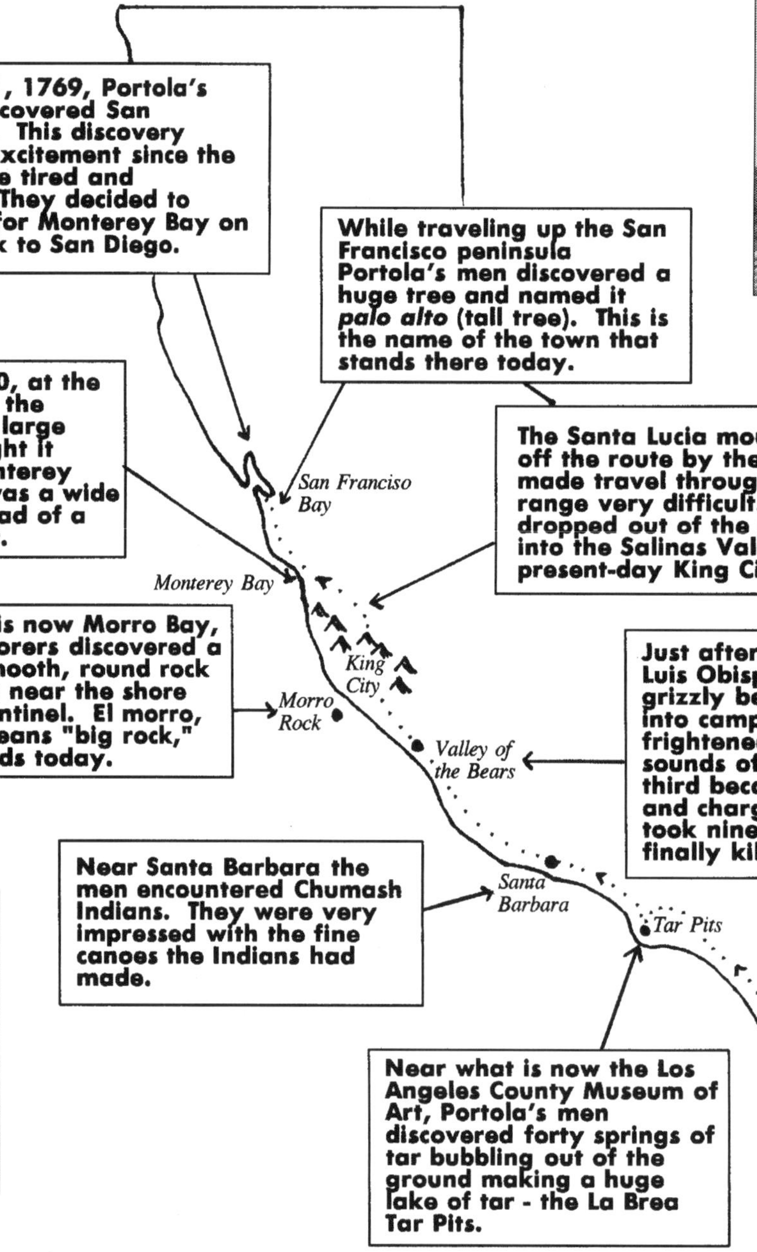

**On October 31, 1769, Portola's expedition discovered San Francisco Bay. This discovery produced no excitement since the explorers were tired and discouraged. They decided to keep looking for Monterey Bay on their way back to San Diego.**

**While traveling up the San Francisco peninsula Portola's men discovered a huge tree and named it *palo alto* (tall tree). This is the name of the town that stands there today.**

**On September 30, at the end of the river, the explorers saw a large bay. They thought it could not be Monterey Bay because it was a wide open curve instead of a sheltered harbor.**

*San Francisco Bay*

*Monterey Bay*

**The Santa Lucia mountains cut off the route by the shore and made travel through the steep range very difficult. The men dropped out of the mountains into the Salinas Valley near present-day King City.**

**In what is now Morro Bay, the explorers discovered a huge, smooth, round rock standing near the shore like a sentinel. El morro, which means "big rock," still stands today.**

*King City*

*Morro Rock*

*Valley of the Bears*

**Just after dawn at San Luis Obispo, three huge grizzly bears wandered into camp. Two were frightened off by the sounds of gun fire, but the third became infuriated and charged the men. It took nine direct hits to finally kill him.**

**Near Santa Barbara the men encountered Chumash Indians. They were very impressed with the fine canoes the Indians had made.**

*Santa Barbara*

*Tar Pits*

*San Diego*

**Near what is now the Los Angeles County Museum of Art, Portola's men discovered forty springs of tar bubbling out of the ground making a huge lake of tar - the La Brea Tar Pits.**

El Morro today.

*February 10, 1770*

*Most Excellent Sir:*

*Seven months ago, on July 15th, I left for Monterey with the few healthy men who had been spared from scurvy, hunger, and thirst, about sixty in total. They looked like skeletons. Father Serra stayed in San Diego to care for the sick.*

*The route was very difficult, especially through the mountains. Sometimes we had to build bridges over gullies so that our animals could pass. After eight days on the trail, we experienced an earthquake.*

*On the first of October, we arrived at the area where Monterey Bay should have been. We saw a great gulf spread out before our eyes. The area was very beautiful. Whales spouted, sea lions splashed, and the white sand of the beach glistened in the sun. However, the gulf did not meet the explorer Vizcaíno's description of a "fine harbor sheltered from all winds."*

*We asked Father Crespi to say the Mass of the Holy Spirit so that Almighty God would give us direction. We determined that we had not yet reached Monterey and continued our journey. By now twenty of our men were very ill with scurvy. Eleven of these had to be carried on stretchers between mules.*

*On the last day of October we sighted Point Reyes and the bay where Cermenho's Manila Galleon was wrecked. We also discovered another large bay that has not appeared on any of our maps. We did not take time to explore it since so many of our men were sick. Supplies were low, the winter rains had started, and the weather had turned very cold. Again we asked for guidance from the Holy Spirit and decided to return to San Diego. It was snowing by the time we reached the mountains. We pressed on, afraid that we would be trapped by the snow.*

*I am of the opinion that the great bay of Monterey has been filled in by sand. When the* San Antonio *returns with more provisions, we will again attempt to find it, but it may be completely gone.*

*In the Service of the King,*

# The Missing Bay

ALTHOUGH HE SEARCHED DILIGENTLY, PORTOLÁ RETURNED TO SAN Diego without finding the object of his search, Monterey Bay. Why? In 1602, Vizcaíno had written a detailed description of Monterey. He said, "We found ourselves to be in the best port that could be desired, for besides being sheltered from all winds, it has many pines for masts and yards, and live oaks and white oaks, and water in great quantity, all near the shore." Perhaps Vizcaíno exaggerated the quality of the port. Perhaps something happened to change it during the 167 years before Portolá followed.

Father Serra did not believe either idea. When discussing the expedition with its organizer, José de Galvez, Father Serra learned that three missions were to be built named for three Catholic Saints: San Diego, San Carlos, and San Buenaventura.

"But, sir," exclaimed Serra, "is our Father St. Francis, the founder of the Order of Franciscan Missionaries, to have no mission?"

Galvez replied, "If St. Francis desires a mission, let him show us his port, and he shall have one there."

Father Serra was certain that St. Francis was to have a mission. He believed God blinded Governor Portolá's eyes so that he could not find Monterey Bay, then directed the men north to discover the long-hidden San Francisco Bay. Scouts reported that there was no way to travel around it as part of it extended very far inland.

Why didn't the explorers think they had discovered the mythical Strait of Anián? Later this idea would be investigated, but at the time the men were disappointed because they could not locate Monterey. Discouraged, they plodded back to San Diego.

Meanwhile, back in San Diego, Father Serra was experiencing his own trials and tribulations.

Governor Portolá and his men accomplished something no other explorer had been able to do in the hundreds of years the Spaniards sailed up and down the coast of California: they discovered San Francisco Bay, one of the greatest harbors in the world.

*Hail Jesus, Mary, Joseph!*

*February 10, 1770*

*Venerable Father and My Dear Sir:*

*Two days after Portolá's men left for Monterey, I founded the mission at San Diego. I planted a cross, constructed a temporary chapel, and rang the mission bells to invite the Indians to come worship with us. While we were not yet able to communicate with them, we gave them small gifts. Little more can be done than to prepare the ground for their eventual conversion and salvation.*

*Shortly after the founding of the mission, the natives noticed how few we were and that we were continually burying a great many. They became very bold and imagined they could kill us all very easily. Suddenly, a great many, all dressed for battle, fell on us and began to steal everything in sight. They even snatched away the sheets that covered the sick. I was praying with Father Viscaíno when my servant dashed into my hut, mortally wounded. I had hardly time to absolve him and help him to meet his end. There I was with the dead man, thinking it most probable I would soon have to follow him, but at the same time praying to God that the victory would be for our Catholic faith without losing a single soul.*

*And so it turned out, thank God. For seeing many of their companions wounded, the Indians all fled. A few days later they returned and asked us to treat their wounds. None of them were killed; therefore, they can yet be baptized. They are all by this time recovered from their wounds, and we are all, since then, living in peace.*

*Our position here is what you can well imagine. But we are not dead yet, thank God. I ask Your Reverence for two things: your blessing, and permission to live here in these parts, relying on Almighty God's protection even if human means might fail. I ask the same for my companion, Father Crespi, who, I feel confident, will not desert me till God chooses otherwise.*

*Your most affectionate and devoted subject,*

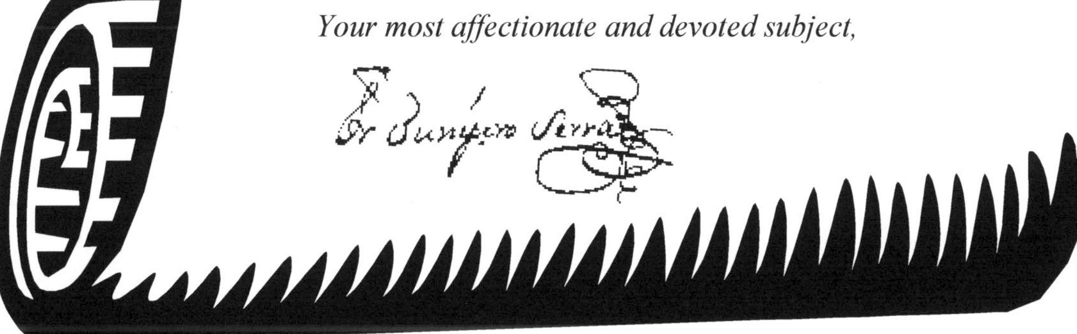

# *Father Serra*

## California's First Catholic Missionary

Born in Spain, José Miguel Serra's greatest desire was to become a missionary in the Catholic church. He accomplished his goal. At age 36, with his new name, Junípero, he sailed for the New World.

On the journey to the New World, Father Serra's strong character showed itself and made his fellow passengers admire him. He suffered from thirst for two weeks without ever complaining. All of the passengers thought they would die in a terrible ocean storm. Father Serra, however, trusted in God to deliver them. He showed no fear but was filled with peace.

In New Spain, Father Serra ran a group of missions in the north called Sierra Gorda. For nine years, he and his assistant taught the Indians to speak Spanish, to raise crops and cattle, and to make Spanish-style clothing. These missions were used as models when new missions were built.

At the age of 56, when many men have ended their life's work, Father Serra headed an effort to bring the Catholic faith to the Indians of California. Father Serra devoted the remaining fourteen years of his life to building nine missions, from San Diego to San Francisco. He died at the age of 70, and is buried at Carmel Mission.

Junípero Serra was a man completely devoted to his duty. His life reflected the scripture, "He that shall humble himself shall be exalted" (Matt. 23:12). His statue is in the National Statuary Hall in the capitol at Washington, D.C., the first choice among Californians, both Catholic and Protestant, for that honor. He has also been recently beatified by the Catholic Church, which is the first step the church takes to declare a person a Saint.

Each state may submit statues of two important historical figures to decorate the rotunda and halls of the U.S. Capitol in Washington, D.C. One of California's submissions, the statue of Junípero Serra, holds a place of prominence in the National Statuary Hall.

# Abandon the Colony?

WHEN GOVERNOR PORTOLÁ AND HIS MEN RETURNED TO SAN DIEGO, smelling like mules because they had to kill and eat their mules on the last leg of their journey, he was worried. He sent his and Father Serra's reports back to New Spain with a small group of men, but the supply ship, the *San Antonio,* had still not returned. Without those supplies, the men would starve. Governor Portolá determined that if the ship did not return by March 19, the colony would be abandoned.

How Father Serra's heart ached as he received this news. He gathered the people to begin a *novena*, or an nine-day prayer ceremony, to St. Joseph, the patron saint of the expedition. On the final day, the Fathers went to the heights overlooking San Diego Bay. A heavy fog hung over the water like a shroud. The hours passed slowly as they strained for a glimpse of a ship. Noon came, but the Fathers did not return to the mission to eat. All hope seemd to fade as the afternoon wore on. The sun, finished with the day's journey, began to sink beyond the horizon. Its orange rays painted the sky, and the fog lifted. Watching and straining, the Fathers finally saw what they were waiting for.

"The ship! The ship!" they shouted excitedly. They clearly saw the white sails, which they called a messenger from God, before darkness fell. The Fathers fell to their knees in thanksgiving while their servants ran to share the news with the rest of the camp. Four days later, the *San Antonio* sailed into San Diego harbor.

The captain of the *San Antonio* had not planned to stop in San Diego; rather, he was heading to Monterey where he thought there would be a colony in great need. Stopping at Santa Barbara for water, he heard that Portolá's group had returned to San Diego. Wanting to be sure, he still tried to go north, but then he lost his anchor and had to return to San Diego.

One historian said about the *San Antonio's* timely arrival, "Can there be any doubt that the missions were founded by the direct providence and will of God Almighty?"

San Diego Mission, the first in the 21-mission chain, was established on July 16, 1769.

Chapter 7

# The First 12 Years

The hand of God was at work as the first settlements were made in California. God protected them through all of the hardships and problems they met. He protected the San Diego Mission from the hostile Indians. He guided Portolá's expedition past Monterey to allow the discovery of San Francisco Bay. Finally, He guided the *San Antonio* to San Diego just in time to prevent the mission from being abandoned.

The next twelve years were hard for the settlements that were finally built in San Diego and Monterey. Twice the men nearly starved. The first time they obtained food in a great bear hunt at a place near San Luis Obispo called *El Cañon de los Osos*—The Canyon of the Bears. Bear meat kept the people alive until supplies could be brought up from San Diego. Plus, the hunt greatly benefited the Indians, many of whom had been mauled and killed by these bears. The grateful Indians sent the soldiers 25 mule loads of dried seeds as a thank-you gift. Later, when a mission was established at San Luis Obispo, the Indians remembered the Spaniards' kindness and welcomed them.

The second famine was ended by the viceroy's attention to the supply ships. (The viceroy was the chief ruler in New Spain.) Communication between New Spain and California was very slow. Even though Viceroy Antonio Bucareli heard that California had plenty of food, he sent the supply ship just to be sure. It was well that he did. At that time California was experiencing the worst famine ever. Men had been living on milk and herbs for several months. Bucareli's good judgment saved many lives.

Viceroy Bucareli was a wise ruler who wanted California to become a settled and prosperous colony. He wanted to send women and families to California. He felt that the society would be better if men had their families with them. A small *pueblo*, or town, developed around Monterey as the first of these families arrived. He also looked for less expensive ways to supply California. When a man named Juan Bautista de Anza approached him with the idea of finding a land route to California, he quickly granted him permission to explore.

# The Overland Route to California

Captain de Anza at San Francisco Bay. Below the horse's nose, his men look over the site of the San Francisco Presidio, where Fort Point currently stands.

In 1773, Captain Juan Bautista de Anza hand-picked twenty volunteers and two missionaries, one of whom was named Father Garcés, a Catholic missionary who had explored the area. Another valuable part of Anza's expedition was an Indian named Tarabal, one of the five Indians from Baja California who had accompanied Portolá on the Sacred Expedition. After losing his wife and brother in the treacherous Colorado Desert, Tarabel met Father Garcés and remained with him for the next seven years. Tarabal agreed to help guide the expedition. Bucareli told Anza to make friends with the Indians and seek their cooperation. He also ordered Anza to look for an overland route to California.

The night before the expedition was to depart, a band of Apache Indians stole more than 100 of Anza's horses and cattle. This caused a delay, but the expedition pressed on. The route from Tubac to the meeting of the Gila and Colorado Rivers was uneventful because the party traveled through familiar territory. At the Colorado River the expedition was warmly greeted by a Yuma, Chief Olleyquotequiebe, whom the Spaniards called Salvador Palma.

Problems started after the Yumas helped the Spaniards across the river. The expedition tried to cross the Colorado Desert but became hopelessly lost in the sand dunes. There was no water and no grass for the horses and cattle to eat. Sandstorms blinded the way. All of the Yuma guides deserted the party.

After six days and fearing death, the expedition returned to the Yuma village. Anza left part of the men and most of the supplies with Chief Palma. With the strongest men, he pushed through the desert. After six days of hard riding, Father Garcés and Tarabal both recognized the area at the foot of the Sierra Nevadas. They guided the expedition through the mountains to the San Gabriel Mission.

The missionaries at San Gabriel were surprised and delighted to see Captain Anza because now more people and supplies could come to California. Anza stayed in California for a short time before returning to Tubac and Mexico City to make his report to Viceroy Bucareli.

# The Anza Expedition

## The First Overland Route to California from New Spain

San Francisco
San Jose
Colorado River
San Gabriel Mission
Imperial Valley
Yuma Village
Colorado Desert
Gila River
Tubac

Captain de Anza traveled from Tubac in what is now southern Arizona to the Yuma village at the junction of the Colorado and Gila Rivers. When he tried to cross the Colorado Desert, he suffered greatly from exhaustion and thirst. Returning to the Yuma village, he rested and then tried the route through what is now the Imperial Valley. After a great struggle, the men arrived at San Gabriel Mission. Anza traveled as far north as San Francisco Bay before returning to New Spain.

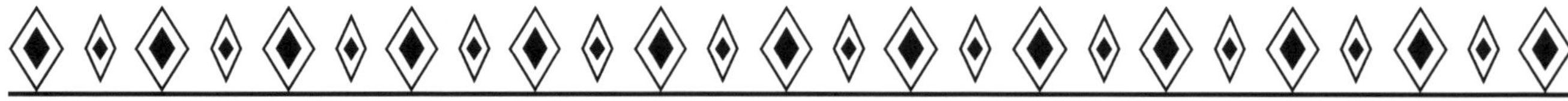

# San Francisco Presidio

VICEROY BUCARELI WAS DELIGHTED WITH CAPTAIN DE ANZA'S route. He authorized Anza to prepare an expedition to build two missions and a *presidio* near San Francisco Bay. He recruited 240 colonists from poverty-stricken families in northern New Spain. One of the families selected for this trip included María Feliciana Gutierrez.

This charming twenty-year-old mother was delighted by the provisions for the journey, all paid for by the government. She looked beautiful in her new linen jacket with fitted waist, green skirt, and high-heeled shoes from Spain. Her black hair was braided with new hair ribbons. María Feliciana chose matching clothes and hair ribbons for her two pretty, dark-eyed daughters. Her husband received a new sombrero, leather jacket, pants, and new boots. As María Feliciana and the other women colonists admired their new finery, the men examined the horses, livestock, guns, and equipment. Everything was provided except money because the colonists were known to gamble.

Just before the expedition left for California, tragedy struck. María Feliciana's husband died. This courageous woman determined to continue the journey with her two young daughters. Captain de Anza agreed to take her. The trip was long and difficult, yet the colonists did not complain. New life in California was worth enduring the temporary hardships on the trail.

Although separate tribes, the Yuma and Mohave Indians lived near each other. Chief Palma's men may have resembled this Mohave Indian, whose body is covered with painted designs.

Yuma Indians met the party at the junction of the Gila and Colorado Rivers. They looked fierce in their black, red, and white paint. Fresh Apache scalps hung from their belts. Chief Palma had a turquoise ring in his nose and gratefully accepted the present Viceroy Bucareli had sent him: a gold-trimmed uniform with a blue coat, yellow vest, black pants, and feathered cap. Chief Palma responded in gratitude, "I have told my people not to steal from you. If they do, I will kill them." Captain de Anza also gave each Yuma coins, tobacco, and glass beads (which were used as money). There was a great watermelon feast. The Yumas had saved 3,000 watermelons from the harvest by burying them in the sand. Chief Palma noticed the lovely

María Feliciana and asked her to be his seventh wife. She said, “No.”

After a few days, the Yumas helped the colonists cross the river. There was a tense moment when the river swept a child off her horse. But Captain de Anza had placed men down river just in case an accident occurred. The little girl was rescued and returned unharmed.

Captain de Anza continued to guide the expedition around the scorching desert and over the snow-covered mountains. Everyone finally reached San Gabriel Mission safely, including several children born on the way.

María Feliciana’s journey ended at the San Gabriel Mission. She won the heart of a young soldier who had come to California in 1769 with Governor Portolá and Father Serra. After the wedding, María Feliciana served as housemother to the Indian girls at the mission until her own family grew too large. Two of her grandsons, Pio Pico and Andres Pico, became governors of California during the Mexican period.

## Indian Attack at San Diego

Captain de Anza’s timely arrival in California was planned by God. While the expedition was traveling over the mountains, the non-Mission Indians near San Diego attacked the mission. Gathering from the surrounding areas, they tried to drive the Spaniards from their territory. The Yumas had been asked to participate, but they had too much respect for Captain de Anza and Father Garcés. They refused. Two attacks were originally planned, one on the San Diego Mission, the other on the presidio. The attack on the presidio failed when the Indians lost their courage.

Shortly after midnight, the mission awoke to sounds of the attack.

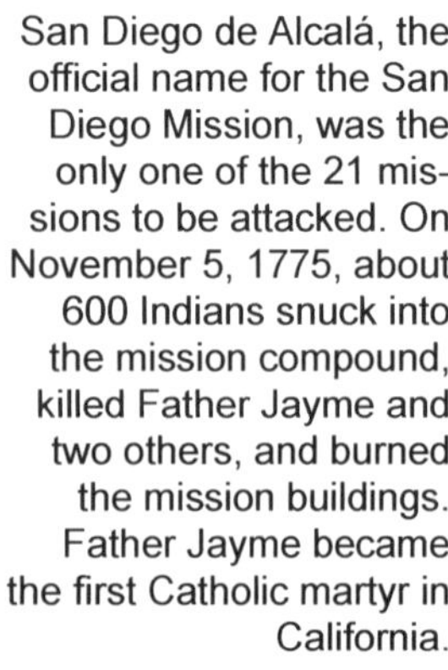

San Diego de Alcalá, the official name for the San Diego Mission, was the only one of the 21 missions to be attacked. On November 5, 1775, about 600 Indians snuck into the mission compound, killed Father Jayme and two others, and burned the mission buildings. Father Jayme became the first Catholic martyr in California.

Father Luis Jayme arose from his bed and greeted a group of hostile Indians with his usual, "Love God, my children." They seized him, dragged him away, and beat him to death. During the battle all the other defenders were wounded. Two more men died.

The presidio was too far away to hear the noise of the attack. Soldiers did not come to help until the next day. They tried to defend the mission against the Indians, but needed more help. Where would that help come from? There were only 70 soldiers in all of California at the time, and they were spread out between Monterey and San Diego. Few could be spared to assist the soldiers at San Diego. Captain de Anza and a supply ship from New Spain had arrived at just the right time, through the providence of God. They saved San Diego Mission.

Instead of destroying the mission, the revolt actually strengthened it. The Indians thought it was impossible to overthrow the Spaniards. They gave up. Everyone agreed that Anza's arrival had turned things around. "Providential," Viceroy Bucareli called it. "Just as if he had come from Heaven."

After the danger was over, Captain de Anza rejoined his expedition. The San Francisco Mission was built in April. In September 1776, after Captain de Anza had returned to New Spain, the presidio at San Francisco was built. The second mission at Santa Clara was founded in January 1777. Finally, Spain occupied the great San Francisco port.

## Juan Bautista de Anza

Born on the frontier of New Spain, Juan Bautista de Anza was a soldier, just like his father and grandfather. When he was only two years old, Apache Indians killed his father. Later, at the age of eighteen, Anza entered the military. He protected settlers against hostile Indian attacks.

Anza was a person of high character and unusual abilities. Dignified with a generous spirit, he was always kind and just to his men. When he was captain of the *presidio* at Tubac, many people came to live there. They were attracted by his justice and fairness.

The dream of finding an overland route to California began with Anza's father. Twice Anza asked the authorities for permission to search for this route. Finally he approached Viceroy Bucareli, offering to pay all costs of the expedition except for the wages of the men. He knew he would be rewarded if he was successful. In September 1773, he received permission to make his expedition.

At the conclusion of the successful expedition, Anza was promoted to Lieutenant Colonel. Each of his men was given extra pay for life. Anza returned to New Spain and continued to serve his country. He later served with honor as the governor of New Mexico.

Chapter 8

# The End of Spanish Expansion

After the San Francisco settlements were built, there was little chance that the colonies would have to be abandoned. The needed settlers had arrived to stay. They brought all of the livestock they would need.

Although California could no longer be easily conquered by a foreign nation, such as England or France, it was not God's plan for it to become a powerful settlement. Viceroy Bucareli planned to send more colonists along the Anza trail. He also planned to build missions along the Colorado River for the Yumas. He was not able to carry out these plans.

Spanish expansion ended twelve years after the Sacred Expedition when a new Spanish ruler received control of California. Viceroy Bucareli continued to govern the more established area of Mexico and Baja California, but Teodoro de Croix received the frontier, including what is now California, New Mexico, and Texas. Although Croix was commanded to visit California as soon as possible, he never did. He paid attention to other areas, especially Texas, and ignored California. Bucareli continued to send the supply ships to California but could do nothing else.

## The Yuma Massacre

VICEROY BUCARELI RECOGNIZED THAT TO KEEP THE ANZA ROUTE open, he would have to make friends with the Yuma Indians. Their help would be necessary for settlers to cross the Colorado River. Anza wrote in his official diary: "On another occasion I have said that if the peoples who dwell along this great river are attached to us we shall effect its passage [be able to cross it] without excessive labor, and that if they are not, it will be almost impossible to do so."

The Yumas asked for a mission. Viceroy Bucareli understood that one should be built quickly. Before he could act, Croix obtained control of the area and changed Bucareli's plans. He finally agreed to build two colonies on the Colorado River but very different from any other

Spanish settlements. To save money, they were a combination of pueblo, mission, and presidio. Trouble began almost at once. The settlers did not bring many presents for the Yumas. Their cattle ruined the crops. When the settlers' provisions were gone, the Yumas charged very high prices for new supplies. Soon the Yuma chiefs began to plot against the colonists. Even Chief Palma joined them.

Father Garcés tried to convert the Yuma Indians to Catholicism. They murdered him.

Meanwhile, Croix had asked Captain Rivera to recruit settlers for a new California pueblo at Los Angeles. Captain Rivera was best qualified for this job. He had led the first land expedition to California with Governor Portolá and later had served as its second governor. Rivera was ordered to find 58 families as well as 25 unmarried soldiers. The settlers would receive land in California, a salary for three years, clothing, food, tools, and equipment for the journey, plus a generous amount of livestock. They would repay this advance out of future earnings.

Soldiers and their families agreed to go to California. But in spite of this generous loan from the government, it was difficult to find civilian families willing to make the journey. After several months of trying, Rivera gave up, even though he was thirteen families short of his goal. In 1781, he began the journey to California over the Anza trail.

When the expedition reached the Colorado River in June, there were more problems with the Yumas. Captain Rivera did not bring gifts, and his cattle destroyed more of the Yumas' crops. The Yumas became very angry. After crossing the Colorado River, Captain Rivera divided his party in two. He sent all of the families and most of the animals on to the San Gabriel Mission. This action saved their lives. He and the unmarried men stayed to rest the remainder of the animals by the river.

The Yumas chose this moment to drive the Spaniards from their land. They destroyed the two Spanish colonies that Croix had built, killed all of the men, and took the women and children captive. They killed Father Garcés two days later. Next, the Yumas crossed the Colorado River and murdered every man in Rivera's expedition, including the captain.

This was the worst disaster to ever occur on the Spanish frontier. Later the women and children who had lived at the settlement at the Yuma village were ransomed and returned to New Spain.

Croix tried to blame Anza for the massacre. He said Anza lied about the trail being safe. Anza, however, had warned the viceroy that the trail could not be used unless the Yumas were friends. Croix had acted too slowly in his attempts to befriend the Yumas. After this, the Anza trail was closed. No more large colonization expeditions could be sent to California.

## Los Angeles Pueblo

THE MARRIED SOLDIERS AND SETTLERS OF CAPTAIN RIVERA'S expedition reached San Gabriel Mission safely. In September they founded the pueblo of Los Angeles. These settlers were not considered a blessing to the colony at first. They had been recruited from some of the poorest families on the frontier. None could read or write. The missionaries complained that they were lazy, but by 1800 Los Angeles's production was second only to San Gabriel Mission.

When we think of California during the Spanish period, we usually think of the beautiful adobe tiled missions with their stunning bell towers. However, these buildings were not built until much later. In 1786 a visitor from France drew this picture of the Carmel Mission. The missionaries, including Father Serra, lived in buildings like these.

## A Look Back

LOS ANGELES WAS THE LAST PUEBLO ESTABLISHED IN CALIFORNIA. Later, one would be attempted near Santa Cruz using convicts as colonists. It would fail.

The closing of the Anza trail by the Yuma massacre was a great blow to Spain's plans to colonize California. No new settlers or livestock could be sent overland to California. Small numbers could be sent by sea but only at great expense. Any real growth would have to come from within. California was strong enough to survive, but not strong enough to become a powerful colony. Population would grow slowly for the next 40 years while California remained a province of Spain.

Events show that God wanted California to be settled but not strong enough to become an independent nation. It was His plan that it eventually become a part of the United States of America.

### The United States of America

While the Spaniards colonized California, the United States of America was born. In 1765, the same year the Spaniards decided to send a colonizing expedition to California to save it from the Russians, Great Britain passed the Stamp Act, requiring the English colonists to put a stamp on all legal documents and newspapers. "No taxation without representation!" the angry colonists cried.

In 1769, the year the Sacred Expedition explored California, Daniel Boone explored Kentucky. The next year, 1770, saw Portolá build a *presidio* at Monterey and British soldiers fire on American colonists in the Boston Massacre. In 1775, Captain de Anza led 240 colonists to San Francisco, while Patrick Henry shouted, "Give me liberty or give me death!"

The English colonies declared their independence in 1776, and the presidio was built in San Francisco. By 1781 the fighting had ended on the east coast as the Americans won their independence from Great Britain. At the same time, many Spaniards lost their lives in the Yuma Massacre.

In less than 100 years, the paths of these two lands would be united forever.

Review Questions

# Unit 3 Roundup

## Chapter 6

1. The Spanish colonization method used the cross and the sword. Explain what these two symbols stood for.

2. Describe the Spanish system of colonization. Use the words *presidio*, *mission*, and *pueblo*.

3. Identify each of these men, and write two or three sentences describing what he did:

   Gaspar de Portolá — Junípero Serra

   Pedro Fages — Captain Rivera

4. Describe the difficulties the Spaniards faced to reach California.

5. **Thought Question:** Would you have wanted to be a member of the Sacred Expedition? Why or why not?

## Chapter 7

1. Identify each of these men, and write two or three sentences describing what he did:

   Juan Bautista de Anza — Viceroy Antonio Bucareli

Tarabel

Chief Salvador Palma

Father Garcés

Father Jayme

2. Why was it so important to find an overland route to California? Who found it?

3. Who was María Feliciana Gutierrez, and what happened to her?

4. **Thought Question**: Look back at Governor Portolá or Father Serra's letters. Pretend you traveled with Captain Anza and write a letter about your adventures.

## Chapter 8

1. What was the Yuma Massacre?

2. How was Los Angeles founded?

## Things to Ponder

Whenever people move from one area to another, they experience difficult adjustments. You might have experienced this. Think about the Spanish missionaries, such as Father Serra, who first left his family in Spain and then his friends in New Spain. He knew he might never see them again. Yet he did not travel to California for personal profit or gain. Think about the sacrifices the Spaniards made when they traveled to California. Would you make them? Why or why not? Collect your thoughts and write a short journal response.

Unit 4

# Spanish Days

The Great Commission

Go ye therefore, and teach all nations,
baptizing them in the name of the Father,
and of the Son, and of the Holy Ghost:
Teaching them to observe all things
whatsoever I have commanded you:
and, lo, I am with you alway,
even unto the end of the world.

Amen.

~~ Matthew 28:19-20

# The Spanish Period

IN ALL, CALIFORNIA REMAINED A territory of Spain for only 52 years. Yet the Spaniards accomplished much in those years. The missions were a very important part of Spain's plan to colonize the New World. Spain wanted citizens who would pay taxes and who would create goods to ship to Mexico and Spain. Above all, it wanted Catholic citizens.

Spanish missionaries came with the earliest explorers, beginning with the second voyage of Columbus. By the time Spain was ready to colonize California, it had over 300 years of experience to draw on. It had learned that the "mission system" was the best way to teach the Indians the Catholic faith as well as other arts of civilization, such as farming, herding, crafting, reading, and writing.

Unit Three briefly talked about the mission system the Spaniards developed to convert the Indians of New Spain to Catholicism. In some areas, such as Mexico City, the missionaries only had to teach the Indians the Catholic faith. But as they moved north to California, the missionaries found that compared with the Spanish way of life, the Indians had very low levels of culture. They realized that to make Spanish citizens, they must also teach the Indians how to farm, sew, blacksmith, and perform other arts, in addition to the fundamentals of Catholicism. In parts of Mexico, the process took about ten years. In California, however, it took much longer.

Since each mission eventually was supposed to become an Indian pueblo, or town, the location was selected carefully. The missionaries wanted the Indian towns to prosper. Each mission was built near a large Indian population. It had to have water for irrigation, good land for farming, and trees for building and firewood. The missions were the first settlements in California and were built on the best land.

In this unit we will learn how the missions thrived in California. We will learn about life on a mission and about the men who ran them. We will learn about some other aspects of Spanish life and about the attempt by the Russians to colonize California. Finally, we will learn how Spain lost its California colonies in the Spanish-American War for Independence.

At first the missions looked very similar to the Indian villages with buildings made of poles and tules, like this one at Carmel Mission. As the years went by, they were replaced with the adobe and tile buildings we can visit today.

Chapter 9

# California Missions

Many miles separated Spain and California. Many miles separated Mexico and California. At first, many miles also separated one mission from the next. If all went well, the missions could expect supplies from New Spain once or twice a year. There were no stores. The missionaries could not run down to the grocery store if they ran out of bread. Instead, they had to grow the wheat, harvest it, thresh it, store it, and when needed, mill it and bake it. The missionaries could not run down to the department store to buy a new set of clothes. They had to raise herds of sheep, shear them, wash the wool, card it, spin it, weave it, then sew a shirt or skirt.

Missions had to be more than training schools for the Indians. They had to be more than churches. They had to more than homes. The missions had to be entirely self-sufficient. That means they had to make everything the Indians needed to live—from clothes to food to dwellings. Everyone worked. Everyone needed to help with the day-to-day tasks.

No two missions looked exactly the same, but they shared some similarities—work areas, arched hallways, and a central patio. Of course each mission had a church, the most important building. Each church had a tower containing bells made in Spain. Bells rang to call people to meals and prayers.

The entire mission was surrounded by a large wall. Usually, Indian villages grew outside of the wall. Non-mission Indians, that is those who were not baptized, could live there and learn about life at the mission. Nearby, the Indians planted orchards of fruit trees and fields of wheat, barley, and other crops. They learned how to farm the land. Mission ranchos, or cattle ranches (called *rancherías*), were built a short distance from the missions so that sheep and cattle would not trample the fruit and vegetables.

The Indians learned many useful trades at the missions. Officials sent masons, potters, mill-makers, carpenters, and blacksmiths from New Spain to teach the Indians these trades. They learned so well that soon the missions became self-supporting.

# A Typical Mission Plan

San Juan Capistrano Mission, drawn before an earthquake destroyed the bell tower, displays some of the common features of most missions.

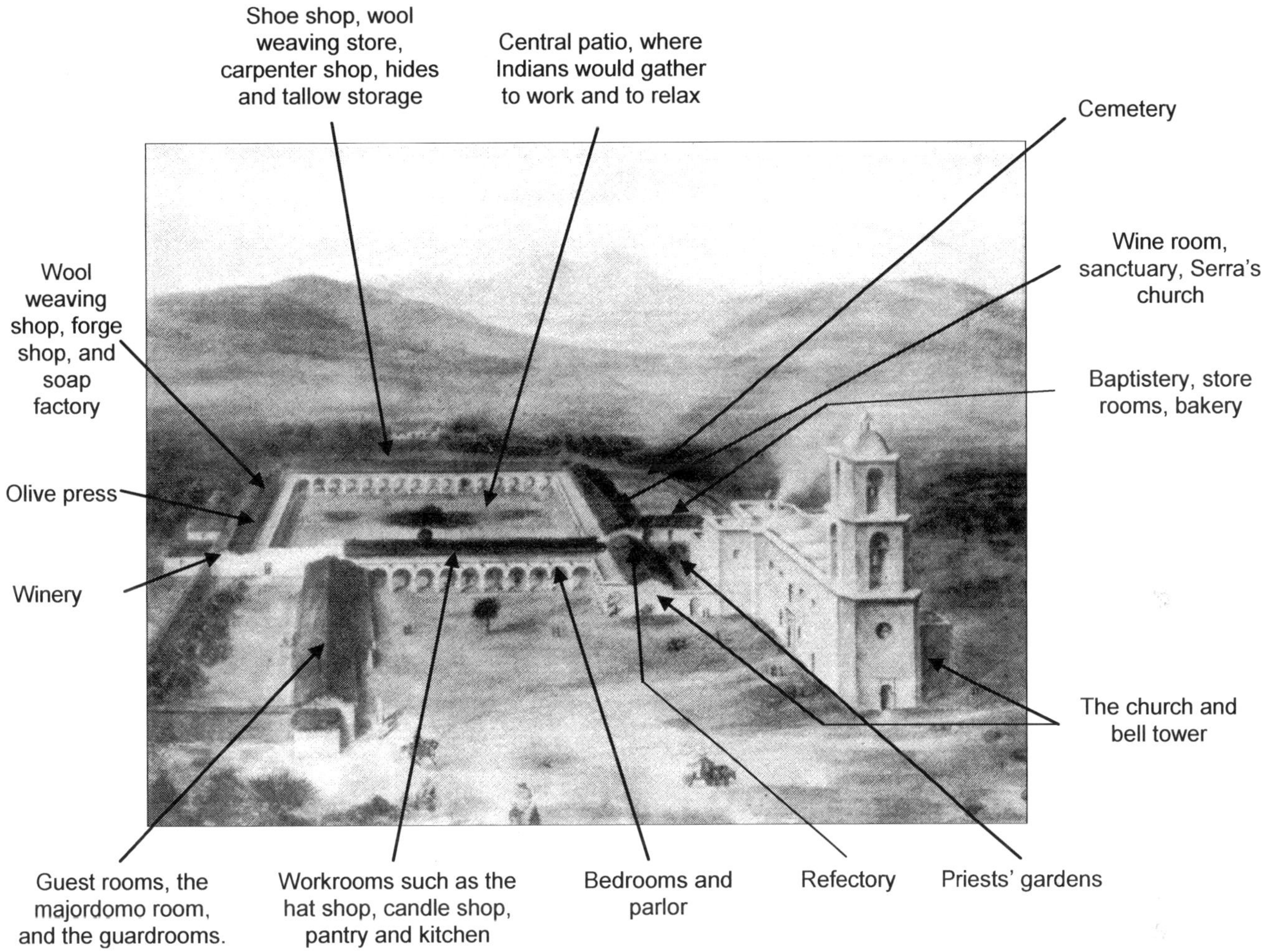

Shoe shop, wool weaving store, carpenter shop, hides and tallow storage

Central patio, where Indians would gather to work and to relax

Cemetery

Wool weaving shop, forge shop, and soap factory

Wine room, sanctuary, Serra's church

Baptistery, store rooms, bakery

Olive press

Winery

The church and bell tower

Guest rooms, the majordomo room, and the guardrooms.

Workrooms such as the hat shop, candle shop, pantry and kitchen

Bedrooms and parlor

Refectory

Priests' gardens

This early drawing of San Gabriel Mission also shows some of the common features missions shared, including the bell tower, orchards, storerooms, outbuildings, and Indian dwellings.

The missions bustled with activity as Mission Indians tended to the day's work.

## Life at the Missions

SINCE THE MISSIONS PRODUCED EVERYTHING THE PEOPLE NEEDED TO live, everyone worked everyday. Not only did the Indians learn useful skills, they also made life easier for others.

Typically, the Indians' day began at sunrise, and the church bells summoned them to morning prayers and Mass, a Catholic church service. At the same time, some of the women cooked big kettles of *atole* that would be ready for breakfast when the service ended. Atole was a mush or porridge made with barley. After prayers, one person from each family came for the family's portion. The thickest parts of the atole at the bottom of the kettle were the best. Children who could say their catechism, questions and answers about the Catholic faith, earned them as rewards.

After breakfast, the missionaries gave out work assignments, which varied depending on the time of year and what needed to be done. Some of the men might work in the fields or shops; others might weave clothing and blankets, work in the blacksmith shop, or make candles; some might tan hides, shear sheep, or care for the livestock. It took many hands to run a mission.

Married women with small children were excused from most of the labor so that they could care for their children. When girls turned about eleven, they went to live in the *monjerio*, a special apartment for girls. A *dueña*, an older woman, taught the girls needlework, their catechism, and other skills Spanish housewives needed to know. Other women worked in the mission kitchens and gardens preparing meals for the thousands of people who lived at the mission.

Indians receiving instruction. At the missions, the men wore cotton pants and the women tule skirts. Both wore colorful blankets around their shoulders, or in colder weather, animal skins.

At noon, the bells rang to announce dinner. Each family sent for their share of *pozole*. Pozole was a stew of ground wheat, corn, peas, beans, and water. After dinner everyone rested until 2 p.m.

From 2 p.m. until 4 or 5 p.m., the Indians completed their work if they had not already done so. Evening prayers followed another meal of atole. The rest of the evening was spent doing whatever the people desired—visiting, playing games, or relaxing. The Indians were allowed to continue any of their old customs as long as they did not conflict with the Catholic faith.

Sundays and festival days were for worship and rest. Meat was served on these special occasions, especially in later years when the missions contained large herds of cattle.

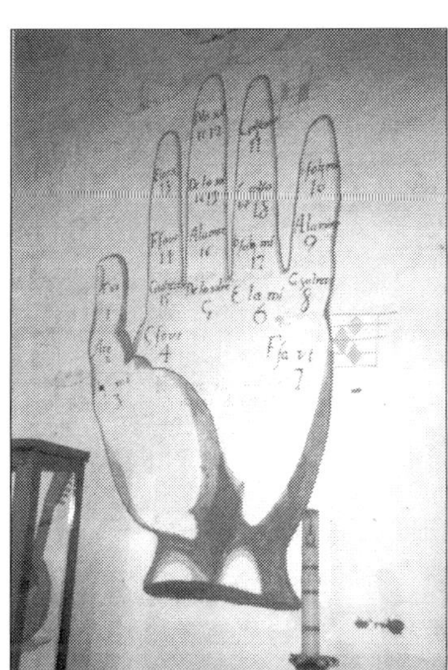

Many visitors to the California Missions commented on how much the Indians loved music. Indians learned to play stringed instruments, such as the violin and cello as well as flute, trumpet, guitar, and drums. Other Indians enjoyed singing. The missionaries thought up clever ways to teach the Indians to read music. In one method, shown in the music book from San Antonio Mission, each note was a different color. To sing harmony, the Indians followed his color. The fathers taught musical notation and scales using the hand painted on the wall of San Antonio.

# California's Mission Chain

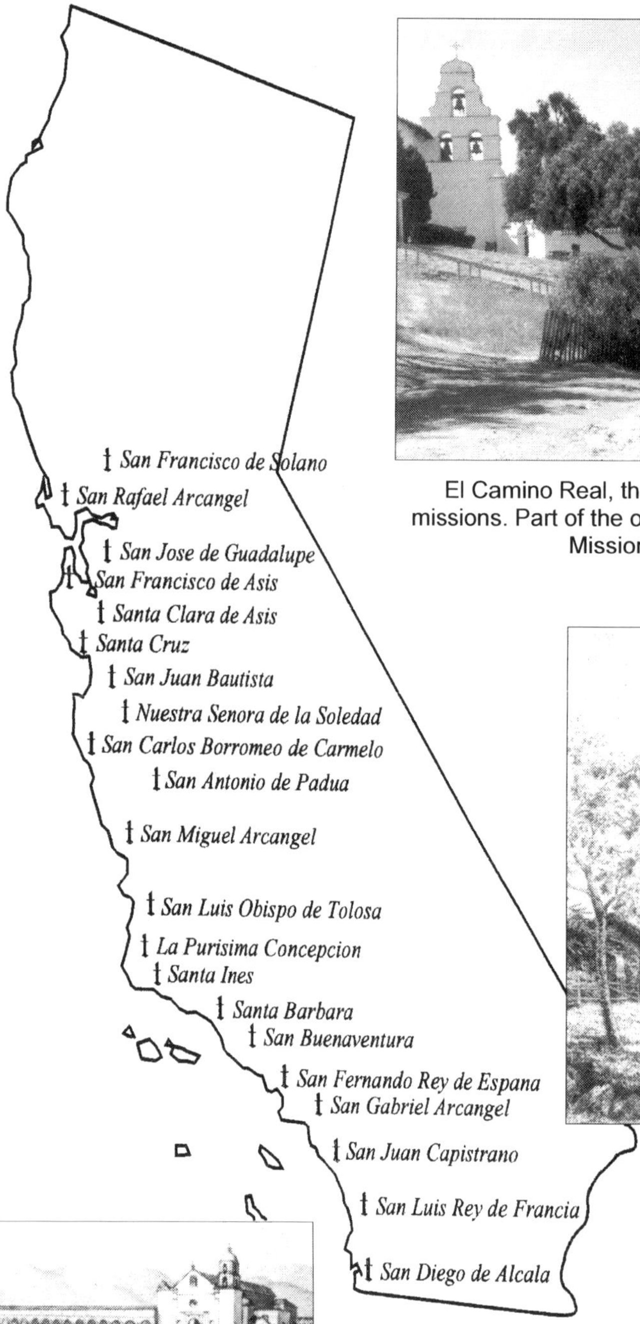

San Francisco de Solano
San Rafael Arcangel
San Jose de Guadalupe
San Francisco de Asis
Santa Clara de Asis
Santa Cruz
San Juan Bautista
Nuestra Senora de la Soledad
San Carlos Borromeo de Carmelo
San Antonio de Padua
San Miguel Arcangel
San Luis Obispo de Tolosa
La Purisima Concepcion
Santa Ines
Santa Barbara
San Buenaventura
San Fernando Rey de Espana
San Gabriel Arcangel
San Juan Capistrano
San Luis Rey de Francia
San Diego de Alcala

El Camino Real, the King's highway, connected the missions. Part of the original road can still be seen behind Mission San Juan Bautista.

Santa Barbara Mission

Mission San Luis Rey

## Leading an Indian to Catholic Faith

AFTER A MISSION WAS BUILT, THE MISSIONARIES TRIED TO PERSUADE the Indians to live there. The Fathers used gifts of beads, trinkets, food, or clothing to attract the Indians. They called these items "the bait and means of spiritual fishing." Once the Indians came to the mission, they were taught the Catholic faith.

By Spanish law, missionaries were supposed to teach the Indians in their own language. This was difficult. First, the Indian's language did not have words to explain concepts like "resurrection," "sin," or "redemption." Second, the Indians at one mission might speak several different languages.

Indians could stay at the missions for several months while they learned the teachings of the Catholic faith. They saw the kind of work the Mission Indians performed. They knew how they would have to live if they decided to stay. When an Indian could demonstrate to the Fathers that his conversion to Catholicism was true, he could ask to be baptized. Baptism was a very important step. Baptized Indians were not allowed to leave the mission without permission from the Fathers. If they ran away, they would be followed and brought back. Once an Indian made a promise to live at the mission, he was not considered free to break it.

After baptism, the Indians were instructed each day. The Fathers illustrated their teaching with songs, pictures, and simple plays. When an Indian was grounded in these teachings, he was allowed to take vacations. If he visited his old village, he tried to persuade his friends to come back to the mission with him. Many Indians followed their friends back to the missions. Mature Catholic Indians were allowed to take communion once they showed they could understand what it meant.

At first, very few Indians were baptized. Not one Indian was baptized for a full year after San Diego Mission was founded. In later years, thousands of Indians asked to be baptized.

This picture shows the first baptism at San Diego Mission.

Chapter 10

# A Closer Look at the Missions

Two missionaries lived at each mission to teach the Indians. These missionaries were well educated. They had left all of the comforts of civilization to live on the frontier. As Franciscan missionaries, they had taken a vow of poverty. They had very few belongings. All of their efforts were directed at making life better for the Indians.

Captain George Vancouver of England, a Protestant, visited California between 1792 and 1794. He told a story that shows how much the Indians loved the Fathers. When Captain Vancouver was at Santa Barbara, he offered the visiting missionary from San Buenaventura passage back to the mission on his ship. The Father gladly accepted. He ordered his Indian servants to return to San Buenaventura with the horses and mules while he went back by sea.

The Indians would not hear of this. They feared for his safety and thought he would perish at sea. They begged him not to go. The missionary prevailed, went with Captain Vancouver, and arrived safely at San Buenaventura. As the party entered the mission, a crowd of Mission Indians greeted them with shouts and excitement. Captain Vancouver thought they were welcoming the foreigners, but they had come to welcome the return of their priest. They greeted him as one who returned from the dead. Captain Vancouver was impressed with this show of love.

Father Duran lived at Mission San José for 27 years. He was fond of music and formed an Indian choir.

## Fermin de Lasuén

FATHER LASUÉN (LA-SOO-EN) WAS THE SECOND PRESIDENT OF THE California missions after Father Serra died in 1783. Father Lasuén became a Franciscan when he was about sixteen. He served at a mission located the farthest north on the Baja Peninsula. Under his administration it became the most prosperous of all fourteen Baja California missions.

Normally two missionaries were assigned to each mission. However, Father Lasuén served in Baja California for five years by himself. Because this hard experience made such an impression on him, when he became president of the California missions, he insisted no missionary should serve alone.

In 1773, when Lasuén was 37, he took over the administration of San Gabriel Mission. He arrived in California during the great famine. Yet by the end of his two-year stay, San Gabriel had become the most prosperous of the California missions. Lasuén was at San Gabriel when Captain de Anza's exploration party arrived in 1774.

After the revolt at San Diego, when Father Jayme was killed, Father Lasuén was assigned to San Diego. He was chosen because he was the most capable of all the missionaries and San Diego was a very important mission. There were no more problems during his stay.

Father Lasuén was 66 years old when he became president of the missions. He served for 18 years. He founded nine new missions and confirmed 9,000 people. He replaced the rude mission buildings of tule and mud with the beautiful tiled adobe buildings we enjoy today. He convinced the authorities to send expert craftsmen from New Spain to teach the Indians.

Lasuén was a gentle, kind man with a firm will. He worked well with everyone, especially the military governors. He died at San Carlos Mission after a short illness. He was 83. His long life was spent in service to his church.

When Father Lasuen oversaw the rebuilding of the California missions, he asked for craftsmen to teach the Indians. They built highly decorated altars like this one at San José Mission. The pillars look like they are marble, but they are really painted wood. Many of the objects in the church came from Spain. Others were created by the California Indians.

# Were the Missions Good?

SOME PEOPLE WONDER WHETHER THE SPANISH MISSIONS WERE GOOD for the California Indians. They wonder if the Indians might have been better off if the Spaniards had never come to California. Yes, the missions were good for the Indians, even though they had their problems.

One major tragedy was the many deaths caused by European diseases. The Indian culture did not have these diseases, and the Indians' bodies could not fight them. In only three months in 1806, one fourth of the Indians living at San Francisco Mission died of measles. Small pox killed hundreds as well. Another health problem arose because so many Indians lived together in the mission—sometimes thousands. Germ theory, the idea that germs cause disease, was not known, and illness spread quickly in the missions. As they learned, the Spanish missionaries did what they could, including vaccinating the Indians, teaching them cleanliness, and moving the missions to healthier areas.

There is no question that the Spanish missions completely changed the Indians' culture. That was the missionaries' goal. They wanted the Indians to become Catholics. They believed the Indians practiced idolatry, and they wanted to save the Indians' souls. In Spain, there was no freedom of religion and no separation between the church and the state. Teaching the Indians Catholicism was part of teaching the Indians to lead a civilized life. Spain spent an enormous amount of money building the California missions to give the Indians a better life.

Photograph by Robert A. Estremo, copyright 2005.

The paternalistic or fatherly attitude of the Spanish missionaries is demonstrated in this statue of Father Serra and an Indian child at San Juan Capistrano Mission.

Spanish society was very paternal. That means that the king acted as a father and treated his subjects as children. Many times Spaniards could not make their own decisions without permission from the king or his representatives—even permission to marry. The California missions were very paternal as well. The Spanish Fathers thought of themselves as actual fathers, looking out for the welfare of their Indian children. They argued that they had to do this to teach the Indians. Unfortunately, it created a dependency—Indians did not learn to think for themselves or learn to make their own decisions. Instead, they relied on the guidance of the Fathers. When the missions closed in the Mexican period and the Fathers left, the Indians had a very difficult time adjusting.

The missions were not perfect—far from it. But even with all of their shortcomings, they did much good in California. The Spanish colonization method was one of most humane in all the world at the time. Other systems pushed the Indians away, but the Spaniards tried to absorb the Indians into their society and make them citizens. Other systems turned the people into slaves, but the Indians at the missions were not slaves. It is true that once they made a commitment to stay, they could not leave without permission, but this permission was easily obtained. It is also true that they had to work at the missions, but everyone had to work to survive. Most of the Indians were happy at the missions. It was inevitable that colonists would come to California. The Indians were fortunate that the Spaniards came first and taught them how to live in the new culture.

The Spanish missions greatly improved the Indians' standard of living. They learned to plant crops and raise cattle rather than rely on hunting and what grew wild. Instead of starving in the winter, the Indians had food year-round. When drought occurred, they could still eat. They learned to use carts and horses to carry heavy loads rather than burden baskets. They learned to use steel tools. This freed them from very hard work. The California Indians gained more food, more comfortable homes, and more substantial clothing.

The missions also provided safety for the Indians who lived at them. In the Indian villages, groups often fought with one another for food, for firewood, or for water. Small parties, especially women and children, were particularly helpless. They received protection at the missions.

The biggest problem with the missions is that they did not have enough time to complete their work. Mexico did not treat the Indians well when it took over California. Under the Spaniards, the Indians profited. With more time, they would have benefited even more.

Imagine a life with no beds. Beds are a simple example of the ways the Indians benefited from the missions, especially older people. Instead of sleeping on the cold, damp, hard ground, they could sleep in a comfortable bed and wake refreshed. Many of the Spanish ideas improved life for the Indians.

# Mission Indians

UNFORTUNATELY, VERY FEW STORIES OF INDIVIDUAL MISSION INDIANS survive. The Spanish missionaries did not keep good records. They recorded births, baptisms, confirmations, and deaths, but they had little time to record individual stories. Thankfully, we do know some.

## Pablo Tac

Pablo Tac was an Indian born at San Luis Rey Mission in 1822. He was very diligent in his studies at the mission school. In 1832, Father Antonio Peyri chose him to go to Spain to further his studies. Pablo Tac describes life among his tribe, the Luisenos, before the Spaniards came to California. He says there was constant war and strife with the neighboring Dieguenos. Men, women, and children were killed as they were sleeping. The villages were burned. He writes

Pablo Tac drew this simple drawing of two men in Indian dress.

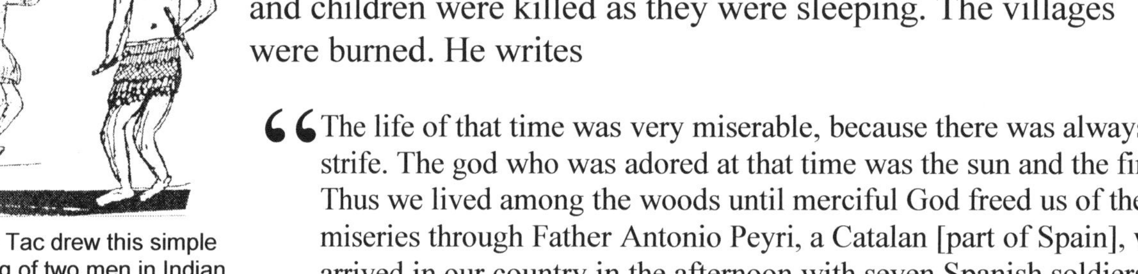

“The life of that time was very miserable, because there was always strife. The god who was adored at that time was the sun and the fire. Thus we lived among the woods until merciful God freed us of these miseries through Father Antonio Peyri, a Catalan [part of Spain], who arrived in our country in the afternoon with seven Spanish soldiers.”

Tac goes on to describe the scene surrounding the Spaniards' arrival. They could not understand each other and had to communicate with signs. The Spaniards gave the Indians gifts and encouraged them to stay. Tac calls that time a "happy day." He says, "O Merciful God, why didst Thou leave us for many centuries, years, months, and days in utter darkness after Thou camest to the world? Blessed be Thou from this day through future centuries."

## Pasquala of Santa Ines

A plaque at Santa Ines Mission tells the story of Pasquala: "On Saturday afternoon Feb. 21, 1824, a senseless and destructive raid was made on this Mission… We are told that a young Indian girl, Pasquala, warned the priest in charge, Padre Francisco Xavier in time...and thus saved Santa Ines Mission from being wiped out...Pasquala's people were of the Tulare Country. Often she had stopped with her kinsfolk at this Mission on their annual journey to the coast for shells and fish. On one of these journeys she became very ill and was cared for at the Mission until she was cured. Pasquala and her family were so grateful that they became Christians. Her father was working in the Mission vineyard when some of his own tribe killed him and carried the girl and her mother back to the Tulares... The mother died four years later. One day little Pasquala heard that the Tulares were about to attack her beloved Mission. That night, she made good her escape and ran while praying to reach Santa Ines... After several tortuous days she staggered into the Mission...

PADRE—PADRE—WAR—WAR

Padre Francisco had been a soldier before he became a missionary. He helped set up the Mission defenses. When the Tularenes appeared with their bows and arrows they set fire to the buildings here at the rear of the church. They were repulsed and fled. The Mission Church was saved.

But Pasquala's act cost her life, for she soon died of a fever contracted when making her escape. It is said that she is buried in the Mission Church."

## Toypurina

Toypurina lived in a village near San Gabriel Mission. She was a sorceress or a medicine woman. In 1785, when she was 24, an Indian asked her to help him destroy the mission. She agreed. On the night of the attack, she told the warriors she had used her powers to kill the missionaries and it was safe to strike. However, the missionaries were very much alive. They leapt up and captured her and the men. They were put on trial.

In the middle of her trial, Toypurina had a change of heart. She asked to become a Christian. In a great act of mercy, Father Miguel Sanchez, the man she tried to kill, baptized her. He gave her a new name: Regina Josepha. To protect her from the anger of the captured warriors, he sent her to Carmel Mission in the north—the one farthest away from San Gabriel.

Toypurina lived at the mission for two years and then married a soldier named Manuel Montero. They had three children. She lived peacefully with her new Catholic faith for fourteen years until she died in 1799 at San Juan Bautista Mission.

### The Lost Woman

In November of 1835, missionaries at the Santa Barbara mission tried to save the last of the Indians living on San Nicolas Island. A storm blew in, and the ship had to leave quickly before it was dashed to pieces on the rocks. Unfortunately, one woman could not be found and had to be left behind. Even more tragic, after bringing the Indians to San Gabriel Mission, the ship sank and could not return for the woman.

In 1850, Father Gonzales heard about the lost woman and paid a man $200 (about $4,500 today) to find her. He could not. Finally after 18 years, a Santa Barbara fur trapper named George Nidever took up the challenge.

His first two attempts to find the lost woman failed, but on the third try he found her, rescued her, and brought her to Santa Barbara Mission.

Although she could not communicate with any of the other Indians, she loved the mission, the horses, and the food. Tragically, she died of dysentery just a few short weeks after her rescue. Her cormorant skirt, bone tools, and water basket burned in the San Francisco earthquake and fire of 1906. A plaque at the Santa Barbara Mission recalls her short visit.

Chapter 11

# California's First Lady

The first twelve years of Spanish rule in California were exciting, difficult years. The next 40 were more peaceful. As the missions grew, four presidios were built at California's best harbors. Spain sent men to govern the territory and soldiers to keep order. In 1782 Pedro Fages (FAH-hayes), who had served as California's second governor, was re-appointed to be California's fifth governor.

Governor Fages was a hot-tempered, but lovable, man. Sometimes called the Stormy Catalan, he was brave, energetic, and devoted to children. He carried sweets for them in his pockets. Self-educated and intelligent, Governor Fages married Doña Eulalia de Callis (Ay-oo-LA-lee-a Day Ca-YEES), the daughter of one of his upper-class friends. At the time of his marriage, he was older than his wife's mother.

After arriving in California, Fages made preparations for Doña Eulalia and their infant son to join him. She must have the very best house that California could provide, so Fages built the Governor's Mansion. This house was hardly a mansion by today's standards, but it was the best Monterey had to offer at the time. Like the other homes, it was made of adobe with a tile roof. The windows did not contain glass, since that was expensive and hard to find, but the floor was wooden instead of hard-packed earth. Fages planted an orchard, grapevines, and a vegetable garden. He filled the mansion with treasures: religious images, embroidered bedcovers, rugs, fine dishes, and silver. He designed the furniture himself and taught Indians how to construct it.

When the home was completed, Governor Fages asked Doña Eulalia to join him in California. At first, his wife refused to leave the comfort of her regal home and her many servants. Her mother, however, persuaded her that her duty was to be at her husband's side.

Doña Eulalia had to ride 2,000 miles from Loreto in Baja California to reach Monterey. Since she was the first lady of status to visit California, the people tried to make her feel welcome. They greeted her at each town with festivities, just like a royal procession. Instead of enjoying the trip however, she found the dry, dusty land and the broiling sun unbearable. After she had given a good part of her wardrobe to clothe the Indians, Governor Fages told her there was no way to replace them. What? No dressmakers in Monterey? What kind of place was she going to? It was pouring rain when the family finally arrived at Monterey. Doña Eulalia ruined her irreplacable chicken skin boots in the mud. When she saw the Governor's Mansion, she was appalled. She did not think it a fitting home for California's First Lady.

Doña Eulalia was never happy with life in California and looked for every opportunity to leave. Once when Fages had to go south on business, he asked the missionaries to look after his wife. She locked herself in her room. Governor Fages, out of patience, returned and forced his wife to obey the Franciscans. But she made him pay for this victory. She threw tantrums at the mission, even in church. It was a huge scandal in peaceful California.

Governor Fages finally grew tired of his wife's complaining about life in California. He asked to be relieved of his command so that they could visit Spain. When permission was granted, Doña Eulalia and her children immediately departed from California. Governor Fages waited for his replacement; then he joined her.

After seven long years, California said good bye to the Stormy Catalan and his even stormier wife. He had been one of California's best governors, who sacrificed his career in his love for his wife.

In 1788 the Spanish King ordered Alessandro Malaspina to visit the Spanish colonies in New Spain, explore, and look for the Strait of Anián. The expedition visited Monterey Presidio in 1791, where the artist of the expedition, José Cardero, drew this picture. Although the Fages had already left California a few years earlier, it shows what Monterey looked like when Doña Eulaliia lived there with Governor Fages.

Chapter 12

# Russians in California

Russian fur traders had discovered many sea otters in the waters near the coast of Alaska. They trapped them and sold the pelts in China, where they were very valuable. Chinese royalty used the fur to make robes and capes and to trim silk gowns. The Russians built a colony at Sitka, Alaska, to hunt sea otters and ship them to China.

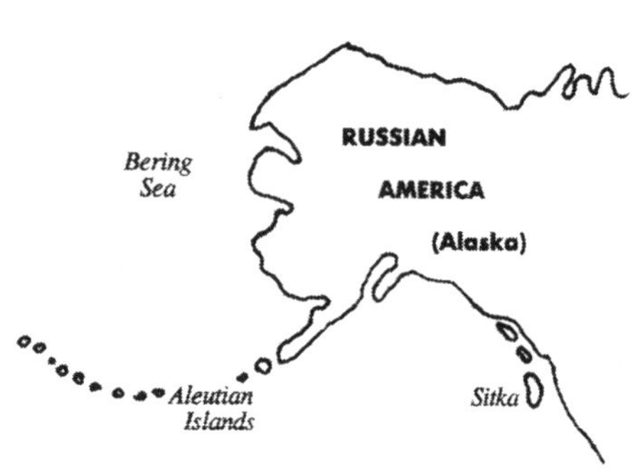


In 1805, Nickolai Rezanov, (NEE-koe-lie REZ-an-off) an ambassador from Russia, traveled to inspect the colony at Sitka. It was in very poor condition. Men were starving. They were eating anything to survive, even eagles and crows. Rezanov bought some food from an American ship, but this would not last long. He decided to travel to San Francisco to try to buy food from the Californians. Rezanov knew that the Californians were not allowed to trade with foreign countries, but his men were starving. He would have to try.

When Rezanov sailed into San Francisco Bay, 15 Californians mounted on horses with silver harnesses rode from the presidio to greet him. They thought Rezanov was on a scientific expedition. Rezanov could not reveal his real mission, but he could not stop thinking of his comrades starving in Alaska.

For several days Rezanov and his men enjoyed California's famous hospitality. Since no one could speak both Spanish and Russian, communication was a problem. Rezanov spoke Russian to the ship's doctor. The doctor translated the message into Latin and spoke with a missionary. The missionary translated the message into Spanish for the benefit of the Californians. When the subject of trade came up, Rezanov was informed that the Californians could not trade with any foreign country. They could sell their goods

Sea otter pelts were valuable.

to Spain only. Rezanov, growing desperate, tried arguing and flattery, but he could not persuade the honest governor to break the law.

Count Rezanov

Rezanov was a 38-year-old widower with two children in Russia. His wife had died a year before he went to Alaska. As the days of Rezanov's stay turned into weeks, he turned his attention to the Commandant's beautiful 15-year-old daughter, Doña Concepción Arguello (Kone-sep-see-OWN Are-GWAY-yo). He learned Spanish quickly and told her of the beauty of the Russian courts. After many visits, the two fell in love. When Rezanov proposed marriage, Doña Concepción, called Concha, quickly accepted.

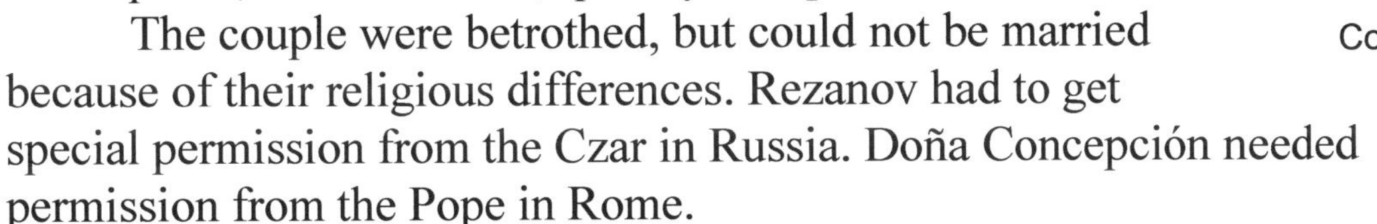

The couple were betrothed, but could not be married because of their religious differences. Rezanov had to get special permission from the Czar in Russia. Doña Concepción needed permission from the Pope in Rome.

After the betrothal, the Californians' attitude towards Rezanov changed. He was no longer a foreigner; he was a member of the family. The law prohibiting trade with foreigners no longer applied. Filling his ship with great quantities of food, he quickly left California to return to the starving colonists at Sitka. He planned to travel to Russia and then Rome to obtain permission to marry Doña Concepción. The fur-trading colony at Sitka was very glad to receive the grain, herring, fruits, and vegetables from California. The starving, scurvy-stricken men quickly returned to health.

When Rezanov left California he had two ideas: to get permission for regular trade with California and to build a Russian colony on the California coast. If Rezanov had been successful, California could have become a Russian country instead of part of the United States. God, in His providence, had other plans.

Doña Concepción waited five lonely years for her betrothed to return. Finally, she learned that his journey had ended in tragedy. Count Rezanov had died. He fell from his horse during his winter journey through Siberia. His last words were of his beloved. He made a young officer promise to return a locket, which had been a farewell gift, and tell her how he died. The young officer kept his promise.

Doña Concepción never married although she had many offers. She cared for others for the rest of her life. She was known for her acts of kindness to families all along the California coast. When she was 51, she entered California's first convent and became a nun. She lived a long life and is buried in Benicia.

## Concepcion de Arguello

By Brett Harte

*Bret Harte came to California in 1854. He wrote many poems and stories about California life, including one about the love shared by Concepcion and Rezanov (Resanoff). This excerpt talks about Concha's long, lonely wait for her betrothed.*

Long beside the deep embrasures, where the brazen cannon are,
Did they wait the promised bridegroom and the answer of the Czar;

Day by day on wall and bastion beat the hollow, empty breeze,—
Day by day the sunlight glittered on the vacant, smiling seas:

Week by week the near hills whitened in their dusty leather cloaks,—
Week by week the far hills darkened from the fringing plain of oaks;

Till the rains came, and far breaking, on the fierce southwester tost,
Dashed the whole long coast with color, and then vanished and were lost.

So each year the seasons shifted,—wet and warm and drear and dry
Half a year of clouds and flowers, half a year of dust and sky.

Still it brought no ship nor message,—brought no tidings, ill or meet,
For the statesmanlike Commander, for the daughter fair and sweet.

Yet she heard the varying message, voiceless to all ears beside:
"He will come," the flowers whispered; "Come no more," the dry hills sighed.

Still she found him with the waters lifted by the morning breeze,—
Still she lost him with the folding of the great white-tented seas;

Until hollows chased the dimples from her cheeks of olive brown,
And at times a swift, shy moisture dragged the long sweet lashes down;

Or the small mouth curved and quivered as for some denied caress,
And the fair young brow was knitted in an infantine distress.

Then the grim Commander, pacing where the brazen cannon are,
Comforted the maid with proverbs, wisdom gathered from afar;

Bits of ancient observation by his fathers garnered, each
As a pebble worn and polished in the current of his speech:

"'Those who wait the coming rider travel twice as far as he;'
'Tired wench and coming butter never did in time agree;'

"'He that getteth himself honey, though a clown, he shall have flies;'
'In the end God grinds the miller;' 'In the dark the mole has eyes;'

"'He whose father is Alcalde of his trial hath no fear,'—
And be sure the Count has reasons that will make his conduct clear."

Then the voice sententious faltered, and the wisdom it would teach
Lost itself in fondest trifles of his soft Castilian speech;

And on "Concha" "Conchitita," and "Conchita" he would dwell

## Fort Ross

SIX YEARS AFTER REZANOV'S visit, the Russians built a fur-trading colony in California eighteen miles north of Bodega Bay. They called it Fort Ross. It was very well fortified and much smaller than the colony Rezanov had planned. Twenty-five to fifty Russian men lived there with an additional 50 to 100 Aleuts, natives of Alaska. A few women also lived at Fort Ross. They were wives of some of the officers or soldiers.

When the Spaniards heard of the settlement, they were very upset. They argued that Russia had broken a treaty that declared that the land belonged to Spain. The argument continued for years.

While officials in Spain and Russia argued, the Californians and Russians at Fort Ross remained friendly. In 1821, the Russians sent a vaccine to Monterey to help fight a deadly disease. In 1823, when the

mission at Sonoma was founded, the Russians sent several ornaments as gifts for the church.

The settlement at Fort Ross was never very profitable for the Russians. When the sea otters began to decline, the colonists tried to farm, but the land around Fort Ross was not very fertile, the Russians were poor farmers, and the fog caused the grain to spoil. Finally, after pressure from the United States, the Russians abandoned their settlement, sold their equipment, and returned to Alaska.

A part of Fort Ross, located near present-day Jenner, has been reconstructed and turned into a state park. It is especially fun to visit during a living history day when men dress up as Russian soldiers and fire their muskets. Other special activities might include a performance by a Russian men's chorus.

With the fond reiteration which the Spaniard knows so well.

So with proverbs and caresses, half in faith and half in doubt,
Every day some hope was kindled, flickered, faded, and went out.

Yearly, down the hillside sweeping, came the stately cavalcade,
Bringing revel to vaquero, joy and comfort to each maid;

Bringing days of formal visit, social feast and rustic sport,
Of bull-baiting on the plaza, of love-making in the court.

Vainly then at Concha's lattice, vainly as the idle wind,
Rose the thin high Spanish tenor that bespoke the youth too kind;

Vainly, leaning from their saddles, caballeros, bold and fleet,
Plucked for her the buried chicken from beneath their mustang's feet;

So in vain the barren hillsides with their gay serapes blazed,—
Blazed and vanished in the dust-cloud that their flying hoofs had raised.

Then the drum called from the rampart, and once more, with patient mien,
The Commander and his daughter each took up the dull routine,—

Each took up the petty duties of a life apart and lone,
Till the slow years wrought a music in its dreary monotone.

* * *

V

Forty years on wall and bastion swept the hollow idle breeze,
Since the Russian eagle fluttered from the California seas;

Forty years on wall and bastion wrought its slow but sure decay,
And St. George's cross was lifted in the port of Monterey;

And the citadel was lighted, and the hall was gayly drest,
All to honor Sir George Simpson, famous traveler and guest.

Far and near the people gathered to the costly banquet set,
And exchanged congratulations with the English baronet;

Till, the formal speeches ended, and amidst the laugh and wine,
Some one spoke of Concha's lover,—heedless of the warning sign.

Quickly then cried Sir George Simpson: "Speak no ill of him, I pray!
He is dead. He died, poor fellow, forty years ago this day,—

"Died while speeding home to Russia, falling from a fractious horse.
Left a sweetheart, too, they tell me. Married, I suppose, of course!

"Lives she yet?" A deathlike silence fell on banquet, guests, and hall,
And a trembling figure rising fixed the awestruck gaze of all.

Two black eyes in darkened orbits gleamed beneath the nun's white hood;
Black serge hid the wasted figure, bowed and stricken where it stood.

"Lives she yet?" Sir George repeated. All were hushed as Concha drew
Closer yet her nun's attire. "Senor, pardon, she died, too!"

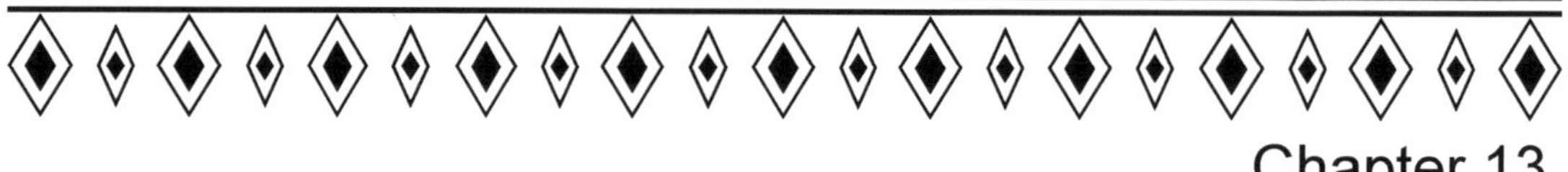

Chapter 13

# Spanish-American Wars

In 1810, Mexico, along with most of the other Spanish colonies, revolted against Spanish rule. At first the rebellion was small, but the fighting grew and continued for twelve years. California remained loyal to Spain. Although not directly involved in the war, it suffered. The supply ships stopped coming, causing a shortage of manufactured goods. This was a severe hardship for the families at the presidios. The missions offered to help the soldiers and supplied them with food and clothing for many years so they would not starve.

In 1818, California heard that some South American privateers with a letter of marque (the Californians called them pirates) had sailed from the Sandwich Islands (Hawaii) to attack California as an act of war. California's Governor Sola ordered the people to prepare for the attack. Valuables were buried and people prepared to escape. Lookouts watched for ships along the coast.

One month later, two privateer ships with hundreds of men entered Monterey Bay. General Hippolyte de Bouchard (Hee-poe-LEE-tay day Boo-SHARD), the commander, sent notice to the governor that the king of Spain had declared war on the Spanish colonies. If California remained loyal to Spain, it would be attacked. Governor Sola replied that the king had declared war on the rebels, not on all of the colonies. California would remain loyal to its king. The privateers returned to their ships. Governor Sola prepared his fifty-five soldiers to fight. He ordered families to flee to safety.

During the battle that followed, one privateer ship was badly damaged by the guns of the presidio. When the men actually landed, Governor Sola ordered his small force to retreat.

There was little of value left in Monterey. The privateers took what they found, repaired their ship, and set fire to the presidio. When Governor Sola returned with over 200 soldiers and many Indians, he saw the retreating ships as their sails disappeared over the horizon.

Bouchard sailed south and attacked the home of the Ortega family above Santa Barbara. (Captain Ortega was the scout of the Sacred Expedition and the first white man to see San Francisco Bay.) No one

General Bouchard

was injured in the attack, but several buildings were burned. Bouchard appeared again at Santa Barbara, San Pedro (near Los Angeles), and San Juan Capistrano. By this time the California forces were ready for him, and he did little further damage.

The presidio at Monterey was rebuilt and improved. No more war ships appeared on California's coast. Nor was California involved in any other part of the Spanish-American Wars for Independence.

After Bouchard and his men left, the Californians discovered one of his crew who had deserted. The young American named Joseph Chapman was kidnapped by Bouchard's men in the Sandwich Islands (Hawaii). This young man quickly became a favorite. There was very little he could not make or repair. He built several flour mills, a church, and a small boat so that the missionaries at San Gabriel could hunt sea otters. He also taught the Spaniards how to fell a tree, splint broken bones, pull teeth, make farm equipment, and make soap.

Chapman married one of the daughters of Captain Ortega, whose home he had helped Bouchard attack. They had five children. He was the first American to live in Southern California.

## The End of Spanish Rule

MUCH WAS ACCOMPLISHED DURING THE 52 years that Spain ruled in California. Presidios had been built at each of the best harbors (San Diego, Santa Barbara, Monterey, and San Francisco). Twenty missions had been built along the coast. Only one more would be built at Sonoma in 1823. Indians learned the Catholic faith and many other useful skills.

In 1821, after eleven years of fighting, Mexico gained independence from Spain. The name "New Spain" was dropped, and the country officially became "Mexico." Communication was so slow that it was not until January 1822 that the news reached California. By April, the Californians were required to swear that they would be loyal to Mexico. All did with no protest.

Spain's empire finally collapsed when her colonies rebelled against her authority. Three hundred years after Cortés landed at Vera Cruz, California passed out of Spanish hands. It officially became a province of Mexico.

It was fortunate for the United States that California remained loyal to Spain. After Spain's empire broke up, its former colonies became independent nations. If California had declared its independence like the other colonies, it too may have become a nation. However, by remaining a part of Mexico, it stayed a weak colony. God had plans for California. It would become a part of a nation that would honor Him: the United States of America.

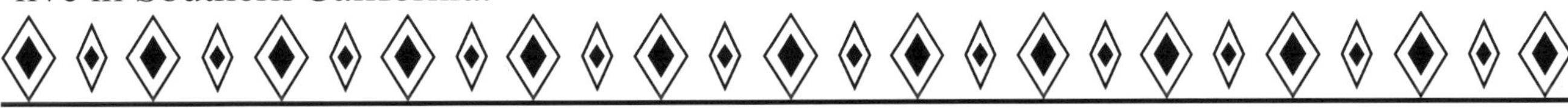

Review Questions

# Unit 4 Roundup

## Chapter 9

1. Describe the mission system. How did it work, and what was its goal? If you do not remember, go back and review Unit 3.

2. The missions were self-sufficient. What does this mean? Why did they have to be self-sufficient?

3. What common characteristics or features did the missions share?

4. Describe a typical day at a mission.

5. Look at the mission map. Which mission is closest to your home? Have you ever visited it?

## Chapter 10

1. What good and bad features do you see in the Spanish missions of California?

2. Were the Indians at the missions slaves? Why or why not?

3. Describe your favorite Mission Indian in two or three sentences.

4. **Thought question:** Do you think it was good or bad for the Spanish missionaries to colonize California and teach the Indians? Explain your answer.

## Chapter 11

1. Who was the Stormy Catalan? Describe him.

2. Who was his wife? Describe her.

## Chapter 12

1. Why did Count Rezanov visit California?

2. Why was Fort Ross built?

3. Why do you think God prevented the Russians from colonizing California?

## Chapter 13

1. Describe California's part in the revolt against Spain.

2. Who was Joseph Chapman?

3. What might have happened to California if it had not remained a colony of Mexico after the Spanish-American Wars for Independence?

## Things to Ponder

Today, many people think the Spanish mission system was very bad and caused great harm to the California Indians. Yet, it caused much good. Thinking in terms of worldview, why might some people scorn the mission system? Ask an adult for his or her thoughts.

Unit 5

# The Mexican Period

For the kingdom of heaven is like a man traveling to a far country, who called his own servants and delivered his goods to them. And to one he gave five talents, to another two, and to another one, to each according to his own ability; and immediately he went on a journey. Then he who had received the five talents went and traded with them, and made another five talents. And likewise he who had received two gained two more also. But he who had received one went and dug in the ground, and hid his lord's money. After a long time the lord of those servants came and settled accounts with them.

~~ Matthew 25:14-19

San Carlos Borroméo de Carmelo Mission, better known as Carmel Mission, fell to ruins when the missions were abandoned during the Mexican period of California's history.

## Mexican Rule

AFTER 52 YEARS, CALIFORNIA PASSED from Spanish hands into Mexican hands. California was glad when the war ended in 1821. "The war years have been hard," the people thought. "The supply ships have not sailed for ten years so we have no manufactured goods. Our soldiers and missionaries have not received their pay. Now that we belong to Mexico, it will take care of us." But Mexico did not take care of California as Spain had.

The 25 years (1821-1846) that California was a province of Mexico can best be described by the word "neglect." Mexico, with problems of its own, ignored its northern colony most of the time. Mexico appointed governors, but most were very poor rulers. After a while the Californians began to think that they could do a better job of ruling themselves. When they tried, other problems developed, especially jealousy between people in the northern and southern parts of the land.

Since the supply ships from Mexico did not sail during the war years, a secret trade began between the Californios and American ships from Boston—called Yankee ships. This helped the Californios get the supplies they needed, and it also opened trade between California and the United States.

In this unit, we will study about life in California during the Mexican period. We will learn about some of the earliest American fur trappers in California, such as Jedediah Smith. We will discuss life on ranchos, or cattle ranches. Finally we will study one of the greatest tragedies in California, the destruction of the missions.

### Revolutions in Mexico

Agustin de Iturbide

While Spain was fighting to save its Mexican territory, a young commander named Agustin de Iturbide (A-goo-STEEN day Ee-toor-BEE-day) helped. Soon he began to agree with the rebel forces and secretly met with them. In the middle of a battle, he and his army switched sides. Instead of fighting for Spain, he turned and fought for Mexico. His actions allowed Mexico to win, and he drove the Spaniards out of the territory. Mexico became a separate country.

Iturbide looked for a new ruler for Mexico, but no one wanted the job. Finally, he became Agustin I, Emperor of Mexico. Long a military man, Iturbide tried to run the country as he ran his army, ordering people around and putting them in prison when they disobeyed. The people did not like this and made Iturbide leave the country. He went to London, but in less than a year, he decided to return. The Mexicans arrested and shot him.

Mexico became a constitutional republic with a constitution similar to that of the United States. It had one important difference, however: the people of Mexico did not govern themselves according to God's law, the Bible.

For the next several years Mexico tried to learn how to govern itself. The people argued about how much power the government should have. Some thought it should be very strong, while others thought the power should be in the hands of the people. There were many revolutions as these arguments continued. (A revolution is change or overthrow of a political system.) During the first 100 years that Mexico was a republic, revolutions occurred, on average, once each year.

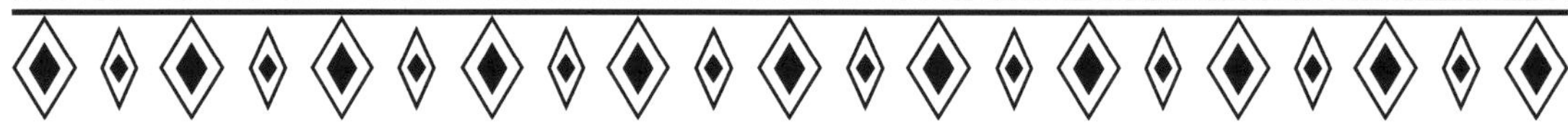

Chapter 14

# The Mountain Men

Very few people lived in California during the Mexican period. With so few people, great quantities of wildlife thrived in all parts of the country. The forests contained several varieties of bears, including the fearsome grizzly. Deer, elk, and antelope occupied the fertile valleys. Mountain lions, wildcats, and coyotes roamed the hillsides while ducks, wild geese, and other fowl teemed in the lakes and rivers. When American settlers came to California, they said that such large flocks of ducks and geese would fly overhead that the sky would darken. A hunter shooting into the flock would be sure to hit a duck since they flew so close together. Whales were frequently sighted in San Francisco Bay along with sea lions and sea otter.

This sounds very inviting to modern Californians, but the early Californians did not agree. When whales spouted in the bay, they smelled terrible. Grizzly bears were greatly feared. They killed people and livestock, as did coyotes and wildcats.

God warns about wildlife overpopulating the land in His Word. When He promised Moses that He would drive the Canaanites from the land of Israel, He said, "I will not drive them out from before thee in one year; lest the land become desolate, and the beast of the field multiply against thee" (Exodus 23:29). It is not safe for people to live in a land that contains great quantities of wild animals.

The large quantities of animals were one of California's greatest resources and should have brought profit to the Californians. The Californians, however, were not fur trappers. It is interesting to note that the Californians failed to develop two of California's greatest resources: furs and gold. All of this wildlife should have attracted other English or American fur trappers; however, the journey to California was very difficult. No fur trapper had ever crossed the Sierra Nevada or entered California from the Pacific Northwest (Oregon). Jedediah Smith, an American and a Christian, became the first mountain man to travel to California. Many others followed him.

Beaver pelts became popular in the mid-1800s, especially to make top hats.

## *Bible-Toter Jed Opens the Way*

A friend drew this picture of Jedediah Smith around 1835, shortly after he died.

WHEN SPAIN SETTLED CALIFORNIA, IT BUILT presidios to protect all of the harbors from foreign conquest. No presidios were built inland. Although ships might arrive by sea, no one expected men to cross the deserts and mountains. One day in the fall of 1826, Jedediah Smith and his men surprised everyone by arriving at San Gabriel Mission. The missionaries welcomed the weary group with a huge meal. As Smith and his men rested from their difficult journey, they entertained the missionaries with exciting stories of their adventures.

Smith and his men had left the Great Salt Lake area, in the present state of Utah, to travel through what is now Arizona and Nevada. Smith was exploring the land, looking for beaver. Beaver fur was very valuable. It was used to make a material called felt. Fashionable men's hats were made from this felt.

Travel south through the desert country had been very difficult. Smith had very few supplies left by the time the exhausted men reached the Mohave Indian villages on the Colorado River. He could not go back. He did not have enough food or water to return to Utah. When Smith learned that it was not far to the missions of California, he decided to travel on to buy supplies and horses. Purchasing some stolen mission horses from the Mohaves and hiring some runaway Mission Indians as guides, he began the journey. Men, horses, and mules suffered from hunger and thirst on the way. Many of the animals died, but the group finally reached San Gabriel.

Discarding the long beaver hair, hatters removed the very short ones from the pelts, pounded them together, and made a material called felt. They fashioned stylish top hats from this felt.

Kindly Father Sanchez, a missionary at San Gabriel Mission, told Smith about one of California's laws. "You will need a passport, or official permission from the governor, to enter California. All travelers in California, including residents, have to carry passports. They are checked at each town. Men who do not have them are assumed to be criminals and thrown in jail. You need to write to the governor and tell him your situation. You and your men are welcome to stay at the mission until you hear from the governor."

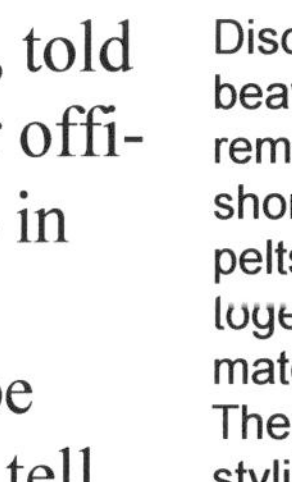

Father Sanchez treated the mountain men well. While they were waiting, he gave them cloth for new shirts since their old ones were tattered and worn from the journey. Smith's blacksmiths made bear traps for the missionaries to use in the mission orchards. At last, Smith was asked to travel to San Diego to see Governor Echeandia (Ay-chay-AN-dee-a).

Smith's arrival in California was a problem for Echeandia. "Why have these men come here?" the worried governor thought. "Are they American spies looking for a way to conquer California? Other Americans are sure to follow this group. They say they are trapping beaver, but who would want to buy beaver skins?" Finally Smith convinced the governor that beaver pelts were valuable in the United States and obtained a passport. But Governor Echeandia told Smith he must leave California by the same way he had come so that he would not see any more of the land.

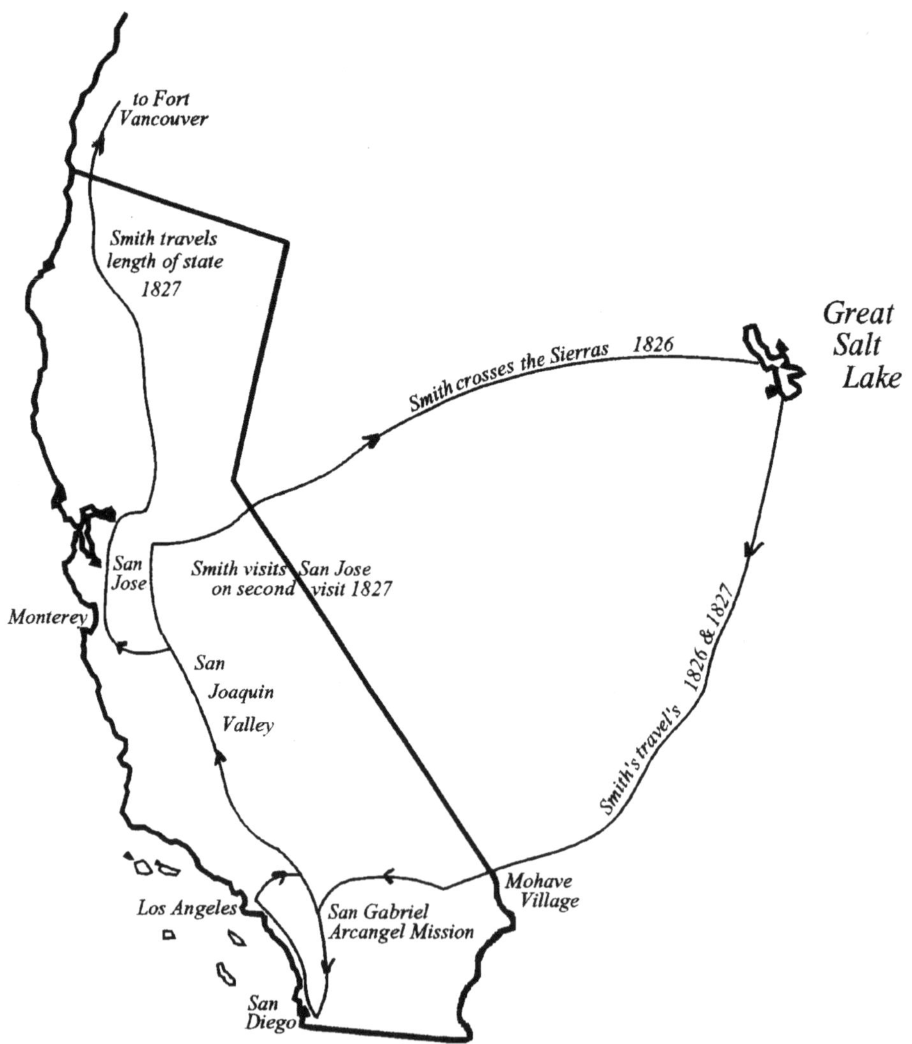


Jedediah Smith was the first American to enter California from the east, the first to cross the Sierra Nevada, and the first to travel the length of the state into what is now Oregon.

## Smith and the Grizzly Bear

JEDEDIAH SMITH WAS THE OLDEST OF THIRTEEN children raised on the Smith family farm in Ohio. The farm was not able to support and educate all of the children, so Smith left at the age of 22 to help care for the family. He became a very successful fur trapper. Many mountain men would spend their season's earnings in drink and wild living. Smith shared his with his family and church. He helped to start his brothers in business and provide for his younger brothers' education.

Smith had many dangerous adventures during the nine years he spent in the mountains. Once while struggling through the wilderness, he heard shouting and excitement behind him. As he ran into the open, he found the problem—a grizzly bear! The bear attacked Smith, broke three of his ribs, and slashed the side of his head.

After dealing with the bear, one of his companions leaned over him and asked, "Captain, what shall we do?"

"One or two of you go for water. If you have a needle, get it out, and sew up the wounds around my head," the injured Smith commanded. The man obeyed, cut his hair, and sewed his scalp.

Then he exclaimed, "I can do nothing for your ear, Captain!"

"Try!" Smith urged, "You must try to stick it on some way or other." So his companion finished the work. Gradually the wound healed, and his ear survived. Smith wore his hair long for the rest of his life to cover the ugly scar. Two weeks later, he was back in the saddle.

Jedediah Smith was a Christian and a man of strong character. He carried his Bible with him on all trips. His friends called him "Bible-toter Jed." This modest, quiet man contributed much to the exploration of California. He opened routes for other trappers to follow from the north, east, and south. Much later, American colonists would travel them as well.

## James Pattie

James Ohio Pattie and his father Sylvester left their home in Missouri and headed west to trap beaver. Later in life he wrote a book about his adventures. Some of his accounts seem more like tall tales, but this is how he described his visit to California.

In September 1827, the men reached the Colorado River. It rained that night, and Indians stampeded and stole their horses. The Pattie expedition suffered greatly as they traveled on foot through the desert. After a month they arrived at the Santa Catalina Mission in Baja California. They were arrested and sent to Governor Echeandia.

Echeandia was even more suspicious of the Pattie group than he had been of Smith, who visited a year earlier. The Californians did not hunt beaver and could not understand why the men thought it valuable. Echeandia threw the men into prison for several months. Sylvester Pattie died, unable to endure such harsh conditions after the hardships of the trail.

An outbreak of smallpox allowed James Pattie to be set free. Sylvester had some smallpox vaccine with him. The governor offered James a one-year passport and payment if he would vaccinate the people of California. Pattie claimed to have vaccinated 22,000 Californios, Indians, and settlers.

The Father at San Francisco Mission offered Pattie 500 cows and mules, along with land for pasturage, as payment for his help. There was a large condition, however. He had to first become a Mexican citizen and a Catholic. "My anger choked me," cried a frustrated Pattie. "I would not change my present opinions for all the money this mission was worth."

Pattie was never paid for his smallpox vaccine. Later he returned to the United States by way of Mexico.

Smith left the narrow coastal strip of land occupied by the Californians. Then he turned north through the San Joaquin Valley and found lots of beaver. By April he had trapped over 1,500 pounds of beaver.

By then, Smith had another concern. The previous spring, before he left his partners at the Great Salt Lake, he promised to return by the summer. If he did not, his partners would worry. Leaving most of his men in California to continue trapping, Smith crossed the Sierra Nevada. He became the first white man to ever cross these mountains. The trip was filled with hardship, yet when Smith wrote about it in his journal, he described it as if it were an ordinary, everyday event.

After the meeting at the Great Salt Lake, Smith returned to California by traveling to the same Mohave village he had visited the previous year. He brought 18 men, horses, and enough supplies for two years. The men built rafts to cross the Colorado River. They planned to cross in two groups. While Smith and the first group were crossing with all of the guns and a small part of the provisions, the Mohaves, who had been watching for the right moment, attacked and killed the ten men in the second group waiting on shore. Smith and his men barely escaped, but they lost all of their horses and most of their food.

The situation was desperate. "We have no other choice but to walk to California," Smith told his men. They journeyed through the desert on foot, relying on Smith's memory of the route. Finally they joined the men he had left trapping in the San Joaquin Valley. But they were hungry too. With no provisions, they were forced to travel to San José Mission.

After enduring weeks of suffering in the wilderness, Smith looked forward to relief at the mission. Instead he was thrown into a filthy jail. He was taken to Governor Echeandia again. This time the governor was certain Smith was a spy. After many conversations and delays, a respected American ship captain agreed to become responsible for the actions of Smith and his men. Smith sold his beaver skins to buy supplies and made preparations to leave. He also bought 150 California horses for $10 each. He intended to bring them to the Great Salt Lake and resell them for $50 each.

Travel along the southern route was impossible due to the treachery of the Mohaves. The horses would not survive the difficult journey over the Sierra Nevada. Smith decided to travel north through California to the Columbia River in what is now Washington. From there he would proceed to the Great Salt Lake over known trails.

In his journal, Smith said the trail was very difficult, especially since he had to lead 150 horses. The group traveled only a few miles each day. On this journey Smith became the first white man and American to travel the length of the state of California. He blazed a trail that would be used by many to enter California from the north.

This God-fearing, adventuresome man met his death two years later at the age of 32. As Smith looked for water during an expedition near Santa Fe, a group of Comanche Indians hid near a water hole waiting for buffalo. Smith did not see them until it was too late. They surrounded him and shot him in the back.

## Joseph Walker

In July of 1833, Joe Walker left Missouri on a fur-trapping expedition. Walker's expedition journeyed to the Salt Lake region and over the mountains to California. He became the first white man to see the beauty of Yosemite, although he did not enter the valley. He also was the first man to see California's Big Trees.

When Walker reached Monterey in November, he received permission from Governor Figueroa to remain in California for the winter. Governor Figueroa (Fee-geh-ROH-a) was one of California's best Mexican governors. His gracious manner was very different from Governor Echeandia's rudeness. By this time, the Californios knew they could not stop the trapping and the men who came to the territory. Instead, they tried to control it. They required all of the trappers to buy licenses which gave them permission to trap.

Walker crossed the mountains at the pass that now bears his name in the southern Sierras. He had suffered greatly from Indians and the desert. Later, he served as a guide to John Charles Frémont on two of Frémont's expeditions to map routes to California.

Although Walker continued to travel throughout his life, he spent many years in California. He came back during the Gold Rush to start a cattle ranch. At the end of his long life he lived with his nephew in Contra Costa County. He is buried in the Martinez cemetery.

Yosemite Valley—the view Walker probably saw.

Chapter 15

# Destruction of the Missions

During the Mexican period, more Californios wanted to own land in California. "The missions have taken all of the rich and productive land," they complained. "We have no place to build our ranchos. It's not fair for the missions to have so much land. They should share it with us." When these complaints reached the ears of the Mexican government, other voices were added. "The church has too much power in California," they said. "Besides, the Indians should not be ruled by the missionaries. All men should be free."

Most of the Californios did not really care about the Indians. Instead they wanted the mission lands. People in Mexico were influenced by the anti-Christian ideas that had caused the French Revolution in the late 1700s. According to these ideas every person should have liberty and equality. No person should be ruled by a king (or missionary); he should be completely free to do as he pleased. The problem with this idea was that the Indians had not learned how to rule themselves. A person will either be self-governed or ruled by others. When the missions ended, the Indians did not gain freedom; they became slaves.

## Destructive Work

The Mexicans and the Californios worked on their plans to destroy the missions for twelve years. Government representatives tried to convince the Indians to move to pueblos, but they did not want to leave. An official traveled to San Miguel Mission and talked about how wonderful it would be if the Indians chose freedom. He stood on a cart in the courtyard and spoke for a long time. Then he asked the Indians to make a choice. Those who wanted to be free should move to the right. Those who wanted to stay with the missionary should move to the left. Almost all immediately chose to stay with the missionary and moved to the left. They did not want to leave.

Mexico finally realized that the missions supported most of the province. They had supported the presidio soldiers for almost 20 years since the government had stopped paying their salaries. If the missions were destroyed, California's economy would be ruined. Mexico dropped the plan to convert the missions to pueblos, but not for long. The mission system ended in 1835 in a process called *secularization*.

The results were disastrous. Some officials in charge of the process were dishonest. They killed the cattle, which were the Indians' property. They enriched themselves from the sale of the hides and tallow (beef fat). Instead of training the Indians as the missionaries had done, many officials forced the Indians to work for them because the land would be worthless without the Indians to perform the labor. For these Indians freedom had turned into slavery.

About two-thirds of the Indians ran away from the missions. Some went to work at the ranchos. They were employed to take care of the sheep and cattle. Some built Indian pueblos using the skills the missionaries had taught them. After a long struggle these prospered. Some sold their land for liquor, then became idlers or thieves. Others moved to the interior, bringing their new skills to the villages in the valley. In the Tulare area, they troubled the ranchos by raiding cattle and horses and selling them to the East. The missions had been destroyed too quickly. With more care, the Indians would have become productive and respected members of California society.

After the missions were abandoned, they quickly fell into ruin, like San Antonio de Padua. President Lincoln restored most of the missions to the Catholic church in the 1860s. Since then, many have been reconstructed.

## Freedom vs. Slavery

There is a great deal of difference between freedom to be able to own property, worship God, and lead a productive life, and freedom to lie, cheat, and steal. The man who governs himself according to God's Word, the Bible, is truly free. The man who uses his freedom to break God's law must be controlled by man's law. In a sense he then becomes the slave of the lawmaker since he is forced to do something he would not do of his own free will. This was the situation with the Indians after the missions were destroyed. The Indians could not govern themselves, so they had to be governed by others.

People who are self-governing do not need many laws. Our forefathers understood this when they wrote the United States Constitution. As more people in our country refuse to govern themselves, our lawmakers are compelled to make more laws to keep order. Only when people turn to the Lord Jesus Christ and obey God's law can they be truly free because "Where the Spirit of the Lord is, there is liberty" (2 Corinthians 3:17). Therefore:

Stand fast therefore in the liberty wherewith Christ hath made us free, and be not entangled again with the yoke of bondage (Galatians 5:1).

## Why Weren't There More Indian *Pueblos*?

Why did so many Indians seem to fall away after the missions were destroyed? Why didn't they build Indian pueblos as the missionaries originally planned? Why couldn't they live on their own as Mexican citizens? The biggest reason for this failure was that the Indians were not taught the Christian principle of self-government under God's law. Individual responsibility was not a part of the California Indians' culture before the Spaniards came, nor was it taught at the missions. The missionaries treated the Indians like children, planning and controlling all parts of their lives.

Before we condemn the missionaries for not teaching the Indians to be self-governing, we must look at the Spanish culture itself. The missionaries were not taught to be self-governing either but rather to obey the pope in Rome (the head of the Catholic church) and the king of Spain. None of the Spanish people were taught individual responsibility. The government was very powerful, centered in the king of Spain and the rulers he appointed. Every aspect of a Spaniard's life was controlled by the government.

All of the Californians had problems learning to rule themselves after Mexico won its independence from Spain. The Indians had the most trouble since they had the least experience with the concept of self-government.

Some Indians continued to live on former mission lands, such as this *rancheria* at San Luis Rey.

## Governors and Revolutions

Life was very chaotic during the 25 years that Mexico ruled California. Mexico did not pay much attention to California, but the attention it did pay was not good. There were several revolutions or forcible changes in California's governmental system. Most revolutions were fought with words rather than with weapons. Even so, some men were wounded or killed.

Mexico appointed governors to try to keep order in California. The first governor was a Californio, and there was peace during his term. Almost every other governor sent from Mexico was either overthrown or had to try to stop a revolution.

The new Mexican government did not have much regard for the colony of California. It began to use California as a prison colony. Men convicted of major crimes were sent to California's presidios instead of Mexico's prisons.

The Californios became very angry with this policy. In 1830, eighty convicts came to Santa Barbara. The Californios sent them to Santa Cruz Island, off the coast. A short time later fifty more convicts arrived from Mexico. Some of these men became the heads of respectable families, but most caused problems for law-abiding Californios. After 1830, Mexico stopped sending large numbers of convicts to California.

It would not be until California became a part of the United States that peace and stability would return to the land.

## General Mariano Vallejo

General Vallejo owned an adobe near Petaluma, which has been reconstructed and opened to the public. This statue stands at its entrance.

GENERAL MARIANO VALLEJO WAS ONE OF THE great Californios. His father, Ignacias, had come to California with Governor Portolá and Father Serra on the Sacred Expedition in 1769. There were very few women or families in California when Ignacias was a young man. At San Luis Obispo, he helped a woman deliver a baby girl. He asked the woman and her husband if he could marry the girl when she came of age, providing she was willing. She was willing, and the wedding took place when she was fourteen. Mariano Vallejo was the eighth child born to the couple.

Mariano Vallejo had the best education that California could provide. At age sixteen he entered the military service. He rose to the rank of Brigadier General by 1840.

When he was 24, General Vallejo married Francisca Benicia Carrillo. The town of Benicia, north of San Francisco, is named for her. They had seventeen children.

General Vallejo was a distinguished leader during the Mexican period, participating in many activities. He owned the largest rancho in California, near the town of Sonoma. He helped to found Petaluma and Santa Rosa with colonists who were sent from Mexico to occupy mission lands. When their plan failed, they faced starvation. Vallejo helped them by giving them food and seed for their first winter.

General Vallejo was a great friend of the Americans. He wanted California to become a territory of the United States. He was a delegate to California's Constitutional Convention in 1849. He was also one of the first state senators.

When General Vallejo retired to his rancho, he devoted himself to horticulture, the study and cultivation of plants. He also supervised the education of his children.

Chapter 16

# Rancho Life

When Spain ruled California it built three kinds of settlements: *presidios* or military bases, *pueblos* or towns, and *missions*. A fourth kind of settlement grew during the Mexican period: the *rancho* or cattle ranches. Spain had made a few grants of land to retired soldiers. These land grants became *ranchos*. The owner of the grant was called a *ranchero*. During the Mexican period the number of ranchos grew rapidly. When the missions were destroyed, much of the mission land was given to Californios to build ranchos. Very little of the land was farmed. Most of it was used to raise cattle. Cattle grew from the old mission herds.

Life on a California rancho was very different from life today. Let's learn about this life as we read a fictional story about a California rancho.

As the sweet strains of mother's *alba* slowly faded, the Martinez *rancho* began to stir. Carlos stretched as he turned over in his rawhide bed. Strips of rawhide, tightly stretched over a wooden frame, made for a comfortable rest. He drifted back to sleep.

"Carlos!" Juanita, his sister, called from the courtyard. "If you don't hurry, Papa will leave without you!"

"I'm coming!" Carlos shouted as he jumped up and pulled on his boots. Today was a special day. It was the annual *rodeo*.

**Spanish Words**

*Adobe*—bricks made of clay and straw
*Alba*—a prayer of thanksgiving
*Bueno*—good, great
*Fandango*—festival or party
*Matanza*—slaughtering
*Metate*—stone mortar, used for grinding
*Presidio*—military fort
*Pueblo*—town
*Rancho*—ranch
*Ranchero*—rancher
*Reata*—long rope to lasso cattle
*Rodeo*—cattle round-up
*Señor*—polite form of address: Mr.
*Vaquero*—cowboy

The rancho house was made with adobe bricks. Bricks were made by molding adobe clay mixed with grass and laying them in the sun to dry. The adobe clay kept the house warm in the winter and cool in the summer.

Thousands of cattle roamed over Señor Martinez's land. These were the descendants of the cattle brought to California on the Sacred Expedition, the Anza Expedition, and before the Yuma Massacre. The few hundred head of cattle had multiplied until they covered the hills. Since there were no fences and the cattle roamed freely over the land, they often got mixed up with cattle from the neighboring ranchos. At the rodeo, they were rounded up, separated, and branded. Señor Cabrillo from the neighboring rancho would be on hand to take his cattle home.

The adobe's large, tiled kitchen was a beautiful place. Beneath colorful strings of drying peppers, onions, and garlic, the Indian servants bustled about preparing the day's meals. Some ground corn on stone mortars called *metates*, while others shaped the coarse flour into thin, flat tortillas. Still others prepared to roast a large ox to feed the hungry crowd that evening. The smell of baking bread from the beehive ovens made Carlos's mouth water.

There was no time to linger, however. He grabbed a tortilla from the hot cooking tile and stuffed it into his mouth as he ran to the stable. An Indian servant had already saddled his horse. Carlos vaulted into the saddle and rode away to join his brothers.

Californios on horseback were a picture of grace and beauty. Later, after the cattle had been corralled, the men and boys would demonstrate their abilities. Juan, Carlos's brother, could pick up a silver dollar from the ground while riding at a full gallop. His daring feats were

Tailing the steer made it more submissive.

often an attempt to impress María, the lovely daughter of Señor Cabrillo.

"Carlos, it's about time you came!" shouted his brother José. "You can ride with Luis. The *vaqueros* need help over by the creek."

Carlos spent the morning and most of the afternoon rounding up the cattle and herding them to the corral. It was hard, dusty work.

"Carlos!" yelled Luis. "One of the cows is breaking away! Go after it!" Carlos urged his horse after the cow that was running away from the herd at full speed. The rancho dogs raced after it. Carlos dashed up to the animal, leaned over in his saddle, grabbed its tail, and jerked to a sudden stop. The cow tumbled over and over on the ground. When it regained its footing, it was tame and willing to be led back to the herd.

"Luis," Carlos asked his older brother when things had quieted down, "how many hides do you think we will get this year?" He remembered the knife he had seen on the Yankee trading ship last year. It had a fine steel blade. If Papa had a good year, perhaps he would buy the knife for Carlos.

"This year will be very good, much better than last year," Luis replied. "Last year there was very little rain, so not much grass grew for the cattle to eat. The heavy rains this year have produced rich clover and wild oats. Papa's herds have grown. There will be many hides this year."

"*Bueno*!" Carlos shouted, thinking about the knife.

The vaqueros herded the cattle back toward the bustling adobe. Papa examined the brand on each cow to separate his cattle from Señor Cabrillo's. Newborn calves bawled as they followed their mothers. The skillful vaqueros branded each one and released it into a corral. Several hundred noisy cattle milled about the fenced yard filling the air with dust and the smell of scorched hair. Carlos helped to count them, using one stone for every tenth animal.

A B C D

E F G H

Cattle Brands

About one-fourth of the herd would be killed at the *matanza* or slaughtering. Some of the meat would be cut into strips and dried. The tallow, or beef fat, would be melted and stored in bags made of cowhide. In the winter, when the weather was cooler, some of the tallow would be used to make candles and soap. Most of the tallow, however, would be sold to the Yankee traders.

The most valuable part of the cow was the hide. After the cows were skinned, workers stretched the hides on poles to dry in the sun and then folded them in half. The dried hides were as stiff as boards. Most would be sold to the Yankee traders, but some would be cut in strips to make fenced corrals, beds, chairs, and *reatas* to lasso cattle. The Yankees took the hides to Boston where they made shoes, saddles, belts, and harnesses. They brought these goods back to sell to the Californios on future trips.

The hard day's work tired Carlos and his brothers. They relaxed under the shade of the long tiled roof that covered the adobe walls outside the weaving room. The looms were silent today because everyone was busy preparing for the evening *fandango*. Inside, their sisters chattered cheerfully with the visiting girls from Señor Cabrillo's rancho. Even amidst the excitement, their hands were never idle. They embroidered pillow cases, bed coverings, and clothing for the family as they talked about tonight's party. Carlos's fifteen brothers and sisters, the Indian servants and their children, the Cabrillo family, plus visitors from other neighboring ranchos would gather for an evening of music and dancing. Everyone was welcome. Californios were very hospitable. Visitors were welcome to stay for a day or a month, it mattered little, in the spare rooms at the rancho.

The fandango began after dinner as the afternoon cooled into evening. Juan

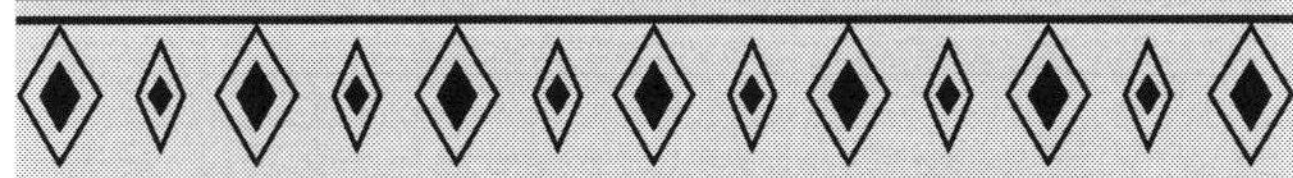

## A Romantic Life?

Life during the Mexican period is sometimes described in very romantic terms. It was said that the people never struggled to make money and spent much of their time outdoors. They were simple in their tastes, healthy, and happy. Some American writers who visited California during this time had a different opinion. One said, "The Californians are an idle, thriftless people and can make nothing for themselves."

The policy of the Spanish government had actually encouraged the people to be idle. California was not allowed to trade with any country other than Spain. Prices for products grown in California were set by Spain. Because these prices were so low, it wasn't worth the trouble to grow crops for export. When California became a colony of Mexico, this situation slowly began to change. Mexico allowed California to trade with other countries. Some rancheros became wealthy through this trade.

The Californios remind us of the man who was given one talent in the parable of the talents (Matt. 25:14-30). Instead of using his talent, he buried it in the ground. The Californios never developed, or even were aware of, the vast resources of California. They enjoyed a simple life and left the resources alone.

Schools were scarce in California during the Mexican period. The larger ranchos sometimes hired teachers for the children. Most parents who knew how to read, however, usually homeschooled their children. They also taught them the doctrine of the Catholic faith and how to run the rancho.

There was one part of California life that was not very pleasant. The country was infested with fleas. They were everywhere. They were especially abundant on the ranchos where there were many sheep, cattle, and dogs and where the homes had dirt floors. Fleas were a problem for many years until modern pesticides and the draining of wetlands greatly reduced them.

Californios wore their finest clothes and danced at the lively *fandangos*.

looked very handsome in his beautifully decorated outfit. Most of the California men dressed royally. María looked equally colorful in her long, full skirt and hand-embroidered vest. She sparkled tonight as she stepped across the courtyard. Her usually braided hair flew loose, covered with a mantle of lace. Her dark eyes flashed when she saw Juan.

Musicians began to tune their violins and strum their guitars. Feet began to tap. Skirts began to sway. The dance was beginning! The young people waited on the sidelines as they watched the graceful movements of the adults. The harmony of guitars and violins floated on the air punctuated by snapping castanets. Soon it was time for the young people to join. María whirled into the center of the patio. Juan quietly moved behind her, threw his hat over her eyes, and darted back into the crowd. Would she keep the hat on or throw it off? If María wore the hat for the rest of the dance, Juan would become her escort for the evening. Carlos was not surprised to see that hat remained securely on her head as she swirled about the colorful dancers. Everybody expected Juan and María to eventually marry, but until then, they were closely watched. They could not be alone until after the wedding.

"Ho," Carlos yawned, leaning against the large cottonwood tree at the edge of the courtyard. "I would rather be riding my horse." Nevertheless, he watched the dancers very carefully, and his feet moved slightly as he tried to mimic their steps. Someday he would be a ranchero like his father. He would have to not only manage a large rancho and be adept on horseback but also be a gracious host and a graceful dancer. It was all part of living in California in the rancho days.

## *Under Mexican Rule*

CALIFORNIA SAW MANY CHANGES DURING THE TIME IT WAS RULED BY Mexico. Mexico, unlike Spain, did not treat the Californians like children, supplying their needs and making their decisions. Californios struggled to learn how to rule themselves during the Mexican period. The results were not very successful. Many Mexican governors were overthrown in revolutions.

California's isolation ended during the Mexican period. It was allowed to trade its hides and tallow for goods from other countries. Fur trappers, beginning with Bible-toter Jedediah Smith, journeyed over mountains that were thought to be impassable. Trade brought many foreign ships to California's shores, while fur trappers broke trails over California's mountains.

Life in California also changed during the Mexican period. The mission system was ended with little regard for the welfare of the Indians. The results were devastating. Many of the Indians worked on ranchos or in pueblos, but others moved to the interior, became idle, or turned to horse-thievery.

Ranchos, or cattle ranches, grew after the missions were destroyed. Many of these new ranchos grew from the mission lands, the lands that were supposed to be given to the Indians. Forming a partnership with the Americans, the Californios traded their hides and tallow, which allowed the rancheros to prosper.

In all, the Mexican period lasted a very short time—only 25 years. Still, it brought considerable change to California.

"For every beast of the forest is mine,

and the cattle upon a thousand hills"

(Psalm 50:10).

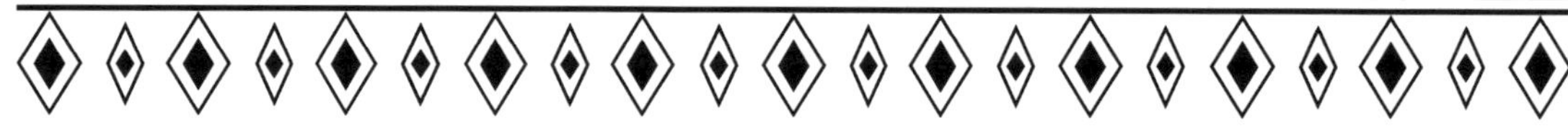

Review Questions

# Unit 5 Roundup

## Chapter 14

1. Describe the changes in California's land between the days of the frontier men and today. Do you think these changes are good or bad?

2. What problems did Mexico have after it became a republic? How did the Mexican republic differ from the American republic?

3. What evidences of Jedediah Smith's Christianity can be seen in his adventures?

4. Jedediah Smith accomplished three "firsts" in his travels to California. What were they?

5. Who were James Pattie and Joseph Walker? Write two sentences about each.

## Chapter 15

1. What is the difference between freedom and slavery?

2. Why were the missions destroyed?

3. What happened to the Mission Indians?

4. Do you think the destruction of the missions was good or bad? Give reasons for your answer.

5. The chapter says the Mexicans *neglected* the Californios. What does this mean? Give examples.

6. Why didn't the Californios govern themselves instead of relying on Mexican governors?

7. How did California become a prison colony?

8. Who was General Mariano Vallejo? Write two sentences about him.

9. **Thought Question:** Can a person ever be truly free? To answer this, you will first have to define "free."

## Chapter 16

1. Describe two things that appeal to you about California ranchos and two that do not.

Unit 6

# The American Settlers

So it shall be on the day when you cross the Jordan to the land which the
LORD your God gives you, that you shall set up for yourself large stones
and coat them with lime and write on them all the words of this law,
when you cross over, so that you may enter the land which the
LORD your God gives you, a land flowing with milk and honey,
as the LORD, the God of your fathers, promised you.

~~ Deuteronomy 27:2-3

People traveling to California and Oregon experienced harsh conditions on the trail. If they could not find water, they suffered from thirst. If their food gave out, they starved. If their oxen died, they walked.

# The California Journey

WHILE CALIFORNIA WAS A PART OF Mexico, hundreds of Americans traveled to the land. In 1845, there were 7,000 Californios, 700 Americans, and 200 other foreigners living in California. In just one year, the number of Americans almost doubled.

The people in California welcomed them. Many Americans became Mexican citizens and received large grants of land. Others refused citizenship because they did not want to become Catholics, as was required. By 1846 this requirement was relaxed, and non-Catholic American citizens could buy land as well.

The early American pioneers were independent, self-governing men. They faced their problems bravely since there often was no one to help them. They were always ready to show kindness to the needy. Evildoers were quickly punished. The pioneers as a group had an unshakable religious faith. They believed that God, in His providence, ruled over the affairs of men and relied on Him for His protection.

In this unit we will learn about California's early pioneers, beginning with John Bidwell, who faced great hardship on the westward trail. We will learn about the end of the Mexican period and how California became a part of the United States.

## Bidwell's Trek to California

In November 1840, a twenty-year-old Missouri schoolteacher read in the local newspaper about a far-off land called California. "The area is very beautiful," the article said. "The authorities will give thousands of acres of land to anybody who will occupy them."

John Bidwell, the schoolteacher, was born in New York but had traveled to Missouri in search of land and adventure. He tried to farm in Missouri, but someone stole his land. Penniless and landless, John Bidwell became very discouraged. Later, when Bidwell became a Christian, he realized that God was using these harsh experiences to train him to withstand tough pioneer life.

He began to think about California. Could it be as beautiful as the newspaper described? A French fur trader named Roubideau said it was. "It's always spring in California," the Frenchman said. "The land is very fertile. Thousands of cattle and horses roam the hills. The Californians are the most hospitable people in all the world. The country is a paradise." Before long, John Bidwell and several others decided to see California for themselves. By the spring of 1841, they were ready to leave.

John Bidwell and his party spent seven wearisome months on their journey to California. They had no maps or trails to follow. They had only a vague idea of their destination. Let's study this journey by reading a fictional, but historically accurate, diary made in part from Bidwell's own journal.

Chapter 17

# First Wagon Trips

## John Bidwell's Journey to California

*May 18, 1841*

Sixty-nine people, including fifteen women and children, are here at Sapling Grove, Missouri, ready to begin the trip to California. John B. Bartleson is our captain. He refused to make the trip unless we named him captain. I was named secretary. There are no trails to California, and no one knows how to get there. We decided to begin our trip with Father de Smet, who is leading a group of Catholic missionaries to the Flathead Indian territory [in present-day Montana].

One of the first landmarks the travelers on the California trail saw is Chimney Rock in Nebraska.

*May 19, 1841*

We started off this morning in single file. The missionaries were at the head of our group with four carts and one small wagon. They were followed by thirteen mule-and-oxen-drawn wagons.

By July 4th, travelers hoped to be at Independence Rock in Wyoming. Sometimes wagon trains would rest, read the Declaration of Independence, or carve their initials in the rock as shown below.

*June 1, 1841*

Wonderful! This evening a new family was created! Isaac Kelsey was married to Miss Williams, the daughter of the Rev. Richard Williams. The ceremony was performed by the bride's father. Now we have five families. Rev. Williams is traveling to Oregon with his family.

*July 8, 1841*

Our progress has been slow since a great deal of our time has been spent hunting and curing buffalo meat. We will need the meat when we travel over the mountains.

*August 7, 1841*

The landscape is beautiful. Today we saw a delightful little lake whose surface was covered with fanciful islands. A river wandered proudly through the valley among willows and cottonwoods until it disappeared among the hills in the shades of the evening.

*August 11, 1841*
Today, after traveling with Father de Smet for the past four months, we said good-bye to him and his company. About thirty-two of our own company became discouraged and decided to go to Oregon instead of California. The rest of us, also thirty-two in number, remained firm. We refuse to be moved from our original purpose of going directly to California. Nancy Kelsey, the wife of Benjamin Kelsey, is the only woman left in our party. Her little six-month-old daughter Ann is the only child.

Father de Smet, a Catholic priest, was a missionary to the Flathead and Nez Perce Indians during the 1840s. Three towns are named De Smet after him in South Dakota, Montana, and Idaho.

*August 19, 1841*
We started early, hoping to find fresh water, but alas! The sun beamed heavy on our heads as the day wore on. We could see nothing before us but extensive, dry plains, glimmering with heat and salt. The sun beating upon the shining plains made us think we could see timber, and wherever trees are found there is water always. We marched forward, but discovered it was a mirage. We hurried back to the river so that our teams would not give out.

If you've ever driven on a road and seen what looks like a puddle of water ahead, you've experienced the effect of a *mirage*. Mirages often trick thirsty people traveling in the desert.

*September 9, 1841*
Unavoidable delays are frequent. Daily, often hourly, the road has to be made passable for our wagons by digging down steep lands or filling gulches. Indian fires hide the mountains and valleys in a dense, smoky atmosphere so that we cannot see any considerable distance. It is hard to break a path through the sagebrush, and sometimes a wagon overturns. We are so near to Salt Lake that the water in the river is too salty for our use, but we have to use it. It does not quench thirst, but it does save life.

The Great Salt Lake in Utah is surrounded by the Bonneville Salt Flats.

*September 15, 1841*
We have decided that we must abandon the wagons if we are to reach California before the snow falls. All hands were busy making pack saddles and getting ready. Everything that could not be packed was thrown away. We started, most of us on foot, for nearly all the animals had to carry

packs. It was but a few minutes before the packs began to turn and fall off. Horses became scared, mules kicked, oxen jumped and bellowed, and articles were scattered in all directions. We took more pains, fixed things, and made a new start. We did better, though packs continued occasionally to fall off and delay us.

**Nancy Kelsey**

The only woman in the Bidwell- Bartleson party to make the journey to California was Nancy Kelsey. She was the first white woman to cross the mountains and enter California. The journey was very hard and dangerous, especially since Mrs. Kelsey also had to care for her young daughter.

Mrs. Kelsey said, "Where my husband goes I can go, I can better endure the hardships of the journey than the anxieties of an absent husband." She bore the struggles of the journey with so much grace that she won the admiration of her fellow travelers.

Nancy Kelsey spent many years in California. In later years she was called Grandma Kelsey. She had trouble seeing and was delighted when people would come and read the Bible to her.

*October 3, 1841*
Our situation is becoming more and more desperate. We are killing our oxen one-by-one for food. Sometimes we cannot find drinking water for days at a time. There is nothing like a trail. When will we reach California?

*October 7, 1841*
Captain Bartleson has been traveling with the mules. I have had charge of the oxen and have been unable to keep up with him. Today, after taking a large portion of the meat, the captain and seven of his men declared, "We are going to California. If you can keep up with us, all right. If you cannot, too bad," and away they started. One of the men would not go with the captain. He said, "The captain is wrong, and I will stay with you, boys."

*October 9, 1841*
We have been able to follow Bartleson's trail for the past few days, but today we came to a sandy waste and could find no tracks. We only have two oxen left. The company has named me captain in place of Bartleson.

*October 15, 1841*
We made camp at the base of a lofty mountain wall [the Sierra Nevada]. I sent out scouts to see if it would be possible to scale the mountains.

The Sierras, seen here near Bridgeport, do look like a "lofty mountain wall," an impassable obstacle to tired travelers.

*October 16, 1841*
The scouts have returned. They say it is possible to climb the mountains, but the way will be very difficult. After we had eaten supper, we saw something coming on the plains. At first we thought it was Indians, but we soon discovered it was the eight men who had left us nine days ago. They were sick and discouraged. We ran out to meet them and shook hands. We put our frying pans on and gave them the best supper we could. Bartleson, who was a portly man when we started from Missouri, was reduced to half his former size. I could not help pitying him. He said, "Boys, if ever I get back to Missouri, I will never leave that country. I would gladly eat out of the troughs with my hogs."

*October 18, 1841*
We traveled about half a mile up the mountain when a frightening sight opened before us: terrible mountains with snow on their summits that never melted with the season. Men went out in different directions to see if there was any possibility of leaving these mountains without going back the way we came. They returned and said it was impossible to continue. We killed our last ox—let this speak for our situation and future prospects!

*October 28, 1841*
We have been eating crows and anything we could kill. One man shot a wildcat. We have no idea how much farther we have to travel to reach California. There seems to be no end to the mountains. Some of the men guess we have at least 500 more miles to travel.

*October 30, 1841*
We had gone about three miles this morning when lo! to our great delight, we beheld a wide valley! [The Sacramento]. This we had entirely missed because of high mountains which blocked our view yesterday.

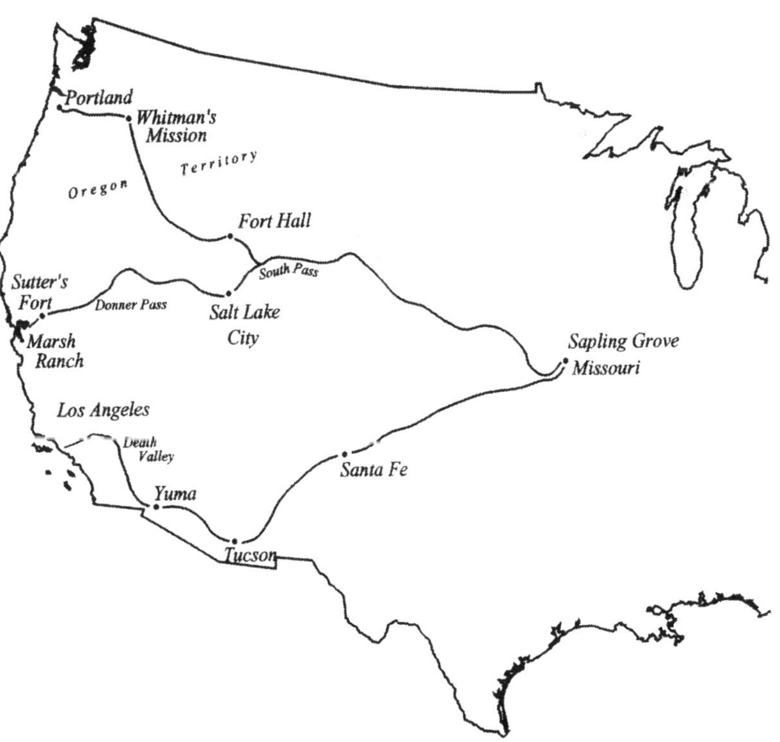

Trails to California developed as more parties followed in the footsteps of the Bartleson-Bidwell Party.

*October 31, 1841*

Today we reached the [Stanislaus] river which we had left in the mountains, joyful sight to us poor famished wretches!!! Hundreds of antelopes in view! Thousands of elk!!! We killed two antelopes and some wild fowl. The valley of the river is very fertile and the young tender grass covers it like a field of wheat in May.

*November 4, 1841*

Our journey is at end! Today an Indian guided us to the home of Dr. John Marsh near the base of Mt. Diablo opposite San Francisco Bay. We are thrilled to find another American. Dr. Marsh killed two bullocks for our half-starved company. We gave him small gifts to thank him for his generosity. We are glad to be here after seven months of hard, dangerous travel!

John Bidwell and his men arrived at Dr. Marsh's *rancho*, Los Medanos, in Contra Costa County.

## John Marsh

Dr. Marsh had come to California with a group of Santa Fe fur trappers in 1836. He had fled to California to escape arrest for selling guns to the Sioux Indians. Before coming to California, Dr. Marsh had begun to study medicine but never finished his course. He tricked the people of Los Angeles into thinking he was a doctor by showing them what they thought was a medical degree. It was really his diploma from Harvard College. Most of the people in Los Angeles could not read and could not tell the difference. Marsh became a Mexican citizen and settled on a rancho near Mount Diablo. He wrote letters urging people to come to beautiful California. John Bidwell read his letters and decided to make the journey.

Bidwell accuses Dr. Marsh of being a very selfish man. Instead of displaying California hospitality, he started complaining about how much money the company was costing him. Half of the men left Marsh's rancho and traveled to the pueblo of San José. They were promptly jailed because they did not have passports. Dr. Marsh got passports for them but charged each man five dollars for something that was free.

Dr. Marsh took part in the Gold Rush and earned about $40,000, a sizable sum for those times. He was murdered in 1856 by a vaquero, or cowboy, after an argument over how much money Dr. Marsh should pay for the branding of his cattle.

## More Wagon Trains

MANY AMERICANS FOLLOWED THE BIDWELL-BARTLESON COMPANY TO California. As more people traveled, the routes became better known. Women and children joined the travelers. The groups had many problems and excitements, but few companies experienced the hardships of the Bidwell-Bartleson company.

### Chiles-Walker Company

Joseph Chiles had traveled to California with the Bidwell-Bartleson party. He left Dr. Marsh's rancho and went to work for George Yount in Napa Valley. Chiles noticed that there was no sawmill in all of California. Trees were plentiful, but all of the boards had to be sawed by hand. He decided to go back to the United States and return over the mountains with sawmill parts. This was an adventuresome idea since he had seen that the Bidwell-Bartleson company could not bring their wagons over the mountains.

Like the Bidwell company, the Chiles company was not able to haul their wagons over the rugged mountains. They buried the sawmill equipment hoping to return for it later. They never did.

### First Wagons Over the Mountains

The Stevens-Murphy company were the first travelers to bring wagons over the mountains in 1844. By the time they reached the top of the Sierra Nevada, snow had begun to fall. The Americans became frightened. If they did not cross quickly, the snow would trap them over the winter. By using all of their oxen, they were able to drag only five wagons over the top of the mountains before the snow became too deep.

Once over the mountains, settlers could fine rest, refuge, and refreshment at Sutter's Fort near Sacramento.

The other wagons contained many things the settlers would need to begin a new life in California. They were very valuable. If they were left unattended over the winter, perhaps the Indians would steal them. Moses Schallenberger, a seventeen-year-old boy, volunteered to stay and guard them. The settlers built him a cabin and left food for the winter. In the spring, Captain Sutter helped to bring the boy and the wagons to California.

## *The Donner Party*

IN 1846, GEORGE DONNER BEGAN THE TRIP TO CALIFORNIA WITH HIS family and several others. The first part of the trip was easy, but in late July, the group made a grave mistake. Several pioneers decided to take a shortcut that was supposed to save them 200 miles of travel. The shortcut quickly turned into a nightmare and cost them one month of hard travel. They began to run out of food, and winter was coming.

In October they reached the Sierra Nevada. Here they made another mistake. The tired pioneers decided to rest for four days at a place where there was grass and water for the horses. While they were resting, it started to snow. The snows were one month early that year. Soon the Donner party was trapped. They had to make a winter camp for four months near what is now Donner Lake.

One group moved into the cabin built for Moses Schallenberger, while others built shabby cabins as best they could. The entire party faced death by starvation or freezing. Two families prayed together each morning. They knew that without God's help they would die. In the middle of December, fifteen people tried to get help. Only seven lived to see the Sacramento Valley.

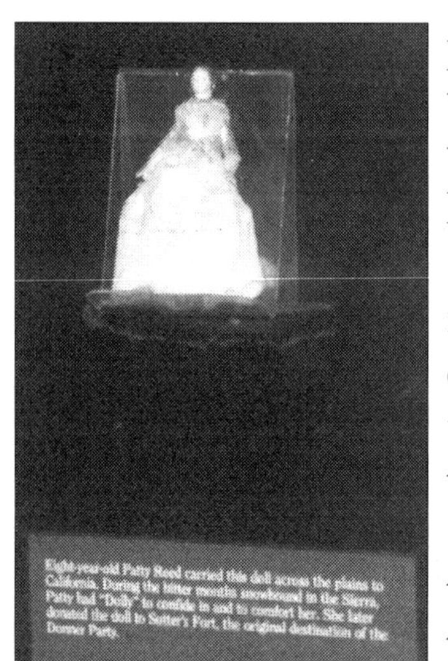

"Dolly," Patty Reed's tiny doll, is displayed at the Sutter's Fort Museum.

When Captain Sutter learned that the settlers were trapped in the mountains, he sent out relief parties. In February 1847, one of the parties got through. The hungry pioneers appreciated these few supplies. Generous people in San Francisco donated $1,500 to equip another rescue party.

Earlier, a man named James Reed had been banished from the Donner company because he had killed a man. He claimed that it was self-defense and had arrived at Sutter's Fort before the snow fell. When he heard that the pioneers were trapped in the mountains, he made a heroic journey to rescue one of the families who had been earnestly praying. They were his wife and four children. Reed arrived just in time to save his family from starvation. Perhaps, as Joseph was unjustly sold into slavery and later thrown into an Egyptian jail so that he could be used by God to save the nation Israel, James Reed was banished so that he could save his family. His daughter, Patty Reed, clung to her doll on the journey to safety. The doll can be seen today at the Sutter's Fort Museum in Sacramento.

Forty-one, or nearly half, of the Donner party died in the mountains. Captain Sutter was most generous in sending out provisions for the relief parties. Without his efforts, the suffering would have been much worse.

# Captain Sutter

John A. Sutter, a very colorful man, was one of the first foreigners to settle in California. Sutter abandoned his wife and four children in Switzerland, as well as many debts, and made his way to the Oregon Territory. In Oregon, he wore a French army uniform and introduced himself as Captain Sutter, claiming he had served in the French army. This was not true, but he was called Captain Sutter for the rest of his life.

Sutter arrived in California in the summer of 1839. He asked Governor Alvarado for 30 square miles of land near the present city of Sacramento. Alvarado informed Sutter that he would have to become a Mexican citizen and a Catholic to receive the land. Sutter was an atheist. He believed that a man should not have to obey any laws, especially not God's law. He thought that each man could work out salvation for himself. These ideas were very popular in France at the time. Today we call this religion Secular Humanism. Nevertheless, at the end of the year Sutter converted to Catholicism to become a Mexican citizen, although he remained an atheist in his heart.

Settlers could buy new provisions at the store in Sutter's Fort. The store has been recreated as part of Sutter's Fort State Historic Park.

Captain Sutter built a home that was well-fortified with guns and cannon. It was called Sutter's Fort and soon began to thrive. When the Russians left California, he purchased their livestock and many other materials on credit. He had thousands of cattle, sheep, horses, and hogs as well as hundreds of acres of wheat and other crops. With all his abundance, he still had trouble managing his money. He continued to live beyond his means as he had in Switzerland, and his debts grew large.

American settlers made Sutter's Fort their first stop after they traveled over the Sierras. Captain Sutter was well known for his hospitality. He never turned a needy person away from his door. He sent rescue parties and provisions to settlers who were trapped in the mountains on several occasions. Many settlers owed their lives to this colorful Californian.

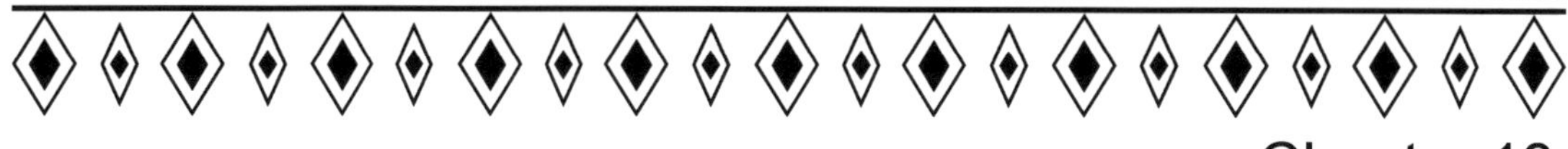

Chapter 18

# The Struggle for California

When American settlers arrived in California, they sent reports to friends and neighbors about the beauty of the land. Soon the United States government began to talk with the Mexican government about the possibility of buying the California territory. This was a large territory that included the present states of California, New Mexico, Utah, Nevada, nearly all of Arizona, and parts of Wyoming and Colorado. But the Mexican government was too unstable to negotiate* for the sale of California. Whenever progress was made in the negotiations, a revolution would bring a new group to power, and the talks had to begin all over again.

**Negotiate:** To bargain, try to reach a deal

**Immigration:** To move to a foreign country.

**Annexation:** To make a part of. To become a territory of.

The United States continued efforts to obtain California through the work of Thomas Larkin. Larkin came to California from Massachusetts in 1832. On the long ship voyage around Cape Horn he met Rachel Holmes, who was traveling to Hawaii to join her husband. When Mrs. Holmes reached Hawaii, she learned that her husband had died. Thomas Larkin sent her a proposal of marriage, which she accepted. The two Protestants could not get married in a Catholic church, so the ceremony was performed on board a United States' ship. Mrs. Larkin was the first American woman to live in California. Her daughter was the first American child born on California soil.

Thomas Larkin

Larkin opened a general store in Monterey. Soon his business thrived. By 1844, he had become one of the leading residents of Monterey and was appointed U.S. consul, which is a position similar to an ambassador. He kept the United States government informed of events in California. He wrote letters encouraging immigration* to California. Many Californians, including General Vallejo, began to favor annexation* to the United States due to Larkin's efforts. If the Mexicans had not started the war with the United States, California might have become a United States territory through simple persuasion.

In 1842, something happened to upset Larkin's efforts to win California peacefully. While Commodore Jones of the United States

Navy was watching the actions of the French and the English along the coast of Peru, he was incorrectly informed that war had broken out between Mexico and the United States. There was no way for him to confirm this rumor since there was no telegraph and it was impossible to communicate with his government. Suddenly, three British man-of-war ships sailed towards California. Commodore Jones thought they were on their way to capture the territory. Jones quickly sailed for Monterey. The British ships were not in sight. Now he wondered what to do. If war had started, he needed to capture the port of Monterey before the British did. If there was no war, it would be very wrong to take the port, and he would be punished. He decided that duty came first. He sailed into the bay and demanded that the Californios surrender to him. They did so with no protest.

The next day, Thomas Larkin convinced Commodore Jones that he was wrong. There was no war. Monterey should not have been captured. Commodore Jones could trust Larkin's word. Jones ordered the American flag to be taken down, apologized to the California leaders, and fired a salute from his ship in their honor.

While the Californians treated the whole affair as a joke, officials in Mexico were not pleased. Commodore Jones remained in California for several weeks attending many fandangos and festivals. Everyone remained friendly to him. The government in Washington formally apologized to the Mexican government for the unfortunate incident. The United States government understood that he had made the best decision with the facts he had available.

Monterey had grown by the time Commodore Jones mistakenly raised the American flag over the Customs House.

**John Charles Frémont**

General Frémont was one of the most restless men to visit California. He was industrious and a remarkable explorer, yet he had weaknesses in his character which would prevent him from reaching true greatness. Frémont was quiet and reserved. He did not like large groups; rather, he enjoyed spending time with his family and close friends. He loved horses and dogs.

Frémont was also quite rash and impulsive. He did not always know how to choose diligent men to work with him. Kit Carson, Frémont's faithful friend, was his guide on early exploring expeditions. On later trips Frémont chose men far less able.

Several times Frémont approached fame and fortune only to lose it at the last minute. He accepted the surrender of the California forces and became temporary governor of California, yet he was sent back East in disgrace and court-martialed because he disobeyed orders. He owned a gold mine at Mariposa containing much wealth, yet he mismanaged it and died a poor man. In 1856 he was the United States presidential candidate of the newly formed Republican party but was defeated by James Buchanan. He was a general in the War Between the States but was forced to resign when he refused to obey President Lincoln's orders.

Frémont's greatest talent was exploring the wilderness areas. The trails he marked and the journals he wrote helped many people reach California and the West.

## The Bear Flag Revolt

JOHN CHARLES FRÉMONT VISITED California twice, in 1844 and again in 1845. On his second visit, he helped the United States conquer California.

The Mexican government, alarmed at events occurring in Texas, ordered all foreigners to leave California within 40 days, or their property would be taken and they would be put to death. The settlers were frightened. When the Americans heard a rumor that California's military governor, General Castro, was urging the Indians to attack them and burn their wheat crops, they became truly alarmed. Frémont promised that he would not leave the Americans while they were in danger.

Frémont was not sure what to do. On the one hand, he had no orders to start a revolt. On the other hand, if a revolt did break out among the settlers, he could not allow it to fail because he did nothing. Frémont did not know it, but Mexico had already declared war on the United States.

In June 1846, the Americans heard that General Castro planned to attack a wagon train of American settlers coming to California. They heard that he planned to kill all the livestock, destroy the provisions, and force the people back across the mountains and plains. He had sent for a band of 100 horses to use in his attack.

The Americans knew they could not stand by while their helpless countrymen were ruthlessly attacked. A group of men captured the horses and brought them to Frémont's camp. Without the horses, the raid was impossible, and the American settlers would be safe. The men then hurried to Sonoma.

Early on the morning of June 14, 1846, the Americans captured the pueblo of Sonoma. They took General Vallejo and his brother, as representatives of the Mexican government, prisoners. That night while the Americans slept, an outlaw named Juan de Padilla tried to rescue Vallejo. Vallejo ordered him to abandon his foolish plan, which would endanger many people. Vallejo said, “I will go with the Americans. People as brave as they are cannot fail to be generous as well.” The Vallejos were held at Sutter’s Fort for several weeks and then released.

Frémont would not allow the men to fly the American flag over captured Sonoma, so one of the men, William Todd, nephew of President Lincoln’s wife, created a new flag. It had a red border, a single star, and the outline of a grizzly bear. The men called it the Bear Flag, and the capture of Sonoma was eventually known as the Bear Flag Revolt. It flew over the pueblo for about a month until it was replaced with the American flag. The original Bear Flag was destroyed in the 1906 fire in San Francisco. In 1911, it became the model for California’s state flag.

The original Bear Flag.

## The Mexican War

The Mexican War had a major effect on California although it started in Texas. American settlers began to arrive in Texas as early as 1821. By 1835, the year before Dr. John Marsh arrived in California, there were 35,000 Americans living in Texas. Very few Mexicans lived in this area. The Texans organized their own government. They were willing to be under the authority of Mexico but wanted to be able to govern local affairs themselves. Santa Ana, a leader in the Mexican army, brought 4,000 men to upset these efforts. He attacked the Alamo and killed every Texan in the fort, including Davy Crockett. "Remember the Alamo!" the people cried. They would not allow Mexico to rule over them after this massacre. Texas became an independent republic. Nine years later, it was admitted to the United States.

Mexico never recognized Texas as an independent republic. Later, when Texas became a state, Mexico declared war by attacking American forces at the Rio Grande, the river separating Mexico and Texas. The war quickly expanded to Northern Mexico, California, and New Mexico. The United States took New Mexico without any fighting. California was conquered by January 1847.

When Mexico would not yield after it had been defeated in the northern territory, United States forces fought until Mexico City was captured in September of 1847. The war was ended by the Treaty of Guadalupe Hidalgo, named for the city in which it was signed, in March 1848. California and New Mexico (which included parts of what are now Nevada and Arizona) became United States territories. The United States paid the Mexican government a total of $15 million for the land plus $3.5 million in forgiven debts.

Chapter 19

# California Becomes American

Commodore Sloat of the United States Navy, stationed in the Pacific, had orders to take San Francisco in the event of war between the U.S. and Mexico. He heard of the hostilities in Texas and sailed to Monterey. Then he hesitated for a few days because he did not want to make the same mistake that Commodore Jones had made four years earlier. When he was satisfied that Mexico really had attacked the United States, he raised the American flag at Monterey on July 7, 1846, and declared that California was now a military territory of the United States. The Bear Flag Republic was dissolved.

A special person raised the American flag over the Sonoma Plaza, Lt. Joseph Warren Revere. He was the grandson of Paul Revere, who fought mightily for the colonies during the War for Independence in 1776.

Some of the California settlers joined Frémont's men to form a military group called the California Battalion. John Bidwell was a member of this group. He said, "We simply marched all over California, from Sonoma to San Diego and raised the American flag without opposition or protest. We tried to find an enemy, but could not."

Most of the Californios were glad to be under the authority of the United States. It had been very difficult to prosper under the misrule of Mexico.

## God's Providence

The hand of God can be clearly seen as California became a territory of the United States. The British had two plans to make California a British province. These narrowly failed according to the will of God.

In the first, Father McNamara, an Irish priest, asked to bring 3,000 Irish Catholic immigrants to California. The Mexican government approved the plan which would give the colonists 13.5 million acres of land. Father McNamara traveled to California to finalize the plan with Governor Pio Pico. Pico approved the plan on July 7, 1846, but he was too late. The American flag had been raised at Monterey that morning, and Mexican authority was ended in California.

The second plan involved the British Navy. The British had military men stationed along the Pacific coast watching events between Mexico and the United States. Admiral Seymour had the same orders as Commodore Sloat of the United States Navy: In the event of war between Mexico and the United States, Admiral Seymour was to raise the British flag over Monterey. Seymour hurried to California to carry out his orders, but fortunately he was too late. When he sailed into Monterey Bay, he could see the American flag flying in the breeze. "Sloat," he said to the American commander, "if your flag was not flying on shore, I should have hoisted [raised] mine there."

Pio Pico was the last Mexican governor of California.

## Sloat's Proclamation

Sometimes when countries are conquered, the citizens are treated badly or even cruelly. Commodore Sloat wanted to reassure the Californians that they would be treated with kindness. He issued a message to the people:

"To the inhabitants of California: The central government of Mexico having commenced hostilities against the United States of America by invading its territory and attacking its troops and these nations being actually at war by this transaction, I shall hoist the standard [raise the flag] of the United States at Monterey immediately, and carry it throughout California. I declare to the inhabitants of California that, although I come in arms with a powerful force, I do not come among them as an enemy of California; on the contrary, I come as their best friend, as henceforward [from now on] California will be a portion of the United States, and its peaceful inhabitants will enjoy the same rights and privileges as the citizens of any other portion of that territory."

The proclamation identified these rights and privileges as:

1. Choosing their own rulers to administer justice.
2. Worshiping their Creator in the way they wished.
3. Prospering in agriculture and trade, since they would no longer have to pay taxes on goods sent from the United States.
4. Keeping their land if they had lawful title to it.

The proclamation ended by assuring the people that the United States military forces would not steal from the Californios. If the military needed supplies, they would pay for them.

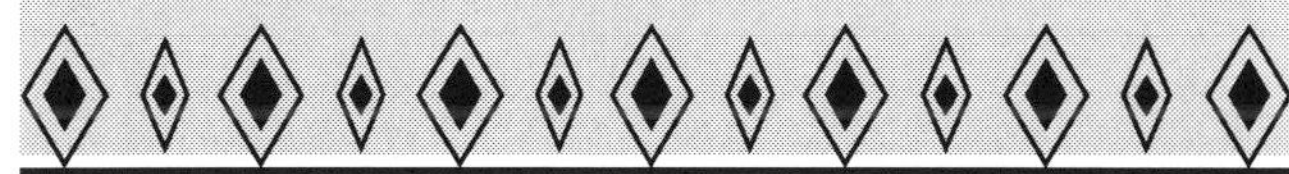

## The Re-Conquest

CALIFORNIA WAS AT PEACE FOR TWO MONTHS. LIEUTENANT Gillespie, one of Frémont's men, was left in charge of Los Angeles. Gillespie did not treat the Californians kindly. The Californios did not like his attitude and, as they had many times during the Mexican period, they revolted. Lieutenant Gillespie had to surrender the town. Soon the whole area south of Santa Barbara was in rebellion, and the re-conquest of Southern California began.

### The Battle of Dominguez Rancho

The Californios won the first two battles. The first was fought at Dominguez Rancho, near Los Angeles. It is sometimes called the Battle of the Old Woman's Gun because the Californios used a cannon that an old woman had buried when she heard the Americans were coming to Los Angeles. The Californios, who were skillful horsemen, moved this gun around quickly during the battle. It was a deadly weapon. Fourteen Americans died in this battle.

### The Battle of San Pasqual

The second battle occurred in December 1846, when more American soldiers came to California from New Mexico. They were led by General Kearny over the long and difficult Santa Fe Trail. General Kearny did not give his company time to rest when they reached California. He rashly attacked the Californians immediately. It had rained the previous night, his ammunition was wet, and his soldiers were tired. The Americans were defeated, and at least seventeen were killed.

At the Battle of San Pasqual, Californios displayed their riding skill during the re-conquest of California. Their lances killed many Americans.

### The Battle of La Mesa

The final battle in California was the re-conquest of Los Angeles. General Kearny came from the south and Frémont approached Los Angeles from the north. After two short battles the Californios scattered. American troops entered Los Angeles on January 10, 1847. Lieutenant Gillespie raised the same flag over the pueblo that he had been forced to lower the previous September.

### Surrender

The Californians chose to surrender to Captain Frémont because of his generosity. Earlier a Californian named Jesus "Tito" Pico had been caught and found guilty of spying. He was sentenced to death. When Señora Pico and his children pleaded, Frémont pardoned him. A grateful Tito Pico remained Frémont's true friend for the rest of his life. The Californios found Frémont to be as generous with them as he had been with Pico. Walter Colton, a naval chaplain who would become *alcalde*, or mayor, of Monterey, called the surrender articles "liberal in their spirit, wise in their purpose, and just in their application."

The Mexican War ended for California in January 1847. It continued in other places for another year. Finally, on February 2, 1848, the war officially ended. A treaty was signed in a Mexican town named Guadalupe Hidalgo. The United States purchased all of the California territory. The American flag has flown over this land ever since.

## A Look Back

MODERN HISTORIANS, TELL US THAT THE UNITED STATES WANTED California so much that it started a war with Mexico just so it could conquer California. Mexico, they say, was forced into a war with the United States against its will.

On the contrary, Mexico provoked the United States: first in Texas, then in California. Mexican officials threatened the lives and property of Americans living in California. When the Texans, of their own free will, asked to become a part of the United States, Mexico declared war, and the United States defended its citizens.

The United States could have conquered California when Commodore Jones mistakenly raised the flag over Monterey. The Californians surrendered immediately. The Mexicans were not in a position to defend Monterey. However, the United States acted justly. It apologized to Mexico for the mistake and restored the port to its lawful owners.

The United States could have kept Baja California and Northern Mexico. It conquered these territories during the Mexican War. However, these lands were not part of the treaty or the $15 million purchase price. They were returned to their rightful owners. It would have been better for California to join the United States by peaceful means. After Mexico declared war on the United States, the peaceful route was closed. And so after 25 years California passed out of the hands of Mexico and became an American territory. Over the next several years American settlers would flock to this beautiful land. They would begin to transform the California wilderness into a great and mighty state.

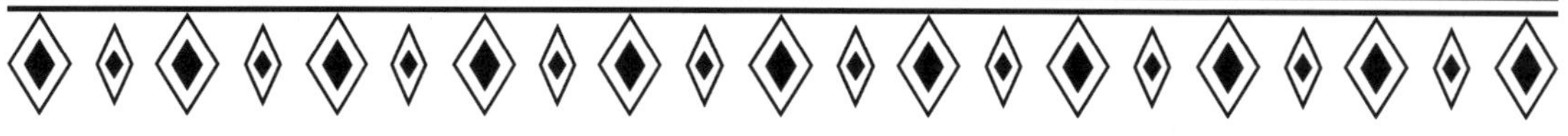

Review Questions

# Unit 6 Roundup

## Chapter 17

1. Briefly describe Bidwell's first wagon train trip to California.

2. How would John Bidwell travel from St. Louis to California today?

3. What were some of the hardships that people on the early wagon trips encountered?

4. Who was Nancy Kelsey?

5. How does the saying, "It's always darkest before the dawn," apply to John Bidwell's arrival in California? Can you think of a Bible verse that applies?

6. Write one or two sentences describing the following immigrant wagon trains:
   a. Chiles-Walker

   b. Stevens-Murphy

   c. Donner

7. Describe John Sutter. How did he help settlers come to California?

## Chapter 18

1. Who was Mariano Vallejo, and what country did he want California to be ruled by?

2. What was Commodore Jones' mistake?

3. How did the Mexican War begin? How did it affect California?

4. What was the Bear Flag Revolt?

## Chapter 19

1. What was Sloat's Proclamation? List at least two of its features.

2. What was providential about the U.S. conquest of California?

3. Was the American conquest of California right or wrong? Defend your answer.

4. How might Daniel 4:17 apply to the American conquest of California?

## Biblical Allusions

Both Nancy Kelsey on page 122 and John Bartleson on page 123 make what is called a Biblical allusion, or a reference to incidents in the Bible.

1. Read Nancy Kelsey's words about staying with her husband wherever he goes, and then the words in Ruth 1:16-17. What is Mrs. Kelsey's allusion?

2. Read Bartleson's comments about eating out of the trough with his pigs, and then read Luke 15:11-32. What is the Biblical allusion that Bartleson makes?

Unit 7

# The Gold Rush

Receive, please, instruction from His mouth,

And lay up His words in your heart.

If you return to the Almighty, you will be built up;

You will remove iniquity far from your tents.

Then you will lay your gold in the dust,

And the gold of Ophir among the stones of the brooks.

Yes, the Almighty will be your gold

And your precious silver.

~~ Job 22:22-25

Hundreds of handbills and advertisements, like this one, lured men from their homes to the California gold fields.

## The Gold Rush

SETTLERS CONTINUED TO FLOCK TO California after it became a territory of the United States. These hard-working and God-fearing men and women planned to make beautiful California their new home. California should have continued to grow slowly as settlers made their way over the mountains. It should have followed the growth of other American territories. Gradually more and more people should have made the journey until California had a large enough population to become a state. But with California, such was not to be the case. God had a different plan for the settlement of this land.

When gold was discovered in California, the trickle of settlers became a mighty river. Within two years, thousands of people had traveled to California. With so many people, California became a state much quicker than other territories.

In this unit we will learn about how gold was discovered at Sutter's Mill near Coloma, on the American River. We will learn about the incredible events that took place as men rushed to California to make their fortune. Finally, we will learn how these events led to the formation of the 31st state in the United States of America.

The California Department of Parks and Recreation remembers the site of the gold discovery and of Sutter's Mill near Coloma. Although Sutter's original saw mill no longer exists, some of the original wood has been salvaged and a reconstruction of the mill has been built a short distance from this site.

Chapter 20

# Gold Discovery

John Sutter stirred the embers and heaped more wood on the parlor fire. Outside the fort, rain thundered against the windows. Warm and snug from the cold January weather, Captain Sutter lit his pipe and leaned back in his chair. He was writing a letter to a friend.

"This has been a good year," Sutter reflected, thinking about the prosperity of his fort. "The American settlers I've hired are hard workers. After the next harvest I will be able to pay all my debts. Maybe I will even be able to send for my family in Switzerland."

Sutter's Fort had indeed prospered. More than 300 American settlers lived in the Sacramento Valley on land that Sutter had sold them. Many worked in his blacksmith shop, blanket factory, wheat fields, and flour mills. Many others traded at the fort's store. Sutter was even building a sawmill to sell lumber to the settlers for their homes. His cattle, horses, and other livestock had grown to be so numerous that he could not count them. Debt, however, continued to trouble the unwise businessman. His love of ceremony and generous hospitality meant that Sutter often spent more money than he had.

"No matter!" Sutter thought cheerfully as he poured himself a glass of brandy. "After next year I will be the most important man in California. I will owe no man anything. Everyone will give me the honor that is my due!"

Captain Sutter's daydreaming was curtly interrupted by a knock on the door. "Mr. Marshall is here to see you, sir," announced his Indian servant. "He says it's very important."

"Send him in," Sutter replied, wondering what could compel Marshall to ride to the fort in the middle of a pounding rainstorm. Were there problems at the new sawmill Marshall was building for Sutter?

James Marshall stood at the door. Rain dripped off his mud-spattered coat and wide-brimmed sombrero, forming puddles at his feet.

"I must speak to you alone," growled the moody millwright.

Sutter shrugged. "Come into my bedroom," he replied. "We will be alone there."

They entered Sutter's private quarters, and Sutter carelessly swung the door closed, but did not lock it. As Marshall began to pull a dirty cloth from his shirt pocket, Sutter's clerk entered the room to ask a question.

"I told you we must be alone!" Marshall exclaimed nervously. "Lock the door!"

Sutter dismissed his servant and locked the door. "Now, Mr. Marshall," he said evenly, "what is all this about?"

"Look here!" Marshall replied as he unwrapped his cloth. It contained several small pieces of metal. "I think it's gold!" he said excitedly. "We found it in the river as we were building the sawmill. There's plenty more. We're rich!"

"Gold!" Sutter repeated as he staggered towards his chair and took a generous drink of his brandy. "Are you sure? What if it's pyrite or fool's gold? Let's test it."

Captain Sutter called for a set of scales, some silver, and performed some tests. "It's gold all right," he said, "and the purest!"

Captain Sutter listened, somewhat dazed, as Marshall told him how he had discovered the gold. "The mill is nearly complete. We discovered that we needed to dig the channel under the waterwheel a little deeper so that it could turn freely. After the men were through digging each night, I gave orders to raise the gate so that the river could wash out as much sand and gravel as possible. In the morning I would walk down, shut the gate, and see what more needed to be done.

"A few days ago on the clear, cold morning of January 24, my eye caught a glimpse of something shining in the bottom of the ditch. I

James Marshall built Sutter's saw mill along a bend in the American River near present-day Coloma. This model, in Gold Discovery Park, shows how it worked.

Marshall built a gate near the river. When opened, the river water ran underneath the mill and turned the wheel in the center. This area is called the "millrace" or sometimes a "tailrace." Marshall found gold while he was trying to make the millrace deeper so the water would turn the wheel.

The top part of the mill, above the platform, contained the saw blade. As the water turned the wheel, a series of gears turned the saw blades. Men pushed lumber through the blades to create planks and boards.

## Sutter's Downfall

John Sutter was not one of the men who prospered during the Gold Rush. He should have become a wealthy man. Instead, the discovery led to his ruin. Sutter's employees deserted him, and his wheat rotted in the fields. People came and built homes on his land without his permission. They also killed his cattle. The land where the gold was discovered never belonged to Sutter. He had built his sawmill without having legal title to the property, so he had no claim to the gold that was found there.

Augustus Sutter, Captain Sutter's son, joined his father in California in the fall of 1848. Augustus took over Captain Sutter's business interests and managed the monumental task of paying off all his debts by the summer of 1849. Finally, Sutter's Fort was sold that fall. Sutter moved his family, newly arrived from Switzerland, to another farm called Hock Farm.

Sutter's debt-free condition did not last long. He continued to spend his money freely on generous hospitality. He drank heavily and squandered $200 to $300 a day, which would be equal to about $4,000 to $5,000 today.

Captain Sutter was never a good businessman. He chose his business partners carelessly. He did not check to see if they were honest men. These partners cheated him out of thousands of dollars.

Finally, in 1865, Sutter was forced to leave California. An arsonist set fire to his house at Hock Farm. Sutter and his wife escaped, but almost everything they owned was destroyed in the fire. Litz, Pennsylvania, became their new home. They lived there comfortably for the rest of their lives. John Sutter died in 1880 at the age of 73.

reached my hand down and picked it up. It made my heart thump for I felt certain it was gold. The piece was about half the size and shape of a pea. Then I saw another piece in the water. I thought it was gold, but it did not seem to be the right color. I trembled to think of it! When I hammered it between two stones, it did not break.

"I returned to my cabin for breakfast and showed my exciting discovery to the men. Over the next few days they picked up more shiny flakes and small pieces. Still unsure whether the metal was really gold or just iron pyrite, I decided to bring it to you to make the final test."

"You did the right thing," Captain Sutter said smoothly, regaining his composure. "We must keep this a secret until the sawmill is finished. Tell the men that I will bring them tools and let them explore the area for a few weeks after their work is done. Instruct them, Marshall, and this is very important, not to tell anyone about the gold! Now, you must be tired and hungry after your trip. I'll have the cook fix you dinner. You may spend the night here and return to the mill tomorrow."

After Marshall left, Sutter thought about this new development. "This is very bad," he thought. "If the people hear that they can just pick up gold from the river bed, they will not stay to work for me. My wheat will rot in the fields. This cannot happen. I must have one more good harvest to pay my debt to the Russians!"

Captain Sutter smoked his pipe, drank his brandy, and planned what he would do. "Gold!" he thought as the rain beat a sharp staccato against the windows. "Will it be a blessing or a curse?"

## Earlier Gold Discoveries

GOLD HAD BEEN DISCOVERED SEVERAL TIMES IN California while it was a province of Spain and Mexico, but God prevented these resources from being developed. If California's rich mineral wealth had been known to the English, French, or Russians, these countries might have fought harder to conquer California.

Reports of gold in California date back to some of the earliest explorers. They said that the soil looked like it might contain gold. Mission Indians are said to have found samples of gold, but the Fathers urged them to keep their discovery quiet for fear that the work of the missions would be upset. In 1842, a man named Francisco Lopez rested in the shade of a tree in Southern California. He dug up some wild onions with his knife and discovered a piece of gold attached to the roots. More gold was found, but the strike turned out to be very small.

Californian landowners during the Mexican period may have known about other gold deposits but kept them secret. According to Mexican law, people only owned the surface of their land. The state or government owned the mineral rights, that is, whatever was underground. This was just one of the many bad laws that prevented California from prospering during the Mexican period. James Marshall discovered gold at Sutter's Mill just nine days before the peace treaty was signed that ended the Mexican War and granted California to the United States, which was not enough time for word to reach Mexico. God, in His providence, kept the riches in California's soil hidden until California was securely a territory of the freedom-loving Americans.

**Don Luis Peralta**

A story is told about Californio named Don Luis Peralta, who had lived in California for many years. When his sons became excited about the discovery of gold, he called them together and said:

"My sons, God gave that gold to the Americans. If he had wanted the Spaniards to have had it, he would have let them discover it before now. So you had better not go after it, but let the Americans go. You can go to your ranch and raise grain, and that will be your best gold field; because we all must eat while we live."

### To the Gold Fields

Captain Sutter tried to keep the discovery of gold a secret, but he could not. The news reached San Francisco in March. By May nearly all the San Franciscan men had left for the gold fields. News of the gold discovery reached Monterey in June, five months after Marshall's discovery. Many people thought the reports were nonsense. They did not believe that the gold could have sat undiscovered for so long. Others began to stampede to the mine fields.

**Reaction to the Discovery:**

"The blacksmith dropped his hammer, the carpenter his plane, the mason his trowel, the farmer his sickle, the baker his loaf, and the tapster his bottle. All were off for the mines, some on horses, some on carts, and some on crutches, and one went in a litter . . [To make] seven dollars a month, while others are making two or three hundred a day! That is too much for human nature to stand."

Rev. Walter Colton, Alcalde of Monterey

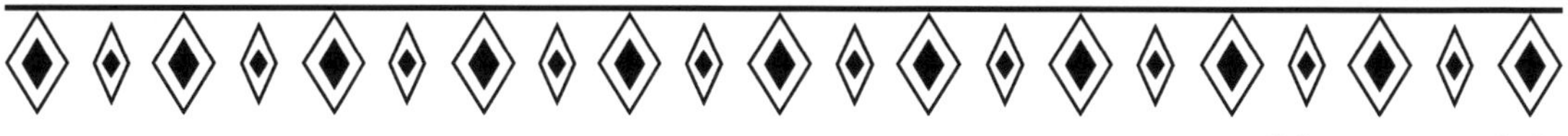

Chapter 21

# Rush to California

News of California's rich gold deposits spread around the world infecting many with gold fever. "In California the ground is littered with gold," the reports said. "All a man has to do is pick it up." In the following year, 1849, thousands flocked to California from all over the world. All hoped to make their "pile," as a large strike of was called, and then return to their homes. Lawyers, doctors, clergymen, farmers, mechanics, merchants, sailors, and soldiers all left their businesses to travel to California. By the end of 1849, more than 115,000 people in California worked in the gold fields.

Thousands of men began to ask themselves, "Where is this place called California?" It was very hard to reach. People could choose three methods of travel: by sea "Around the Horn," as travel around Cape Horn at the tip South America was called, across the Isthmus of Panama, or overland across the plains. Travel by each method had its own advantages and hardships.

## Around the Horn

This mode of travel was generally chosen by men who lived along the eastern coast of the United States. The trip from New York could take six to nine months. Because it was summer south of the equator, this trip was pleasant in 1848. The most dangerous part was rounding Cape Horn. It took a skilled captain to guide the ship around fog-shrouded rocks or treacherous icebergs. The main problem with travel by sea was the boredom, but usually people kept their humor and made the best of the situation.

## By Way of the Isthmus

In 1849, it took three to six months to travel across the Isthmus of Panama. This is the narrowest piece of land between the Atlantic and Pacific Oceans. Voyagers took a ship to the Atlantic side of Panama, and then hired natives to take them up the Chagres River by boat and over the mountains by donkey. Once in the city of Panama, on the Pacific side of the isthmus, travelers had to wait for a steamer bound for California. Usually there were more people waiting to board the ship than there was room. Many people became ill with fever and died while waiting in the overcrowded city. Others became discouraged and returned home. In later years more steamers made the trip between Panama City and San Francisco, and the trip became faster.

At the time of the Gold Rush, people did not realize that mosquitoes carried yellow fever. While traveling through Panama, many people were bitten by mosquitoes, got yellow fever, and died. When the United States built the Panama Canal, it spent great effort to get rid of the disease-bearing mosquitoes to make travel safe.

## Across the Plains

Overland parties of travelers began the trip to California in April or May of 1849, when the grass began to grow. Horses, cows, and oxen ate the grass for food so that the travelers did not have to bring extra supplies for them. Travelers followed the trails that Captain Frémont had marked. They experienced many hardships. With so many people on the trail, the grass and water quickly disappeared. Sickness and disease, including cholera, followed. Hundreds of grave markers lined the trail. Historians estimate that one tenth to one fifth of the people who started the journey to California died on the way and only one-third of the wagons crossed the mountains.

Overland travelers carried all of their belongings in covered wagons and sometimes walked alongside. At night the wagons were parked in a circle, and the women prepared meals on open campfires. Horses and mules grazed outside of the circle until dark when they were herded inside for protection. Each man took a turn standing guard.

Other overland travelers made their way across the southern part of the United States. One of the most famous of these wagon trains was the Lewis Manly party.

# Manley and Rogers of Death Valley

GOLD FEVER SEIZED LEWIS MANLY, A YOUNG MAN OF 19. MANLY began his trip as a driver in a wagon train, and then joined another group containing women and children. They pursued the southern route towards Los Angeles.

In less than a week, this new party became lost. Instead of retracing their steps, they decided to travel due west and make their own trail. Each day their situation grew worse until provisions were exhausted and the children cried for water.

The suffering people decided that there was only one action to take. Two of the strongest men would go ahead to get food and water, while the party waited ten days for their return. Lewis Manly and a strong Tennessean named John Rogers were chosen to make the journey. As they set out, the prayerful words of Mrs. Bennett rang in their ears: "God bless you and help you to bring food to my starving children."

Manly and Rogers made the perilous trip over the desert without water or food. Only the thought of starving women and children urged them on. Finally, they reached a stream of clear water, a mountain summit, and a beautiful meadow in California. Quickly, the two men gathered supplies and started on the return trip.

Other men may have given up the trip. "What's the use?" they may have thought. "Our friends are probably dead by now anyway." To their honor, these thoughts did not take root in Manly and Rogers. With great suffering, the men trekked back to the camp.

As the settlers were rescued, one turned and said, "Goodbye, Death Valley!" This is how the desert was named.

The first sight to greet their eyes when they finally arrived was the dead body of their captain. Would any be left alive? A shot from Manly's rifle announced the men's arrival. People crawled out from under wagons and shouted, "The boys have come! The boys have come!" Since Manly and Rogers had taken twenty-six days instead of the planned ten, many of the party had already left camp. Those who remained owed their lives to the brave and unselfish Lewis Manly and John Rogers.

## Mining Methods

ONCE IN CALIFORNIA, THE EAGER MINERS MADE HASTE FOR THE MINES to establish a claim. A claim was a small area of land that the miner called his own. No other man could work the claim until the miner gave it up. Miners used three methods to find gold.

### Panning

Many miners panned for gold using a pie pan, a large bowl, or sometimes an Indian basket. They scooped dirt and water into the pan and swirled it around. Then most of the dirt and water would be thrown over the side, and the heavier gold sank to the bottom.

### Cradle

Gold mining methods improved with the introduction of the cradle, which looked like a baby cradle. A grate covered its opening so that rocks could not enter. Miners poured dirt and water through this opening. The mixture would travel along the cleat-covered bottom while a man rocked it. Heavy gold got trapped between the cleats, while the dirt and water washed out the other end. Two men were required to operate this device, one to pour in the water and dirt, and the other to rock the cradle.

### Long Tom

When the long tom was introduced, even greater quantities of gold could be mined. This device had cleats like the cradle but was much longer and did not need to be rocked. Miners poured water and dirt into the elevated end of the long tom. Gold was trapped between the cleats while the dirt and sand passed by.

This scene shows all three early mining methods. A man pans for gold in the left front, another uses a cradle (sometimes called a rocker) above him, and the men in the right front use a long tom. In later years mines and sluices (the long device at the right) developed to take more gold from the land.

Chapter 22

# Miners and Mining Life

Some miners made fabulous strikes. John Bidwell, who came to California in the first wagon train over the plains in 1841, found his gold at a place later named Bidwell's Bar. He never revealed just how large his strike was, but it allowed him to build a very large farm near Chico. John Sullivan, a former oxcart driver, took $2,600 worth of gold from Sullivan Creek in a very short time. One miner found $1,500 worth of gold in one pan. A boy named John Davenport found $2,700 worth of gold in only two days.

While many found riches, most people found very little. Those who thought they could just pick the gold up from the ground soon found that mining was hard work. They were not prepared for the change in living conditions or for the new climate. A miner had to stand for hours in icy water, fresh from the melted snows of the Sierras. In the summer the weather was extremely hot, with very little breeze. The weather, change of lifestyle, and diet caused many miners to become sick. Many would not live to return to their families.

At the end of a weary mining day, the miner still had housekeeping chores such as cutting wood for the fire and preparing dinner. There were very few women in the camps, and most miners had no help with these chores. One woman in Nevada City, Mrs. Phelps, found that her cooking was much appreciated by the miners. She made dried apple pies which sold for $1 each. The pies sold as quickly as they were made. Soon Mrs. Phelps made more money baking pies than her husband made mining for gold.

On Sunday miners rested from the demands of the mines. Some washed and mended their clothes or wrote letters home. Others amused themselves with foot races and shooting contests. Even though there were few ministers in the gold country at first, many miners set aside Sunday as a day of worship.

Life in the mines could be very colorful. Let's learn more about Gold Rush times by reading a fictional story written by a California history student.

**The Biggest Nugget**

The biggest gold nugget found in California weighed 195 pounds and was valued at $45,535. (Today it would be worth over one million dollars.) According to the story, it was found by a man who was chasing his mule (some stories say a cow). The man knocked off a piece of stone to throw at the straying animal. This stone turned out to be a chunk of gold weighing fourteen pounds.

## *Life in the Mining Camps*

by Tonya Christl (age 12)

James was awakened by the chattering of dozens of languages. He stretched and lazily rubbed his eyes. On any other day the valley walls would be echoing with the clang of picks and shovels, but today was different; it was Sunday, "holiday" in the mines.

James quickly got up and pulled a clean shirt over his head. Then, stuffing a few ounces of gold dust in his pocket, he hurried to join the other miners on their way to the center of the camp.

Immediately, James noticed a change. When he had heard news of a rich strike in this area and had hurried to journey here, he had been shaken by the scattered tents and crudely built cabins in the town called "Bedbug." Now he was surprised to see a completed mercantile and many small shops lining the street. Everywhere he looked he saw miners meandering through shops as construction workers hurried to complete what appeared to be another mercantile.

James passed a tall, lanky German. The German was shouting in a sharply accented voice and waving a large lock in the air. "Dis lock is duh miracle of duh universe. I'll vager you any amount of gold dust dat no man here can open dis lock in two minutes time."

Just then a short, stocky Italian pushed his way through the crowd. He whispered something to Pierre, who became very excited. The giddy little Frenchman was always expecting to find his fortune around the next corner, and now his well-kept mustache bounced in excitement as he watched the Italian open the lock with ease. The Italian nudged Pierre, "Better make a bet. I'll go halves with you." Pierre shoved his way to the front of the mob and placed a large bag of gold dust on the table. The German dropped twenty Spanish doubloons beside it.

"Start now!" Pierre rushed to open the lock. He pushed a small notch in the back as he had seen the Italian do. He pulled and tugged but the lock wouldn't budge. "Your two minutes are up!" the German shouted. Pierre lowered his head and trudged back through the crowd. The Italian had been an accomplice,* and many hours of digging and panning had been lost.

James and the other miners felt sorry for their friend. However, inside they were secretly glad that it had not been their own misfortune.

> *Accomplice: One who helps another commit a crime.

*Quid: The amount of tobacco a man could comfortably chew at one time.

As the sun began to set, James noticed a stream of miners heading towards a large tent on the outskirts of the camp. He sauntered over and found that inside a miners' ball was in full swing.

A tall, gangly man stood in a corner with a fiddle cocked carelessly over his shoulder, sawing away. He shifted his quid* of tobacco and called out in a loud, nasally voice, "Now gents, since we ain't got no ladies we'll have to have a ball without them. Turn your rears this way." The miners roared with laughter and obliged. "All you gents with canvas patches on the seats of your pants is ladies for the night." A new outburst of laughter followed this announcement.

Embarrassed by the patches that dubbed him a lady, James blushed as he was swung off the floor by another miner. Roars of laughter echoed through the room, and the walls shook with the commotion.

On towards morning, a man burst into the room and shouted above the racket of the dancing miners, "Everybody out! Dawn's a bustin'!"

The miners poured out into the streets and once again the valley walls echoed with the clang of picks and shovels. But in the back of every miner's head was the nagging thought, "Is there really a fortune for me somewhere deep in these hills?"

A miners' ball

## The Sabbath Story

WHILE MANY MINERS CONTINUED THEIR WORK ON THE LORD'S DAY, one miner refused to break the fourth commandment and was blessed for it. Elihu Anthony was a blacksmith and a pastor. He came to California in 1847. Immediately upon his arrival, he began conducting Sunday services in San Jose. When news of the gold finds reached Rev. Anthony's ears, he joined the rush.

One Sunday, his partners decided that working on the Lord's Day would be better than sitting around idle, especially since there were no churches in the mines. They found a quantity of gold and thought they had made a good decision. Rev. Anthony, however, refused to work on Sunday. He spent the day with his Bible, in the shade of a tree.

The next day Rev. Anthony asked his partners if he could work under a boulder in the area they had worked on Sunday, instead of working with them. They agreed. Rev. Anthony found several hundred dollars worth of gold nuggets under the boulder. He had obeyed the Lord, rested his body, and received the Lord's blessing for his obedience.

Later, as more men arrived at the gold fields, Rev. Anthony held periodic worship services in the mines until ordained men were available. He gave up mining and used his blacksmith talents to make picks for the miners. He sold these for three ounces of gold each ($48).

"Remember the Sabbath day to keep it holy. Six days shalt thou labor and do all thy work, but the seventh is the Sabbath of the Lord thy God. In it thou shalt do no work."

(Exodus 20:8-9).

Chapter 23

# What the Gold Rush Brought

The Gold Rush brought many changes to California. Within two years the population had increased tenfold. Peaceful California was changed into a thriving, bustling community. Sleepy Yerba Buena (Spanish for "Good Herb") became the commercial giant San Francisco. Quiet Sacramento became a busy supply city. Stockton, originally called "Tuleburg," arose from the tule marshes.

The Gold Rush brought some good changes to California, while others caused problems. We will briefly discuss some of these changes.

## Inflation

**How much is that worth?**

To quickly convert Gold Rush prices to today's, multiply by 20.

Inflation is an increase in the supply of money. Usually governments cause inflation by printing more paper money. Inflation also accompanies most large finds of gold. Increases in the supply of money created big problems in California during the first few years of the Gold Rush.

Imagine you had $20 to spend. You decide to spend your money on a toy. As long as you have only $20, the toymaker cannot raise his price for the toy. If he decided to charge $25 for the toy, you would not buy it because you only have $20.

Next, imagine you found $5 so that your supply of money has increased to $25. The toymaker quickly realizes this and raises the price of his toy to $25. You can still buy the toy; however, it now costs you $25 instead of $20. The increase of your money supply has not allowed you to buy more goods; instead, it has caused prices to rise.

This is what happened during the Gold Rush. When the miners found great quantities of gold, California's money supply was expanded, or inflated. This caused huge increases in the price of goods. Butter sold for $1 a pound and boots sold for $18 a pair. These sound like today's prices, not those of 150 years ago. Common shoes that could be bought in Boston for $.75 sold for $8 to $12 a pair. For a time eggs sold for $1-$3 apiece. Picks and shovels ranged from $5 to $15 each, while poorly constructed cradles brought $50 to $80. Following the Gold Rush, prices in California increased one hundred to several hundred percent. From about 1854 to about 1874 there were several recessions, or downturns in the economy, while the effects of inflation were undone.

## Gambling

The gambling halls spared no expense to make their surroundings inviting to the miners.

Gambling was another result of the newly found gold. Large gold finds were exciting and produced instant wealth. Since there were no social institutions in the gold country to discourage gambling, such as churches or families, it flourished. Many men spent their Sundays gambling away their week's earnings. The work of many months could be lost in one game. A man who had spent months mining enough gold to buy a farm back home could find himself so poor that he did not even have enough money for his return passage. In later years when families joined the men in the mines and churches were established, gambling greatly decreased.

## Christian Ministers

The Gold Rush also brought Christian ministers to California. The first minister to arrive in San Francisco was Timothy Dwight Hunt. Rev. Hunt was a missionary to Hawaii. When news of California's gold deposits reached Hawaii, most of Rev. Hunt's congregation joined the rush to the gold fields. Since there was hardly any congregation left in Hawaii, Rev. Hunt decided to go to California with his flock. He arrived in November 1848.

Rev. Isaac Owen

The city of San Francisco hired him to be the City Chaplain for one year. His job was to hold regular church services in Portsmouth Square. Before the year was over, so many other ministers from a variety of Christian denominations had arrived that Rev. Hunt resigned his position. All of the pastors worked together to bring Christianity to the people of California.

The first years in California were hard for the Christian ministers. Many families suffered hardship to bring the gospel to the land. Rev. and Mrs. Isaac Owen began the long, tedious journey across the plains. When they arrived in Benicia, across the bay and north of San Francisco, they learned that Rev. Owen had been assigned to Sacramento. Since the oxen were too worn out to pull the wagons any farther, they hired a boatman to take their goods up the Sacramento River. The boat overturned and sank. All of the precious goods that had been hauled over miles of prairie, plains, and mountains sank to the bottom of the river.

The Owens arrived at Sutter's Fort in December 1849, and stayed there while a house was built for them. In January the Sacramento River flooded, submerging the city. The new parsonage was destroyed. Mrs. Owen and the family was sent back to San Francisco. Here tragedy struck the Owen family for the third time. Their precious baby daughter died. Isaac Owen ministered in California until his death in 1866.

The missionaries who came to California believed that God caused the Gold Rush not to enrich men with gold, but rather to enrich them with Christianity. Men from all over the world could be converted in California, and then bring the Good News, the message of peace and pardon through the gift of Jesus, back to their own homeland. In this way California was the most important mission field at the time.

### Law and Order

When the miners arrived at California's gold fields, they found themselves in a country with very few laws. But most of the miners were Christians from the United States. They knew how to be self-governing using the Bible as their rule-book. They formed their own government.

In the early years of the Gold Rush before 1851, there was very little crime. Miners could leave thousands of dollars worth of gold dust in their tents without fearing that it would be stolen. When crimes did occur, the miners formed courts of law. A man accused of a crime would be tried by a jury of twelve men. If guilty, the jury would determine his punishment. Crime increased when foreigners and other men arrived, who did not govern themselves according to the Bible

As more miners arrived in California, cabins replaced tents. This replica of a miner's cabin in Gold Discovery Park is quite dusty and dirty—just like the original dwellings.

### Prosperity

The Gold Rush was the beginning of events that turned sleepy California into one of the wealthiest and most productive areas of the world. The miners found California to be a rich and beautiful land. They realized that its greatest wealth was not in gold but in the land itself. Men sent for their families, bought farms, and started businesses. In a short time agriculture produced more wealth than gold.

## The 31st Star

CALIFORNIA'S POPULATION RAPIDLY INCREASED AFTER THE DISCOVERY of gold, and the people realized that they needed a government to provide law and order. California was a military territory from 1846 until it was sold to the United States at the conclusion of the Mexican War in 1848. During this time the Mexican laws, such as they were, were used to govern the land.

When a land becomes a part of the United States, as California did at the end of the Mexican War, Congress is supposed to provide a territorial government. This government makes sure the mail is delivered, organizes courts of justice, and provides civil or military protection if needed. When enough people have moved to the territory, they can ask to become a state.

Congress would not provide a territorial government for California because the legislators were afraid. In 1849 there were 15 Northern states that did not allow people to be kept as slaves (called free states) and 15 Southern states that did. If California became an organized territory, soon it would want to become a state. If it chose to be a free state, the Northern states would become more powerful than the Southern. Many Southern congressmen did not want the North to become powerful because then they would lose their states' rights. Congress postponed making such an important decision.

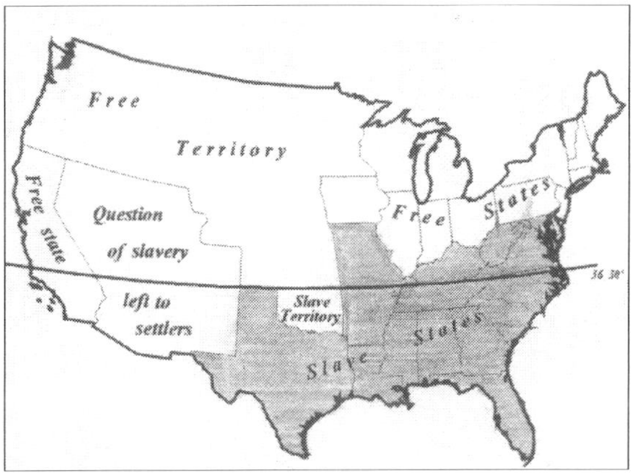

When California became the 16th free state, the balance between slave and free states would be forever destroyed. Eleven years later the Southern states tried to leave the Union. North fought against South in the War Between the States. At its end, slavery would no longer be permitted in the land, and the federal government would rule over the states.

Finally, the Californians realized that if they wanted a stable form of government, they would have to form it themselves. General Bennet Riley, the military governor, asked the people to choose delegates, or representatives, to meet in Monterey in September of 1849.

### Constitutional Convention

On September 3, 1849, 48 delegates from all over California met in the upper floor of Colton Hall in Monterey. These men came from a variety of nations. Although most of them were Americans, Californios from the South, miners, and pre-Gold Rush settlers were all represented. Very few of the representatives knew each other. Their only plan was to prepare a constitution for California. General Vallejo, Thomas Larkin, and Captain Sutter were some of the men chosen as delegates to the Constitutional Convention.

## California's First Constitution

The constitution written in 1849 is not California's present Constitution. A new constitution was written in 1879, completely replacing the old. Although the original constitution did have some limitations, it contained many wise provisions which the current one does not:

1. Legislators could not vote to increase their own salaries. Any pay raise would not take effect until after the voting legislators' terms had expired (Article IV Sec. 24).

2. No lottery could be authorized by the state, nor could lottery tickets be sold (Article IV Sec. 27).

3. The state was not allowed to set up banks. Private persons could establish banks, but the state could not exercise control over them (Article IV Sec. 34).

4. Paper money was not allowed in the state. Gold and silver coins were the only money that could be used. The state government could not print paper money to replace gold that it did not have (Article IV Sec. 35).

5. The state government could not spend more money than it had. The amount of the debt the state could incur was strictly limited (Article VIII).

6. Common schools were supported by the sale and rent of certain land set aside for that purpose. Also, money from estates of people who died without wills or heirs was added to this fund. People were not taxed to build or support the first public schools (Article IX Sec. 2).

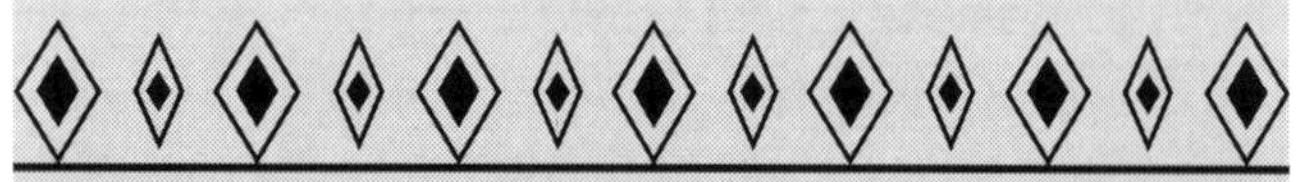

A constitution is a written set of laws that tells the government what it can and cannot do. The U.S. Constitution gives rules of the national government and says all states have powers not reserved for the federal government. Therefore, each state needs its own constitution to put limits on this power.

The delegates to the convention did not forget their need for God's guidance in their work. "Recognizing the fact that there is need of more than human wisdom, in the work of founding a state under the unprecedented condition of the country," the minutes of the first meeting record, "the delegates voted to open the session with prayer" led by Rev. Samuel Willey and Father Antonio Ramirez.

First the delegates had to decide whether to form a state or territorial government. They chose state, and California became the first state to seek admission to the Union without first being an organized territory.

Next, they talked about slavery. All the delegates, including many from the Southern states, voted to prohibit slavery within California's borders.

The convention finished its business in October. Copies of the constitution were distributed among the people. In November 1849, the people approved the new constitution almost unanimously.

### Statehood

William Gwinn and John Charles Frémont were elected as Senators and brought the new constitution to Washington, D.C. They asked that California be admitted as the 31st state. Since California had already decided the slavery issue for itself,

Congress accepted the constitution. California was officially admitted to the Union on September 9, 1850.

One month later, the mail ship *Oregon* steamed toward the port of San Francisco with flags waving from every mast and sporting a huge sign. City businesses closed, and people watched the ship until they could read the sign: "California is a State!"

The entire city exploded in a grand celebration. Bells rang, men cheered, women and children laughed with delight. Messengers were sent from San Francisco to carry the news to the rest of the state. They galloped away, shouting and singing. As they passed a town or a rancho, people ran out to see what all the excitement was.

"California is admitted to the Union!" the rider shouted as he raced by. Looking back, he saw men shaking hands and throwing their hats into the air. Cheers followed him as he raced on to share the news with others. People all over the state were grateful to be a part of the Union. Peter Bennet, the new governor of California, appointed November 29, 1850, as a solemn day of thanksgiving and prayer for the new state of California.

## A Look Back

FOR SEVERAL HUNDRED YEARS, California remained the possession of the Indians. Spain claimed it for 52 years and Mexico for 25. During all this time, thousands of people lived in the land. All this changed in 1850. Once a part of the United States, California's population grew to millions and its economy to one of the most prosperous in the world.

### The State Seal

California's constitution directed that a state seal be designed to be used on all official documents. It contains thirty-one stars to represent the states in the Union at the time California was admitted.

Minerva, the Roman goddess of wisdom, is in the foreground. According to Roman mythology, one day Jupiter, the chief of the gods, had a great headache. It was finally relieved when the goddess Minerva sprang from his forehead, fully grown. She symbolizes the fact that California joined the Union fully formed without ever having been an organized territory.

A grizzly bear is at her feet beside a miner, cradle, and bowl to symbolize the great mineral wealth of California. Beyond them, ships in the bay symbolize commercial greatness while the Sierra Nevada rise in the distance. The motto "EUREKA," which means "I have found it!" appears at the top of the seal.

**Other state symbols include**

**Flower:** California poppy

**Tree:** California redwood

**Bird:** Quail

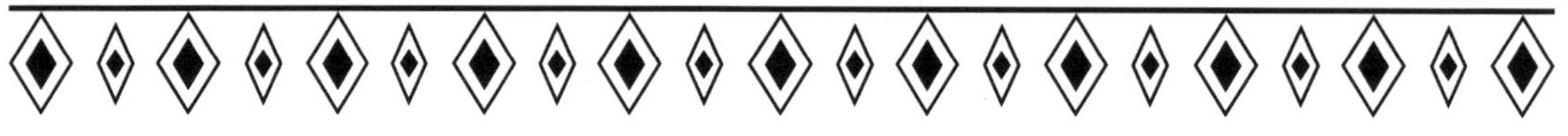

Review Questions

# Unit 7 Roundup

## Chapter 20

People to know—Write a sentence describing each of the following:

John Sutter James Marshall

1. Describe the way gold was discovered in California. Who made the discovery?

2. Explain why gold might have been found during the Spanish or Mexican periods but kept a secret.

3. What was providential about the timing of the gold discovery?

## Chapter 21

1. Describe the three ways people traveled to California. Which way would you choose and why?

2. Why should Lewis Manly and John Rogers be considered heroes?

3. **Thought Question:** Why are the people who rushed to California called "forty-niners"?

## Chapter 22

1. Describe different ways to pan for gold.
2. Why do you think Mrs. Phelps made more money selling apple pies than her husband did mining for gold?
3. How was the Rev. Anthony rewarded when he obeyed the fourth commandment?

## Chapter 23

1. What is inflation, and what does it cause?
2. Why did the first Christian ministers come to California when gold was discovered?
3. Describe the hardships of the Owen family.
4. How was law and order a result of the Gold Rush?
5. The Christian ministers believed God caused the Gold Rush for what reason?
6. Why didn't the U.S. Congress provide a territorial government for California?
7. Describe California's first Constitutional Convention.
8. **Thought Question:** On what day did California become a state? What do we call this holiday?

Unit 8

# Beginnings & Endings

On this rock I will build My church,

and the gates of Hades shall not prevail against it.

And I will give you the keys of the kingdom of heaven,

and whatever you bind on earth will be bound in heaven,

and whatever you loose on earth will be loosed in heaven.

~~ Matthew 16:18-19

The Gold Rush brought Christian ministers to California, and churches soon followed.

## *Great Changes*

THE PERIOD AFTER THE GOLD RUSH WAS a time of great change for California. Thousands of men flocked to its shores. The gold seekers were not looking for a home; rather, they were looking for quick riches and wealth. Lawlessness and crime flourished between 1850 and 1856.

What could tame this throng of people? Christianity could. Many of the Americans who came to California were Christians. After they decided to stay in California, they sent for their families. They built homes and churches and began to take dominion over their society. San Francisco, as the leading city of the new state, contained the first churches. Later churches were built in most of the gold-mining towns as well as in Sacramento, Stockton, and other cities in Northern California.

In this unit we will look at the changes that took place between 1850 and 1870. We will see how San Francisco became a law-abiding, prosperous city. We will see how the great ranchos of the state turned into smaller farms and homes as the Californios became American citizens. Finally, we will see what happened to the California Indians and how some were absorbed into California society while others suffered as they clung to their old way of life.

Since many men came to California without their families, they appreciated letters from home. Whenever a ship entered San Francisco Bay, long lines formed at the Post Office. Those who received letters rejoiced.

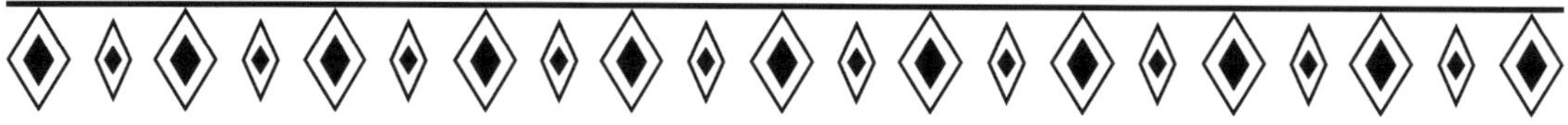

Chapter 24

# The Taming of San Francisco

In 1847, fewer than 500 people lived in the sleepy pueblo called Yerba Buena. Within three years, the name changed to San Francisco, and the population grew to 50,000. Men from all over the world thronged to its port. Portsmouth Square, the town plaza, bustled with men from Asia, Africa, the Pacific Islands, Europe, South America, and of course, America. All wore their native clothing and spoke their native languages, creating a very colorful scene. Very few women lived in San Francisco in these early days. Most of the men were very young, around age twenty-five.

San Francisco's early boarding houses were not very comfortable.

The population of San Francisco increased so quickly that the men could not find houses. Some men stayed at boarding homes. Rough boards set into walls served as beds. Luxuries like sheets, pillows, or mattresses were not available. Sometimes a few coarse blankets were used by all the men. As soon as one fell asleep, his blanket was given to another. These boarding houses were often very uncomfortable places in which to live. They were infested with fleas and lice. Other men formed mess-companies. They pitched tents, bought a skillet or coffee pot, and took turns cooking. Soon thousands of tents dotted San Francisco's hillsides.

San Francisco men dreaded wash day because there were very few women to help with this task. Men had to do it themselves or pay someone else. Often it was less expensive to buy new clothes than to pay to have them washed.

The men of early San Francisco were quite rowdy. They cared little for California and felt no responsibility to become good citizens. Some men were Christians, but there were many temptations in San Francisco. Early San Francisco is a good example of how quickly Christians can fall away from their duties and into sin without the restraining influence of God's Word: "Therefore we must give the more earnest heed to the things we have heard, lest we drift away" (Heb. 2:1).

Gambling thrived in early San Francisco. The gambling houses were truly magnificent, the most richly decorated buildings in the city. Musicians filled the air with their sweet strains. Beautiful women served drinks at the bar. Often homesick young men would go to these gambling houses at night rather than sit in their dark tents and dream about home. They were easily caught up in the colorful excitement and often gambled or drank the night away.

Before the Gold Rush, few people came to California by way of San Francisco. Most came to Monterey, the capital during the Mexican period. In 1848, Yerba Buena Cove looked like the top picture.

The Gold Rush brought thousands of people to San Francisco Bay since it was the closest harbor to the mines. Sailors abandoned their ships in the bay and tried to find their fortune in gold. The picture at the bottom shows Yerba Buena Cove in 1849.

Yerba Buena Cove no longer exists. Looking for more land, the early Californians filled the cove with sand from other building projects. It is now San Francisco's financial district—the area around Montgomery St.

## The Houses of God

God sent His ministers into the unruly city of San Francisco, beginning with the Rev. T. Dwight Hunt, who became the City Chaplain. Many other ministers followed.

Rev. O. C. Wheeler, a Baptist minister, arrived in February 1849. He began preaching in the home of Mr. Ross, a leading San Francisco businessman. But after four Sundays there were only six people attending the service.

Mr. Ross grew discouraged about the low attendance and said to Rev. Wheeler, "I guess you'll have to give this up, Parson."

"Give what up?" asked the preacher.

"Oh, this preaching and Sunday School," Mr. Ross replied. "It's no use. The pressure is too strong—you can't make it go."

Rev. Wheeler stated, "I will give up the effort in your house if you say so, but I shall get another place. I didn't come here to give up but to succeed, and I shall do it or die!"

Four weeks later the house overflowed with people listening to the service. By August, six months after Rev. Wheeler's arrival, the First Baptist Church of San Francisco was dedicated. It was the first Protestant building in California.

The Methodists sent Rev. Isaac Owen to Sacramento, as discussed in the previous unit, and Rev. William Taylor to San Francisco. One day shortly after his arrival, William Taylor planned to preach Sunday afternoon on Portsmouth Square.

"What!" exclaimed his friends, "That's where all the gamblers are! Why, if they don't like what you say, they will shoot you on the spot. No one will take any notice other than a brief announcement in tomorrow's paper that a preacher was killed on the square!" William Taylor knew the danger, but he was determined to go anyway.

Later that afternoon, Rev. Taylor arrived at the Plaza, seated his wife and another woman on a bench, and borrowed a carpenter's workbench for a pulpit. One of his friends, thinking Rev. Taylor needed protection from the sun, went across to Brown's Hotel to borrow an umbrella.

"I won't give an umbrella to a preacher," was the haughty answer, "but if I had some rotten eggs, I'd give them to him!" William Taylor was safe from the eggs. Eggs cost nine dollars a dozen, and the man could not afford to throw them at the preacher.

Standing on the carpenter's bench, Rev. Taylor began to sing in a deep, rich voice:

*Hear the royal proclamation*
*The glad tidings of salvation,*
*Published now to every creature,*
*To the ruin'd sons of nature,*
*Lo! He reigns, He reigns victorious*
*Over heaven and earth most glorious,*
*Jesus reigns!*

By the time Rev. Taylor finished all seven verses of the song, a crowd of 1,000 curious men surrounded him.

"Gentlemen," he began, "your favorite rule in arithmetic is the rule of 'loss and gain.' In your tedious voyage around the Horn, or your wearisome journey over the plains, or your hurried passage across the Isthmus, and during the few months of your stay in California, you have thought of nothing other than how much money you will lose or gain. Now, I want to ask you a question using your favorite arithmetic rule. I want you to use all of your mathematical power and skill to figure out the answer: 'What is a man profited if he shall gain the whole world, and lose his own soul?'" (Matt. 16:26).

Every man was completely orderly and attentive. The gamblers did not interfere. This was the first of over 600 sermons that Rev. Taylor preached on the streets of San Francisco between 1849 and 1856. He refreshed the Christians in California and encouraged them as God redeemed sinners in the land of gold and crime.

The winter of 1849-50 was very cold and rainy, one of the worst on record. People had poor shelter and since prices were so high, they also had a poor diet. There was much suffering. Many men died. San Francisco's early ministers banded together and formed the Strangers' Friend Society to provide relief for the sufferers. The Reverends Hunt, Taylor, and Wheeler, along with their congregations, participated in this ministry.

Presbyterian, Episcopalian, Congregationalist, and many other ministers also came to San Francisco. By 1852 there were thirty churches in the city. All of the ministers supported each other's ministry. They put aside church differences and worked together to help the people of California. On Monday mornings they met together, prayed for each other, and offered encouragement.

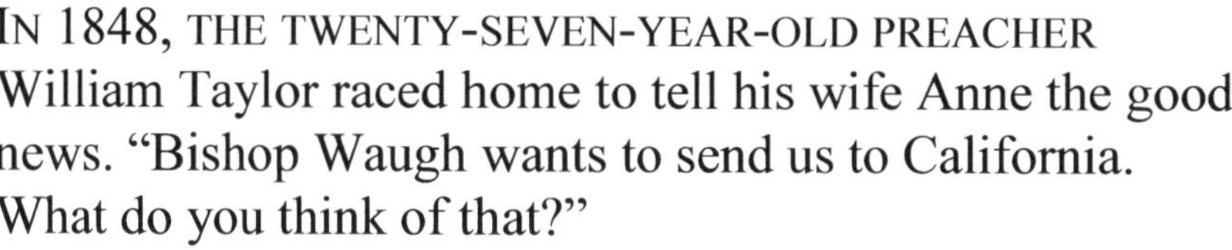

# William Taylor

IN 1848, THE TWENTY-SEVEN-YEAR-OLD PREACHER William Taylor raced home to tell his wife Anne the good news. "Bishop Waugh wants to send us to California. What do you think of that?"

Mrs. Taylor made no reply but ran upstairs to her room. She returned in a few minutes, smiling and said, "Yes, I'll go with you to California."

"How did you settle the question so quickly?" asked Rev. Taylor.

Anne replied, "I went upstairs and kneeled down and said, 'Lord, Bishop Waugh wants to send us to California. Thou knowest, Lord, that I don't want to go, and see no possible way of getting there (the Taylors had two small children and were expecting a third). But all things are possible with Thee, and if it is Thy will to send us to California, give me the desire to go.' In a second or two He filled and thrilled my whole being with a desire to go to California." Thus the Taylors sailed from Baltimore, Maryland, to California. Their daughter, Oceana Taylor, was born off Cape Horn.

An incident that happened on the voyage shows the character of William Taylor. One Sunday in the South Pacific while Taylor was reading the Bible, he heard an excited cry, "A shark! A shark!" Everyone ran to see the huge monster. Many tried to catch it with baited hooks, but the shark bit them off. Finally it was harpooned and drawn aboard. Colonel Myers, returning from the excitement, came back to Rev. Taylor as he sat, still reading the Bible. Rev. Taylor continues the story in his book *California Life Illustrated*:

"Did you not see the shark?" Colonel Myers asked.

"No, sir," said I.

"Why not?" said he, with great surprise.

"I was engaged," replied I, "in reading the word of the Lord, which to me is of more importance than shark killing, especially on the Sabbath." Rev. Taylor continued to explain, "Colonel, if I was talking to a king on important business, and if in the middle of the conversation I ran off over some small excitement, like a shark killing, wouldn't I be showing great disrespect? I have just been reading a message from and talking to the Great King. If I were to run away to see a fish killed on this His holy day, I would not be treating the Lord with courtesy."

In addition to words, Taylor ministered to the Californians through deeds. He formed a Bible Society to give people Bibles and Christian literature. He ministered to men in the city's filthy hospitals by writing and sending letters for them, talking about their spiritual condition, and tending to their bodily needs. Hospital reform followed through his efforts.

William Taylor also started a ministry for sailors called Bethel. He thought that sailors who heard the gospel in San Francisco could spread it throughout the world. He fearlessly spoke about the evil practice of *shanghaiing*, where men were kidnapped and forced to serve as sailors on the ships.

William Taylor courageously spoke out against the evils of San Francisco, especially gambling and drinking, yet he became a friend to the gamblers. If one died and wanted a Christian burial, his friends called William Taylor to perform the funeral service. Taylor would faithfully warn the gamblers of their dangerous path. He won their admiration and confidence.

His preaching was very successful. One man said, "I am a gambler, and I did a first-rate business, and made money here, till these preachers came to the city. But this fellow [Taylor] is hallooing at the people here every Sunday, and has broke up my business. I can't get a decent living."

During the seven years William Taylor spent in California, he faithfully proclaimed the Word of God. He confronted men with their sin and called on them to repent. He held and controlled a crowd using a combination of humor and sternness. Sometimes he spoke to 20,000 men at a time.

Rev. William Taylor left his ministry in California in 1856, but his life's work was just beginning. San Francisco had become a more settled, law-abiding city, but most of the world still needed to hear the gospel. Taylor spent the next 40 years bringing the gospel to every continent. He crossed the equator 37 times on his missionary tours. In 1884, at the age of 63, he became the Missionary Bishop of Africa. He established 36 mission stations in the Congo to bring education and the gospel to the natives.

Rev. Taylor finally retired at the age of 75. He spent the last six years of his life in Southern California.

## Fiery Judgment

FIVE SERIOUS FIRES BURNED SAN FRANCISCO BETWEEN 1850 and 1851. Some were deliberately set to act as distractions for men committing crimes. The flimsy tents were quickly consumed along with filth and garbage piled up around homes.

The most destructive fire was May 3, 1851. Most of the city burned. William Taylor called this fire a judgment from God and urged the citizens of San Francisco to turn from their wicked ways.

The last great fire occurred in June 1851. By this time the San Franciscans had learned some lessons. They rebuilt the city with fire-proof materials instead of canvas tents. They constructed sewers to dispose of garbage. Fire-fighters were organized, and reservoirs were built throughout the city.

The city continued to grow, and more land was needed. There was very little level land available. The city of San Francisco contained many large hills of sand. Some of these sand hills were leveled at great effort and expense. One man built a house on a street which was later lowered. He had to build a "basement" to his house and it became two stories. Soon after, the city lowered the street again, and the man had to turn his home into three stories. The extra sand was thrown into Yerba Buena Cove, filling in the bay. Some of the most valuable buildings in San Francisco are built on what used to be mud-flats.

The city of San Francisco continued to grow and improve. City streets were made of dirt, which quickly turned into mud during the rainy season. When these streets were planked with wood, it became much easier to travel in the winter. Wharves jutting out into the bay became streets. The city sold the new waterfront land very high prices.

## The Vigilance Committee

CRIME WAS A MAJOR PROBLEM IN EARLY SAN FRANCISCO. ONE historian has estimated that there were 1,000 murders between 1849 and 1856, only one of which was brought to justice. The people got together in 1851 to punish some criminals and banish others, but the effects of their efforts were short-lived. Honest men were unwilling to take time away from their business and devote themselves to solving the crime problem.

By 1856, the situation began to change when men sent for their families and settled permanently. Churches thrived. Gambling was outlawed in 1855. The people of San Francisco began to take responsibility to make it a safe place to live.

They had much to accomplish. San Francisco's government was very dishonest. City leaders took bribes and rarely brought criminals to trial. Crime truly paid. Even the voting procedures were corrupt. Ballot boxes were stuffed. In this illegal practice, voting boxes were filled with ballots pre-marked for a particular candidate. This candidate would always win since there were more pre-marked ballots than honest votes.

James King of William was the editor of a newspaper called the *Daily Evening Bulletin*. Since James King was a common name, he added his father's name "of William" so he would not be confused with other men. Mr. King, according to Rev. Taylor, was a Christian. He began to attack the evil in the city by writing about it, sometimes very rashly. Soon he had many enemies. When he revealed that one of the city supervisors, a man named James Casey, had served time in the New York State Prison, his life was in danger. One evening as James King of William walked home from work, Casey shot him. King died several days later.

The men of San Francisco had finally had enough. They organized a group called the Committee of Vigilance. Soon 6,000 of the best citizens had become members of the committee. They arrested Casey, gave him a fair trial, found him guilty, and sentenced him to be hanged. Hanging was the required punishment for murder in those days. The sentence was carried out at the same time James King of William was buried.

The Committee of Vigilance worked for six months to cleanse the city. After trials, it hanged ten men and banished many others. When the committee disbanded, 8,000 men marched in a parade to show their support for its efforts.

## Was it Right?

In the United States people are governed by law, not by men. No man can randomly decide what is right or wrong. He must obey the laws set forth in the Constitution as well as the laws in the Bible. In San Francisco, evil men set the law aside. They used their positions for their own gain. The men of the Vigilance Committee believed it was their duty to restore the rule of law and reclaim the government from men who were abusing their power.

Sometimes it is hard to determine the rightness or wrongness of a question that is covered by the dust of time. In this case it is sometimes helpful to examine the opinions of godly men who lived at the time being studied. Let's see what the San Francisco ministers of the 1850s thought about these actions.

Every minister save one supported the committee's actions. Rev. William Caldwell Anderson, a San Francisco pastor, said, "It seems hard to let the people rise and yet it is necessary here. We have no law—no power in our courts—all is in the hands of gamblers and villains."

Rev. William Taylor said, "Violent outward remedies [to crime and wickedness] are sometimes necessary, as it is necessary to cut off a growing cancer; but the root is still there, and it will grow again. The individual hearts composing society, must be regenerated by the grace of God, and thus the purified fountain will send forth a pure stream. 'The good tree will bring forth good fruit'" (Matt. 7:17). He said that the efforts of the Vigilance Committee cleared away the wickedness of the city, but to achieve true and lasting reform, men must repent and turn from their evil ways.

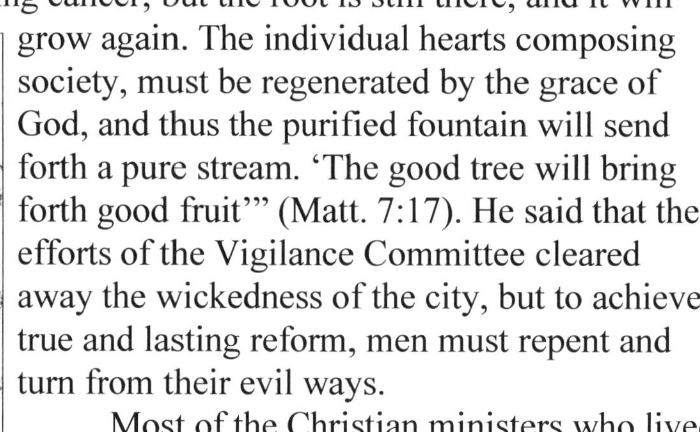

William Coleman speaking to the crowd from the balcony of the Graham House.

Most of the Christian ministers who lived in San Francisco at the time believed that the actions of the Vigilance Committee were regrettable but right. They knew that the citizens of San Francisco had the obligation to reclaim their city's government, but they also knew that no lasting reform could be expected unless men repented and governed themselves according to God's law. They approved the orderly actions of the Vigilance Committee. But they also taught the people of San Francisco about the Lord Jesus Christ so that they would live their lives in a way that would please Him.

## William Coleman

WILLIAM COLEMAN CAME TO CALIFORNIA IN 1849 to seek his fortune in the gold fields. He quickly found he was not suited to gold mining and became a merchant in San Francisco, buying goods from incoming ships and selling them to other people. After James King of William was murdered, William Coleman led the Vigilance Committee. He hated mobs and worked to make the committee orderly and upright. Coleman insisted that, although the committee was technically outside the law, its duty was to uphold the law.

When the committee disbanded in August 1856, Coleman went back to business. He worked hard and became a millionaire. In 1877, 21 years after he headed the Vigilance Committee, more trouble came to San Francisco. Unemployed troublemakers accused the Chinese in the city of taking away their jobs. They threatened to riot and burn the Pacific Mail Steamships that brought the Chinese to San Francisco. The police and the military did not have enough men to stop the rioters, so they asked William Coleman to organize a committee of citizens to help them. Once again Coleman laid aside his work and organized the people.

Coleman did two things which saved many lives. First, he had his men buy up all of the guns in town so that they would be in the hands of honest men and not available to the rioters. Second, he issued his own men hickory sticks for weapons instead of guns. The rioters were stopped with no loss of life because of Coleman's wisdom. The citizens of San Francisco, the governor, and other authorities were very grateful to the honest and morally upright William Coleman.

An incident towards the end of Coleman's life shows his integrity. After he had invested in a new business project, the government changed one of its policies, causing Coleman to lose his entire fortune. He became bankrupt and owed thousands of dollars. According to the law, he was only required to pay forty percent of the money he owed; however, Coleman worked very hard for four years and paid back every cent. The effort broke his health, and he died one year later at the age of 70.

Chapter 25

# End of the Ranchos

As San Francisco changed from a lawless to a law-abiding town, many other changes occurred between 1850 and 1870 in California.

When the United States signed the treaty ending the Mexican War, all Mexican citizens, or Californios, became American citizens. Furthermore, the United States agreed to protect the property of these new citizens. All Californios could keep their land if they had lawful title to it. However, determining which titles were lawful became a real challenge for the Americans.

A bullock's head fastened to a tree could mark the boundaries between rancheros' land during the Mexican period.

During the Mexican period of California's history, land was given freely to whoever wanted it. The boundaries of the land grants were poorly defined and sometimes overlapped neighboring ranchos, so both rancheros claimed the same property. This was not a problem since land was used only to raise cattle. If cattle wandered onto a neighbor's land, they would be sorted out at the next rodeo.

In the confusion following the Gold Rush, many Americans decided to make California their home. Oftentimes they built farms on land that they thought was vacant but really was already owned by a ranchero. The United States finally set up a Land Commission to resolve these problems.

The Land Commission had the difficult task of examining each claim to see if it conformed to Mexican law. Some were invalid because the land had not been granted by a person with the proper authority. One of Captain Sutter's land grants was disallowed for this reason. Others were rejected because the Californios had not obeyed Mexican law and lived on the land for at least a year. A few were outright frauds. The Land Commissioners spent four years, from 1852 to 1856, examining the records. Their decisions were generally fair; although due to the problems they faced, undoubtedly they made some mistakes.

Rancheros could appeal the commissioners' decisions to the U.S.

District and Supreme Courts. When they did, it took 15 or 20 years to establish legal ownership. Meanwhile, lawyers had to be paid. Many rancheros gave their lawyers part of their land to pay for legal fees.

### Californios Prosper

In spite of the problems with the land grants, the Californios prospered as American citizens in the years following the Gold Rush. They were close to the gold fields and found large strikes in the early days. Their property values increased after the Americans came, so they could sell all or parts of their property at higher prices. Of course, they had to wait until the Land Commission decided that the titles were lawful. Rancheros also became very wealthy by selling their cattle. During the Mexican period, cattle were valuable only for their hides, which sold for $2 apiece. After the Gold Rush, cattle were sold at very high prices to feed hungry miners.

What did the rancheros do with all of this newly acquired wealth? Some of it was spent on lawyers as the rancheros defended their land titles. Most, however, they spent on rich living. Rancheros bought fancy clothes and furnishings, and they threw elaborate parties. They did not save much for the future.

By 1856, most of the surface gold had been taken from the mines, and mining got harder. As the miners switched to other methods of taking gold from the ground, the gold, or money supply, decreased, or deflated. We have seen in our study of the Gold Rush that as gold was found, the money supply increased since gold is money. This increase is called inflation. It causes prices to rise. Deflation is the opposite of inflation. It results when the money supply, in this case gold, decreases. It causes prices to fall. Since most of the rancheros had saved nothing for the future, they had problems getting through these hard times. Cattle prices dropped, and many Californios were forced to sell more of their land to pay their debts.

### Storms and Drought

In November 1861, California experienced an extremely severe rainstorm. This storm was the worst in California's history. Rain poured for fifteen days. Fifteen more days of downpour followed in December. When the skies finally cleared in January 1862, much of California was

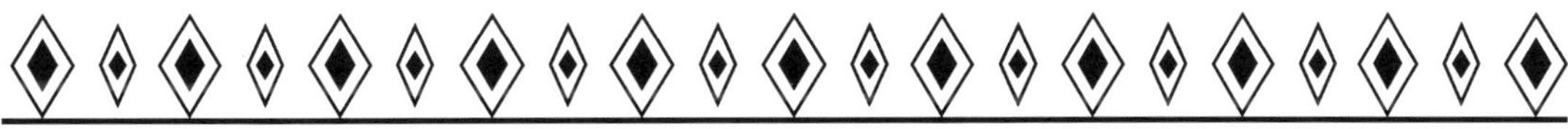

devastated. Rivers and streams had overflowed and ruined thousands of homes. Entire valleys were under water. Entire towns were swept away. Trees were uprooted, and vineyards and orchards were destroyed. When the flood waters finally receded, the land was covered with a residue of sand.

The rains caused much grass to grow in 1862. Cattle grew fat on it and sold at record prices. However, this was the Californios' last chance with the ten talents the Lord had given them. Most still did not store up their wealth for the future.

A severe drought followed the huge winter rains. It rained only once during the two years, 1862 and 1863. After the grass withered, the cattle had nothing to eat. They died by the thousands. Once-prosperous ranchos filled with white, sun-bleached bones. Normal rainfall did not occur again until 1865, four years after the downpour.

Most of the ranchos were broken up after the drought. Californios lost their cattle and had to sell their land to pay their debts. The few that had used their money wisely invested in sheep and began to raise sheep instead of cattle. Some Californios worked for the sheep ranchers, while others worked for farmers or turned to other pursuits. By 1900, very few of the ranchos remained. Instead, the land was dotted with farms run by enterprising Americans, some of whom were former Californio rancheros.

Some Californians of the time saw the demise of the ranchos as the work of God. Benjamin Hayes, a judge from Los Angeles, said, "The finger of Providence [God] seems to mark the decay of the old California families." When asked why, he added, "We must not judge, but the Indians have suffered great crimes and injustices from the later Mexican governors and people."

The next generation of children did not grow up on ranchos; instead, they lived on farms or in towns and were educated in American schools. One Californio, Romualdo Pacheco, became governor of California in 1875. Others prospered in various ways as they joined the new American society.

Some of General Mariano Vallejo's land claims were disallowed by the Land Commission. He also had many problems with squatters and other lawless men who came to California at the beginning of the Gold Rush. Yet, in later years General Vallejo said:

> The inhabitants of California have nothing to complain of in the change of government, for even though the rich saw themselves robbed of thousands of horses and cattle, the condition of the poor has been improved. Formerly an ordinary education was obtained with great difficulty while today it would be hard to find any place where educated people do not abound.

Chapter 26

# Decline of the Indians

After the missions were destroyed during the Mexican period of California's history, hundreds of ranchos were established. Some former Mission Indians lived and worked on the ranchos, especially in the southern part of the state. Many of these Indians realized the Spanish goal of becoming citizens. They became productive members of California society, sometimes marrying Californios.

At the same time, the Indians living in California's interior experienced great hardship. In 1833, most of the Indians in the San Joaquin Valley died from malaria after fur trappers from the Hudson's Bay Company in Oregon brought this deadly disease to California. When the missions were destroyed, some of the Mission Indians moved to the valley and lived in the deserted villages.

As food became scarce, the valley Indians caused trouble for the ranchos. They stole horses from the ranchos and traded them for supplies with people in New Mexico. Violence increased. John Marsh, who owned a rancho across the bay and east of San Francisco, wrote letters to the local newspapers complaining about these thefts. Both Californios and Indians were often killed when the rancheros tried to stop these thefts or recover their horses. This stealing continued after California became a state and caused great conflict between the settlers and Indians.

After the American conquest, the army tried to protect settlers from Indian raiding. Calls for help came from Sonoma, Monterey, Los Angeles, San Luis Obispo, and San Diego. Indian raiders made traveling very dangerous. They continued to raid livestock and killed anyone who challenged them.

The Indians had a chance to prosper at the beginning of the Gold Rush. Labor was in short supply, and the Indians could find jobs working for gold miners or farmers. Many did and soon learned to demand to be paid in gold or silver. Indians panned for gold and traded for food and clothing. But, as more gold seekers came to California, the demand for Indian labor fell off. Captain Sutter, who employed many Indians on his Hock Farm, explained that the Indians would work for a week and then rest for a week. This could be a big problem during a harvest when the crop needed to be gathered quickly, as there would not be time to find more workers. Indians would also spend much of their earnings on alcohol. Often the Indians were not reliable workers.

Troubles increased as the Gold Rush brought thousands of Americans and foreigners to California. In 1850, the Modocs in Northern California attacked a group of 80 in a wagon train that had just camped for the night. The Indians surprised and massacred all but one in the group, including the women and children. The place was later named Bloody Point. A year later the Modocs tried to murder another group of immigrants passing through the same territory. The army arrived just in time to stop them.

As more people came, more problems occurred. Violence erupted, especially in the southern mines. Whites killed Indians, and Indians killed whites. The army could not keep order. Something had to be done.

## The Treaties

Before the U.S. purchased the California territory after the Mexican War, its policy towards the Indians was called "removal." Indi-

An Indian rancheria, or village, near Riverside in Southern California. This picture was taken in 1890.

ans were encouraged and forced to move to lands farther west. In California, there was no more "west." To stop the conflicts and violence between the Indians and the settlers, the federal government sent three commissioners to California to make treaties with the Indians.

By 1852, these commissioners made 18 treaties with 139 tribes. The Indians were to receive one-third of all the land in California and supplies to help them become self-sufficient. According to the U.S. Constitution, before a treaty can go into effect, it must be ratified, or approved, by the U.S. Senate. The Senate voted unanimously to reject the treaties.

## The Reservations

Instead, the federal government began the reservation system, which was similar to the Spanish missions. Agents taught the Indians agriculture. By 1857, nearly one-sixth of the California Indians were living on the reservations. In later years, the number increased to almost half. Like the Spanish missions, the reservations were supposed to be temporary. Unlike the Spanish missions, they were run by very corrupt men who were more interested in making money than in helping the Indians.

Before the War Between the States, Captain (later General) Ulysses S. Grant was stationed at Fort Humboldt in Northern California, in present-day Eureka. His job was to protect the settlers from hostile Indians. After Grant became President of the United States in 1870, he asked Christian churches to run the Indian reservations. They added Christian training to the Indians' education. They were successful in bringing the gospel to the Indians as this testimony from the Hoopa Valley Reservation shows:

> "The outpouring of the Holy Spirit in our midst continues with increasing power. Sunday night, the 22nd of February, 1874, 35 declared themselves on the Lord's side, and applied for membership in the Church, making a total to date of 541."

The young members of the Indian tribes were the first to receive Jesus Christ by faith. Later, the older members believed as well.

Other Californians, especially Christians, worked to better conditions for the Indians. They set up schools and tried to assimilate, or absorb, the Indians into American culture.

## John Bidwell and His Work

NOT ALL OF THE INDIANS LIVED ON RESERVATIONS. IN FACT, during the early years, most of them did not. Some lived in villages located on the ranchos. A group of Chico Indians, the Mechoopdas, lived on Rancho Chico, owned by John Bidwell.

Annie Bidwell was the daughter of a high-ranking Washington, D.C, official. She was 29 when she married John Bidwell. President Andrew Jackson and future President Ulysses S. Grant attended their wedding. After they moved to California, they continued to host distinguished guests.

John Bidwell came to California in 1841 on the first overland wagon train. He took part in the Gold Rush and found a rich strike of gold at a place later named Bidwell's Bar. He also opened a successful store at Bidwell's Bar to trade with the miners. John Bidwell used the money he made during the Gold Rush to purchase Rancho Chico, a large ranch near present-day Chico in Northern California.

General Bidwell had seen Indians treated harshly and determined to do something to help them. He invited the 250 members of the Mechoopda tribe to live at Rancho Chico. He protected them from other hostile Indians and settlers, and paid them to work on his ranch. He built homes and other buildings for the tribe and employed a doctor to look after them.

In 1868, at the age of 56, John Bidwell married Annie Kennedy. They had met when General Bidwell was visiting Washington, D.C., as a California Congressman. Bidwell gained more than a wife in Washington, D.C.; he also gained a new life. Through the influence of his godly fiancée and a Christian church, John Bidwell gave his life to the Lord. He had always been strict in his moral life, but now he professed faith in Jesus Christ as his Lord and Savior.

When Mr. and Mrs. Bidwell returned to Rancho Chico in California, the General took his new wife to see the Indian village on his land. Annie Bidwell immediately became his partner in the care of the Indians. She taught them how to speak English, using pictures and how to do arithmetic, using pebbles and sticks for numbers. She taught the women to cook, bake, and how to keep house. Later she taught the Indians to read, sing, and make clothes. The Indians called her the "little white mother."

General Bidwell built a church in the center of the Indian village and taught the people to know the Living God. He often worshipped with them at this church. After he and his wife died, the village became the property of the Indians.

## The End of the Indian Culture

MANY MODERN SCHOLARS BLAME THE AMERICANS FOR THE demise of the Indian culture. They say that the American settlers drove the Indians from their land, brought diseases which killed many, and destroyed villages just to rid the land of the Indians. While these accusations are true in part, many happened before California became a territory of the United States. But these accusations present an incomplete picture of what really happened to the California Indians.

Although the Indian way of life essentially ended by 1870, individual Indians benefited. Their standard of living greatly increased. They had regular food and shelter and opportunities for education. Indian women especially benefited.

The Sherman Institute (originally Perris Indian School) was built in 1872. It was the first boarding school built outside a reservation specifically for Indian children. Students learned agriculture and domestic science. The school still exists and operates today.

The most important benefit the Indians received was hearing about the Living God and having the opportunity to turn their lives over to Him. Jesus Christ is the King, and this world is His kingdom. The Indians had an opportunity to leave their ungodly religion and live in a way that pleased their Lord.

## A Time of Change

CALIFORNIA SAW MORE CHANGES IN THE 20 YEARS BETWEEN 1850 and 1870 than at any previous time in its history. San Francisco rose, the ranchos declined, and the Indians changed. California would continue to grow and prosper over the next several years as Christians flocked to its shores and began to take dominion over the land.

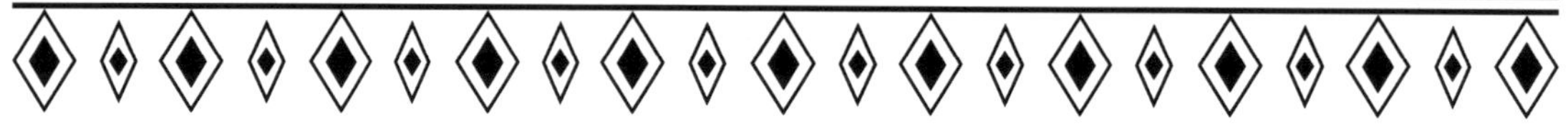

Review Questions

# Unit 8 Roundup

## Chapter 24

1. Describe early (1850-1856) life in San Francisco.

2. Name the first Christian ministers to come to San Francisco, and describe how they helped tame the city.

3. How many men listened to William Taylor's first sermon on Portsmouth Square? How many men do you think would listen to him today? What does this tell you about modern San Francisco?

4. Why were there so many fires in early San Francisco?

5. Why was the Vigilance Committee formed, and what did it do?

6. **Thought Question:** Do you think the actions of the Vigilance Committee were right or wrong? Explain your answer.

## Chapter 25

1. What were some of the problems the Land Commission experienced with California property?

2. How did the Gold Rush affect the Californios?

3. What providential event caused the break-up of many ranchos?

4. **Thought question:** Read Matthew 25:14-30 and tell how it applies to the Californios.

## Chapter 26

1. Write two or three sentences describing the conflicts between the settlers and the California Indians.

2. How did Annie Bidwell minister to the Indians of Rancho Chico?

3. In what ways did the California Indians benefit from contact with the Americans?

Unit 9

# Linking to the Union

“The Yankees are a wonderful people—wonderful!
Wherever they go, they make improvements.
If they were to emigrate [move] in large numbers to hell itself,
they would irrigate it, plant trees and flower gardens,
build reservoirs and fountains and make everything beautiful and pleasant,
so that by the time we get there,
we can sit down at a marble-topped table
and eat ice-cream.”

~~ General Mariano Vallejo

And let us not be weary in well doing
for in due season we shall reap
if we faint not.
~~ Galatians 6:9

## Religion Motivates

AS WE LOOK BACK OVER OUR STUDY OF California history, one thing is clear: the people who lived there were motivated by their religion. What they did depended a great deal on what they believed.

California Indians lived in the state for hundreds, perhaps thousands, of years. Yet they made almost no improvements to the land because their religion forbade change. Oftentimes the land did not produce enough food, but the religion of the Indians would not allow them to improve their food-gathering methods.

The Spaniards came to California as a result of their religion. They believed they were commanded to bring Catholicism to the natives of California. However, the Spaniards were very dependent on the government to provide for their welfare. During the fifty-two years of their stay, they were able only to sparsely settle a thin strip of land near California's coast.

The twenty years that Mexico ruled California were lawless years as religion was largely set aside. The Californians were influenced by ungodly, humanistic ideas like those that caused the French Revolution.

The Americans brought Christianity to California along with Christian ideas, such as community and self-government. Men and women worked hard to turn California into a prosperous home. The Americans made more improvements to California before 1900 than the Indians, Spaniards, and Mexicans combined, as they followed God's law using the Bible as their standard.

In this unit we will continue to study the Americanization of California. We will begin with California's part in the War Between the States, the war that almost destroyed the Union. We will study various methods of transportation, especially the transcontinental railroad which connected California to the East. Finally, we will study the beginnings of Los Angeles and see how this Mexican pueblo transformed into a great and mighty city.

### Civil War Generals in California

Many famous generals spent time in California prior to 1861. They included:

- **William T. Sherman**—a San Francisco banker.
- **Henry W. Halleck**—an engineer who came to California to inspect the Pacific coast defenses in 1847. Was a delegate to the first Constitutional Convention and a member of a law firm for six years.
- **Joseph Hooker**—a captain in the Mexican War. Retired for ten years and lived on a ranch near Sonoma. Ended retirement and became known as "Fighting Joe Hooker."
- **Philip H. Sheridan**—a railroad surveyor who came to California in 1855 to map a railroad route from Oregon to California.
- **Ulysses S. Grant**—an army Captain stationed at Fort Humbolt, near present day Eureka. Later became president of the U.S.
- **David G. Farragut**—a naval captain at Mare Island where his wife started the first Sunday School in Vallejo. Later became an admiral.
- **Albert S. Johnston**—commanded the United States forces on the Pacific. Resigned to join the Confederacy.

Chapter 27

# Early Transportation

Little did people realize that when California became the thirty-first state in 1850, it would trigger a series of events that would bring about the most severe trial our country has ever faced: the War Between the States, also called the Civil War.

Californians remembered Thomas Starr King in the National Statuary Hall in Washington, D.C. In 2006, the California legislature voted to replace his statue with former president Ronald Reagan's.

California's part in the war was very minor in one respect, and very major in another. All states were required to send a certain number of soldiers to serve in the Northern armies. California was excused because the cost of getting to the east was too high. Many Californians offered their services anyway to other states to help make up their quotas of men. The "California Battalion" fought about 50 battles, mostly in Virginia, with the men of Massachusetts. Other Californians fought with the men from Washington Territory, but most showed their loyalty in other ways.

Thomas Starr King, a Unitarian minister, was a very strong supporter of the Union. (A Unitarian is not a Christian. Unitarians deny the trinity and do not believe that Jesus Christ is God.) King tirelessly supported the Union by collecting money for the Sanitary Commission, an organization similar to today's Red Cross. Of all the money raised for the Sanitary Commission during the war, about one-fourth came from California. Additionally, this money was gold since California's first constitution did not allow paper money. Gold was a real help to the Northern economy. Ulysses S. Grant, later President of the United States, declared, "I do not know what we could do in this great national emergency were it not for the gold sent from California."

### Better Transportation Needed

The War Between the States made Californians realize they needed better transportation to connect them to the Union. The Gold Rush had brought many people to California, but they worked very hard to get there. They had to cross a wide ocean, formidable mountains, or scorching deserts. In this day of instant satellite communication and space shuttles, it is hard for us to imagine how isolated California was.

A trip by freeway that takes us one hour today would have taken five days by oxen in the middle 1800s. Many ideas were tried to link California to the rest of the Union.

## The Panama Railroad

In 1855, a railroad was built across the Isthmus of Panama, making this route safer and faster. Travelers were not as likely to be exposed to disease like the dreaded yellow fever and could make the trip to California in about four weeks. This was still too slow for the men in California hungry for a word from their families.

## The Camel Corps

Californians tried many ways to speed communication with the rest of the United States, some more interesting than others. In 1857, mail was carried by camels. Camels can travel twice as far and four times as fast as mules on the same amount of water. They can also find their own food along the way so that they can carry more goods instead of food. But these unusual animals posed their own unique problems. They smelled awful. They had a very bad temper and would spit when angry. Further, they frightened other livestock, such as horses and cows. They could not be brought into towns without creating quite a disturbance. This clever experiment was not a great success.

For a very short time, camels delivered the mail.

## Stage Coach

In 1858, people began to make the trip to California on Butterfield Overland Express stage coaches. The coaches traveled along the southern route, through Arizona and into California near the place where the Yuma Massacre occurred during the Spanish period. The trip took only twenty-five days to reach San Francisco, but it was very uncomfortable for passengers. Sometimes as many as fifteen people had to ride in and on top of the small stagecoach. The bone-jolting ride, terrible food, and danger from Indian attack discouraged many from making the trip. When the war broke out, the route had to be changed so that the stage coaches traveled through Northern territory, and weather became a hardship. The Union feared that the Butterfield Overland Express would be captured by the Confederacy and used for its benefit.

## *The Pony Express*

THE PONY EXPRESS WAS BEGUN BY THE FIRM OF Russell, Majors, and Waddell to deliver a letter from San Francisco to Missouri in just ten days. They gathered eighty of the finest young riders in the West to ride between 190 stations to deliver the mail. Each young man had to be slightly built to ride a horse such a long distance. Even though the riders traveled light, they were required to carry their Bibles with them at all times.

**All Pony Express riders were required to sign the following oath:**

"I do hearby swear, before the Great and Living God, that during my engagement, and while I am an employee of Russell, Majors & Waddell, I will, under no circumstances, use profane language; that I will drink no intoxicating liquors; that I will not quarrel or fight with any other employee of the firm, and that in every way I will conduct myself honestly, be faithful to my duties, and so direct all my acts as to win the confidence of my employers. So help me God."

One famous Pony Express rider was a man named Buffalo Bill. His section of the journey was filled with hazards from unfriendly Indians and bandits. On one journey he heard that bandits intended to rob him, so he hid the mail under a pouch filled with blank paper.

Soon the road agents found him and demanded, "Hand over the money or we will shoot you!"

"No!" shouted Buffalo Bill. "My job is to protect the mail!"

When the bandits pointed their guns at him, Buffalo Bill began to remove the fake pouch slowly, pretending that he did not want to give it up. Then suddenly he threw it in the face of one of the men, shot the other, and raced off. He arrived at the next station ahead of time and the mail was safe.

Another famous Pony Express rider, Pony Bob Haslam, holds the record for the longest ride. He arrived at the relief station and found that Indians had stolen all of the horses. He had no choice but to go on, even though his horse was very tired. When it came time to change riders, his replacement was ill, so Pony Bob had to ride this man's stretch as well. He had to ride 185 miles before he could rest. His rest was short, only nine hours, before he was called to duty again. When he reached the first station on the return trip, he found that Indians had killed the station master and stolen all of the horses. There was no other rider to continue the trip. When he finally reached his own station, the brave Pony Bob Haslam had ridden a total of 380 miles.

The Pony Express riders faced many dangers. Battling icy streams, hungry wolves, and hostile Indians, they faithfully served their country by carrying the mail.

## The Coming of the Railroad

BEFORE THE SPANIARDS CAME TO CALIFORNIA, WHILE INDIANS STILL roamed the hillsides, explorers searched diligently for a short cut to Europe called the Strait of Anián. Cabrillo searched for it and found California instead. The Englishman Drake looked for it but had to sail around the world to return to England. It was never found since it did not exist. Still the dream persisted.

In the 1850s, men began to think about making a "Strait of Anián" to link Europe and Asia by building a railroad across the United States. Products could be shipped from Europe to the United States, transferred to the railroad, and then shipped from California to Asia. One of the earliest dreamers was an engineer named Theodore Judah.

Judah was more than a dreamer; he was also a hard worker. He developed the first plan for a railroad to connect California to Missouri across the towering Sierras and the burning deserts beyond. At first men called him "Crazy Judah" and laughed at his grand plan. Undaunted, Judah spent many years and much of his own money to map a route. So great was his care that this was almost the exact route that the railroad would eventually follow.

Next, Judah tried to find the money to build the railroad. He was not very successful since the amount needed was enormous. He traveled to Washington, D.C., to try to convince Congress to lend him the money. Congress was willing to build a railroad through U.S. territory but debated about the route it should take. The War Between the States had not yet begun, but in a way storm clouds were on the horizon, and people new it was coming. The North approved Theodore Judah's route since it went through Northern territory. The South, however, would not.

Judah returned to Washington, D.C., again in 1862 after the war had started. Now there was no Southern opposition to the railroad route since the South had seceded* from the Union, and there were no Southern congressmen. Additionally, great amounts of silver had recently been found in Nevada. A railroad would help to bring this silver to the United States Treasury. Congress passed a railroad bond in 1862 to provide the money for this great undertaking. The money would be a loan which the railroad would have to repay out of future earnings.

*Secede* means to pull out or separate—in this case, the Southern states left the Union.

Judah joined four Californians, called the Big Four, to form the Central Pacific. They would start building in California. Another company, the Union Pacific, would start building from Omaha. The two companies would race to see who could build the farthest. The rewards were huge. In addition to the loan from the federal government, each

A thousand foot wall of granite named "Cape Horn" had to be conquered. Chinese men were lowered in baskets over the edge of this wall. For many weeks they patiently chiseled out a narrow ledge. After a foothold was gained the ledge had to be blasted out to accommodate the train track.

company received large grants of land on alternate sides of the rail line, in a checkerboard pattern. When the railroad was completed, the land could be sold at huge profits. If successful, the railroad builders could become very wealthy men.

But the hardships they faced were vast, especially for the California side. All tools and equipment had to be shipped from the East around Cape Horn at great expense and time. Thousands of men must be found to do the sometimes dangerous work. The biggest challenge was crossing the Sierras.

Progress was slow at first. Only eighteen miles of track were laid in 1863. Twelve more were laid the following year. Since the federal government would not pay any money until at least 40 miles of track were laid, the Central Pacific ran out of funds.

When the War Between the States ended, interest in the railroad revived, and construction began in earnest. Immediately, the Central Pacific encountered a big problem: it could not find enough men willing to work on the rails. Charles Crocker solved this problem by employing a group of Chinese. The Chinese were very willing and hard workers. Soon 2,000 were employed. At its peak, 15,000 Chinese worked to build the Central Pacific Railroad.

Fifteen tunnels had to be driven through the solid granite of the Sierra Nevada. Picks and shovels were of little use in this hazardous work, and blasting powder only discolored the rocks. A substance called nitroglycerin was developed to blast through the mountains. This substance was very dangerous, and sometimes the men were blasted along with the rock. Trestles (bridges) had to be laid across chasms, valleys, rivers, and streams.

An historical marker marks the site of China Wall, near Truckee, which was built by hand to shore up the rail tracks above it.

Snow was another worry. The spring thaws of 1867 and 1868 caused the ground to melt. All of the work had to be redone. Avalanches occurred suddenly and swept workers to their deaths. Crocker built snowsheds to protect the trains and allow the work to continue. Thirty-seven of the forty miles of track crossing the summit of the mountains were covered with snowsheds.

The biggest challenge was the summit tunnel. While only fifteen miles in length, it was through the hardest rock yet encountered. Crocker sank a shaft through the middle of the tunnel and had thousands of men work from both ends and the middle in twelve hour shifts around the clock. The men could cut only eight inches a day. It took a full year just to complete the summit tunnel. This was the last tunnel drilled by hand in the United States.

Holes were drilled in rocks and then filled with blasting powder to create the tunnels.

The mountains were finally conquered, and the work continued over the flat, desert land with temperatures reaching 120 degrees. The Chinese workers from the Central Pacific raced against the Irish workers from the Union Pacific to see how much track each side could lay before the line was complete. On the day before the track was joined at Promontory Point in Utah, Crocker bet that his men could lay ten miles of track in just one day. Displaying their skill, loyalty, and teamwork, the Chinese workers did it, and Crocker won his bet.

## The Link is Complete!

Five hundred men from the East and the West gathered at Promontory Point, Utah, on May 10, 1869, to watch the joining of the rails. The rain poured and they had to slosh through mud to reach the tracks. Two trains, one from the Central Pacific, the other from the Union Pacific, sat on the unfinished tracks, nose to nose. A band played in the icy wind. Chinese workers brought the last railroad tie, made of polished California laurel.

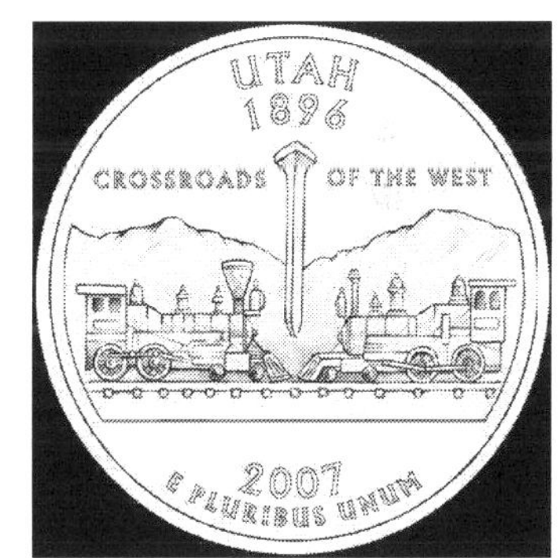

The Utah state quarter remembers the driving of the golden spike, which is kept in the Stanford University Museum.

A long nail called a spike, made of solid silver from the Nevada silver mines, and a second spike of silver and gold from the Colorado mines were driven in place. Finally, Leland Stanford, California's governor and president of the Central Pacific, drove the last spike made of pure California gold. The inscription on the last spike said, "May God continue the unity of our country, as this railroad unites the two great oceans of the world."

Telegraphic dispatchers quickly spread the word to the east and west coasts. In Washington, D.C., a magnetic ball above the capitol dropped as a signal that the rails were complete. Cannons fired in San Francisco. The whole nation celebrated as California, Utah, Nevada, and Colorado were joined together just 100 years after the gentle Franciscan missionary, Junípero Serra, set foot on California soil.

## Theodore Judah

THEODORE JUDAH CAME TO CALIFORNIA IN 1854 TO BUILD A railroad in the Sacramento Valley. Soon he thought about building a larger railway linking the east and west coasts. He worked hard, and after he met the Big Four, it seemed his dreams would come true.

Judah had many problems with the Big Four. He was a Christian, the son of a minister. His code of honor and ethics often clashed with the devious ways of the Big Four, especially with Huntington. Since the Central Pacific would receive more money per mile for track laid in the foothills, the Big Four tried to say that the foothills started just seven miles east of Sacramento, in the flat Sacramento Valley. Judah objected to these tactics. Soon he and the Big Four were at odds.

Judah planned to return to Washington, D.C., to complain about the policies of the Big Four and to try to get financing from other sources to continue building the railroad. He died shortly after he arrived in the East from a cause that his railroad would one day eliminate.

As Judah and his wife Anna arrived in Aspinwall on the Isthmus of Panama, torrential rain fell. Gallant Judah found an umbrella and started escorting women and children from the scanty shelters of doorways to the waiting ship. Anna knew he was tired and pleaded with him to stop, but he replied, "Why, I must do this, even as I would have someone do for you. It is only humanity."

Theodore Judah's monument.

When Judah and Anna finally arrived in their cabin aboard ship, Judah fell ill, shaking with fever. He had contracted the dreaded, almost-always-fatal, yellow fever. He died eight days later, never seeing the completion of his dream.

Judah was not recognized for his accomplishments until nearly 60 years after his death. In April 1930, the employees of the Southern Pacific Railroad Company dedicated a monument to him. It can be seen in Old Town, Sacramento.

## The Big Four

### Charles Crocker

Charles Crocker, a Sacramento dry goods merchant, actually built the railroad. Although he had little experience in rail construction, he learned along the way. Those who knew Crocker described him as, "boastful, vain, stubborn, tactless, and bull-like." He said, "I used to go up and down that road like a mad bull, stopping along wherever there was anything amiss, and raising Old Nick with the boys that were not up to line."

### Leland Stanford

Leland Stanford, a former grocery store merchant, was the figurehead of the Big Four, the man most in the public eye. He was governor of California during the War Between the States and later California's senator. When the Stanfords' only son died, they built Stanford University in Palo Alto.

### Mark Hopkins

Mark Hopkins owned the Huntington-Hopkins Hardware store in Sacramento along with Colis P. Huntington. He managed the accounts of the Central Pacific Railroad, paid the bills, and kept the records. Hopkins was a quiet, thrifty man, affectionately called Uncle Mark. He was thin, especially compared to his partners who all weighed over 200 pounds. He was a vegetarian and refused to smoke, drink, gamble, or curse. Even when he was worth millions, he paid $35 a month to live in a simple cottage, walked to work, and gardened for relaxation. He and his wife Mary had no children.

### Colis P. Huntington

Colis P. Huntington was the moving force behind the Central Pacific Railroad. At one point he was the most powerful man in California and Nevada. Although born in poverty, Huntington learned to support himself. By the time he was 14, he had earned and saved $100, about $2,500 today. Huntington rented a small office in New York while he obtained materials and supplies to build the railroad. People who knew him called him "a hard and cheery old man, with no more soul than a shark, scrupulously dishonest, and ruthless as a crocodile."

# What the Railroad Brought

AFTER THE RAILS WERE JOINED AT PROMONTORY POINT, THE BIG Four were treated like heroes. California expected to profit greatly from the railroad. Merchants expected that people would flock to the state, land would become more valuable, and businesses would prosper.

Unfortunately, such was not to be. Instead, the Suez Canal in Egypt was completed the same year as the transcontinental railroad. It was less expensive to ship goods using the Suez Canal than the transcontinental railroad.

After the initial rush of families rejoining relatives in California, passenger demand fell off. Instead of people coming to buy California's products, manufactured goods from the East flooded California's markets at prices it could not beat. The citizens of California benefited from this competition because they could buy merchandise for less money; however, some businesses faced tough times during this period of adjustment.

The Central Pacific began to call itself the Southern Pacific Railroad. It became a mighty power in California. The Southern Pacific continued to build railroads in California until it controlled all lines. When the Big Four planned a rail line through a town, they would approach the town leaders and ask for land and money or threaten to bypass the town. San Bernardino refused to meet these outrageous demands and was bypassed. Instead, the town of Colton a few miles from San Bernardino, was built to house the railroad terminal.

When the railroad was completed, people could order nearly anything from the Sears, Roebuck catalog, including this brand new house.

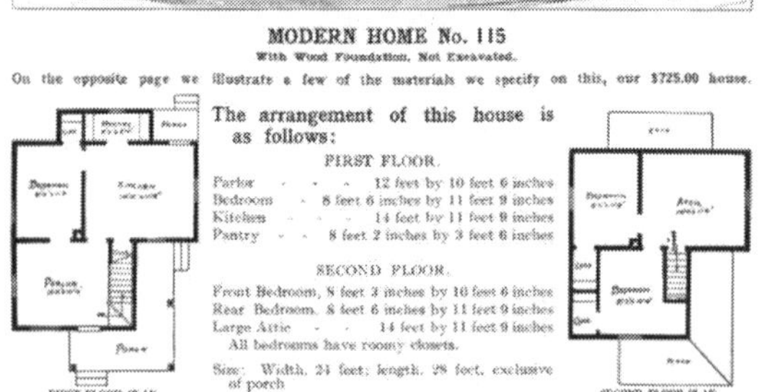

MODERN HOME No. 115

With Wood Foundation, Not Excavated.

On the opposite page we illustrate a few of the materials we specify on this, our $725.00 house.

The arrangement of this house is as follows:

FIRST FLOOR.

| | |
|---|---|
| Parlor | 12 feet by 10 feet 6 inches |
| Bedroom | 8 feet 6 inches by 11 feet 9 inches |
| Kitchen | 14 feet by 11 feet 9 inches |
| Pantry | 8 feet 2 inches by 3 feet 6 inches |

SECOND FLOOR.

| | |
|---|---|
| Front Bedroom, | 8 feet 3 inches by 10 feet 6 inches |
| Rear Bedroom, | 8 feet 6 inches by 11 feet 9 inches |
| Large Attic | 14 feet by 11 feet 9 inches |

All bedrooms have roomy closets.

Size: Width, 24 feet; length, 28 feet, exclusive of porch

FIRST FLOOR PLAN.

SECOND FLOOR PLAN.

For the next 35 years, the Southern Pacific controlled most of the people in the local, state, and federal government, as well as many of the newspapers. People were willing to elect corrupt officials to positions of leadership. These leaders were then bought and controlled by the Southern Pacific Railroad.

In spite of the many abuses brought by the railroad, it also brought many good changes to California. Land that would have remained idle for many years was brought into production. In the late 1880s more immigrants came to the state, especially to the south. But for many years, the railroad was considered a mixed blessing.

# What the Engines Said

By Bret Harte

Bret Harte, a famous California poet, wrote a whimsical poem at the opening of the transcontinental railroad. It records a fanciful conversation the two trains had when their tracks met at Promontory Point, Utah:

What was it the Engines said,
Pilots touching, - head to head
Facing on the single track,
Half a world behind each back?
This is what the Engines said,
Unreported and unread.

With a prefatory screech,
In florid Western speech,
Said the Engine from the WEST:
"I am from Sierra's crest;
And if altitude's a test,
Why, I reckon, it's confessed
That I've done my level best."
Said the Engine from the EAST:
"They who work best talk the least,
S'pose you whistle down your brakes;
What you've done is no great shakes,-
Pretty fair, - but let our meeting
Be a different kind of greeting.
Let these folks with champagne stuffing,
Not their Engines, do the puffing.

"Listen! Where Atlantic beats
Shores of snow and summer heats;
Where the Indian autumn skies
Paint the woods with wampum dyes,-
I have chased the flying sun,
Seeing all he looked upon,
Blessing all that he has blessed,
Nursing in my iron breast
All his vivifying heat,
All his clouds about my feet
Every shadow must retreat."

Said the Western Engine, "Phew!"
And a long, low whistle blew.
"Come, now, really that's the oddest
Talk for one so very modest.
You brag of your East! You do?
Why, I bring the East to you!
All the Orient, all Cathay,
Find through me the shortest way;
And the sun you follow here
Rises in my hemisphere.
Really, - if one must be rude, -
Length, my friend, ain't longitude."

Said the Union: "Don't reflect, or
I'll run over some Director."

Said the Central: "I'm Pacific;
But, when riled, I'm quite terrific.
Yet to-day we shall not quarrel,
Just to show these folks this moral,
How two Engines - in their vision -
Once have met without collision."

That is what the Engines said,
Unreported and unread;
Spoken slightly through the nose,
With a whistle at the close.

Officials and workers celebrate the completion of the transcontinental railroad.

Chapter 28

# Los Angeles and the South

For many years after the Gold Rush, Southern California and Los Angeles remained a Mexican pueblo. The southern rancheros became wealthy by selling their cattle to the gold miners. The Californios spent this newly found wealth on imported rugs, New England furniture, and pianos from Germany as well as silk gowns and costumes that cost thousands of dollars. Even their horses were ornamented in expensive silver bridles and hand-carved saddles. Fiestas and fandangos became more elaborate and extravagant.

## City of Demons

Los Angeles, the center of this wealth and activity, had a reputation for wickedness unequaled in the entire state. Crime greatly increased after the San Francisco Vigilance Committee banished criminals from that city. Many traveled to Los Angeles. Every night pistol shots would be heard. Horse stealing, robbery, and murder became commonplace.

During the 1850s and 1860s, Christian ministers tried to establish a church in Los Angeles. One after another, they failed. In 1854 Rev. James Wood tried to start a church but could only find sixteen

worshipers. Rev. Wood was shocked by the violence in Los Angeles. He compared it to Sodom and Gomorrah in his sermons. He left within a year, saying the City of the Angels was really "a city of demons."

The Angelinos, not used to governing themselves, did not set up effective legal institutions—laws and courts. In contrast to San Francisco, Los Angeles was ruled by the mob. In the ten years following the Gold Rush, twenty-four people were lynched. In a lynching, a person accused of a crime is hung without the benefit of a fair trial. These lynchings were nothing more than murders.

## American Farmers

By 1860, many Americans who were disappointed in the mines came south and started farming. Orange groves blossomed as wells were dug to tap underground sources of water. Farmers dug irrigation canals from nearby rivers to water the fertile ground. El Monte was the first American town in Southern California. It quickly established the first Protestant church as well as schools and farms. Communities such as Compton, Santa Ana, and Riverside followed. Bull and bear fights were outlawed, and the first Los Angeles baseball team was founded. After the terrible drought of the early 1860s, the ranchos began to be sold, and more American farms appeared. By the early 1870s, the Los Angeles pueblo was beginning to look more like a Yankee town. Church steeples appeared across the horizon. On Sundays families traveled from their farms to spend the day worshiping the Lord.

When the railroad linking California with the rest of the United States was completed, the people of Los Angeles realized that they must be a part of the rail system to grow and prosper. They approached the Big Four to ask for a rail line. The Big Four demanded that the city pay the Southern Pacific Railroad a huge fee plus give them control over a short rail line that connected Los Angeles with the harbor at San Pedro. With this demand, the Angelinos would no longer have free access to the harbor; rather, they would have to pay whatever rail rates the Southern Pacific charged to ship freight. Los Angeles agreed, and the railway was completed in 1873, but the stage was set for continued conflict between Los Angeles and the Southern Pacific Railroad. New towns continued to blossom, including San Fernando and Pomona.

## Emigrant Trains

With the completion of the line, emigrant trains replaced the covered wagons and brought more people to California. These emigrant trains were boxcars with cooking facilities. Families would load all of their possessions and ride to California. The journey took about ten days and was much more comfortable than the earlier wagons, especially over the mountains.

> Author Robert Lewis Stevenson rode on an emigrant train. This is part of how he described them:
>
> I suppose the reader has some notion of an American railroad-car, that long, narrow wooden box, like a flat-roofed Noah's ark, with a stove and a convenience, one at either end, a passage down the middle, and transverse benches upon either hand.

Word of the beauty of Los Angeles and the wonderful climate of Southern California began to spread. Promoters, called boosters, sang the praises of the paradise called California. But in 1881, their efforts backfired. The Angelinos had succeeded in talking the California Editorial Association into holding its annual convention in their fair city. Newspapermen from all over the state were finally going to get the chance to see for themselves if the stories they heard about the beautiful climate were true. As the newspaper men stepped onto the street, a freezing Sierra wind attacked them. Looking up they could see icicles hanging from the roof edges. A few days later the entire coast was whitened with snow. It did no good to protest that this weather was very unusual (which it was). The newspapermen wrote that Los Angeles was just like any other California town—except that it was largely populated by liars.

## Competition

The boosters continued to entice Americans to Los Angeles, especially those from the Midwest, and the land blossomed with a patchwork of farms as more Americans made their way to Southern California. Then in 1885 the Southern Pacific, which had controlled most of the railways in California, had its first taste of competition: The Santa Fe Railway also built a line to Los Angeles. A year later, the two companies were locked in a rate war.

On March 6, 1886, the Santa Fe advertised in the Los Angeles Times, "Down! Down! Down! Today we offer lower rates ... than any competitor!" The Southern Pacific, quick to accept the challenge, began cutting its rates to and from Kansas City. Fares plummeted from $100 to $15, then to $10, $8, $6, $4, and finally to just $1. Imagine traveling to London, England today for just $20, and you will have some idea of how great a bargain this was. Californians and Midwesterners, who had no prior plans to travel, quickly grabbed up the tickets and packed their bags. Rates continued to stay low, about $5, for several weeks.

Midwesterners poured into California throughout the summer of 1886. Many fell in love with the land and determined to stay. This set off another frenzy, this time in real estate. Everyone began buying up land and reselling it to make a profit. One story tells of a older woman from Pasadena taking a carriage ride in the country. A real estate agent offered her a lot for $50. She said that she didn't mind "making a little investment" and bought it. Later that day as she returned, the same man asked her if she would be willing to sell the lot. She would "for a fair price." The agent offered $200, and the lady went home to a fine dinner.

Land prices increased 400 to 500 percent. This would be the same as a $200,000 home selling for $1 million. New towns were laid out and sold in a carnival atmosphere. Burbank, Fullerton, Monrovia, Whittier, Inglewood, and Hollywood soon made their appearance. The madness was not to last, however. The real estate bubble burst in 1888, and prices fell with a resounding crash. Many people lost fortunes. Newly-laid out town sites became deserts once again.

After the crash, as life returned to normal, Los Angeles became a fine city with paved streets, colleges, churches, and street lights. The Mexican pueblo of 10,000 people had become an American city of 50,000. The city was set to boom again and again until it would become the Queen of the South.

People eagerly wait to buy lots at an auction in Imperial, California, in 1904. For many years, this kind of scene was repeated all over Southern California as people tried to buy property.

## An Unusual Migration

SOUTHERN CALIFORNIA DREW MORE IMMIGRANTS IN WAVES OVER the next several years. At first the very wealthy were drawn to the land, including several millionaires. The next wave, from about 1900 to 1920, brought people in medium circumstances. From 1920 to 1930, lower middle class people arrived, and in the final wave, from 1930 to 1945, the working class made Southern California their home. This is exactly backwards from the way that other areas had been settled, including Northern California. Because of the resources brought by wealthy immigrants, improvements in the land began immediately, causing Southern California to skip the frontier stage of development entirely.

In other regions of the country, people from neighboring states and territories spilled over and settled new lands. Settlers from Illinois overflowed into Wisconsin and Iowa, for example. Southern California's immigration was quite different. People from all over the United States and the world made the land their new home. Travel by railroad was not so harsh, so many older and retired people also made the journey. Because of this diversity in immigrants, Southern California's culture blended many different customs. Most of the newcomers who came to Southern California after 1880 were Christian, god-fearing, respectable, and conservative. They reflected the make-up of the rest of the United States, which was largely Christian at the time. Nearly everyone went to church on Sunday. Sermons were reprinted in the daily newspapers. Christians lived quietly and prosperously as they transformed Southern California into an American land.

## Growth and Change

GROWTH AND CHANGE—THESE WORDS BEST DESCRIBE THE years in California during the last part of the nineteenth century. Oddly, the War Between the States had a great effect on California even though the state played a very small part in it. California's statehood upset the balance in the Senate and started the slide toward secession. California supplied the gold to keep the Union currency stable. California also supplied generals, many of whom made the state their home prior to the war.

But the greatest effect the War Between the States had on California was the construction of the transcontinental railroad.

The Big Four, using the plans drawn up by Theodore Judah, managed the monumental task of building the railroad over the Sierra Nevadas. The rails were completed in 1869.

After some short term problems, the railroad brought prosperity to California. When the Southern Pacific Railroad was forced to compete with the Santa Fe, fares were greatly reduced. People could afford to come to California from all parts of the United States. Southern California benefited the most from this migration. So many people came to Southern California, so fast, with so many resources, that it skipped the frontier phase of development completely.

California's growth has been very unusual. Usually people move into a new territory gradually, but the Gold Rush brought thousands of people and filled up the land in a very short time. Normally a land becomes a territory first and then a state, but California became a state immediately. In other areas people of the working class come to a new land before the very wealthy. In California, exactly the opposite occurred. Finally, other lands were usually settled by people overflowing from adjoining states. In California, however, people came by railroad without settling the neighboring territories. One territory next to California, Arizona, did not become a state until 1912, more than sixty years after its neighbor.

Most importantly, the Christian faith continued to grow in California. Immigrants built churches as soon as they came to the new land. Southern California was filled with Christians. Christianity would form a foundation for the state to grow and change during the next several years.

By the early 1900s, when this picture was taken, Los Angeles had grown to a prosperous city.

Review Questions

# Unit 9 Roundup

## Unit 9 Introduction

1. How did religion motivate people to come and settle California?

2. What part did California play in the War Between the States?

3. Name some generals who lived in California before the war.

## Chapter 27

1. What early methods of transportation were used to bring people and goods to California? What was the common problem with all of these methods?

2. Would you have liked to have been a rider on the Pony Express? Why or why not?

3. Why was Theodore Judah called "Crazy Judah"? Do you think he was crazy?

4. Write a short description of each of these men:

   Theodore Judah

   Mark Hopkins

   Charles Crocker

   Colis P. Huntington

   Leland Stanford

5. Describe some of the hardships in the construction of the transcontinental railroad.

6. Did the railroad help California to prosper? Explain.

## Chapter 28

1. Describe the early days in Los Angeles.

2. What event in 1885 brought many Midwesterners to California? How does this event illustrate the benefits of competition?

3. What was unusual about the migration to Southern California?

4. What effect did Christianity have on the growth of Southern California?

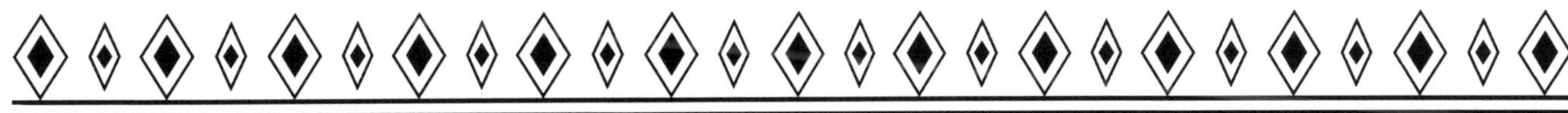

Unit 10

# Californians Take Dominion

"Then God blessed them, and God said to them,
"Be fruitful and multiply;
fill the earth and subdue it;
have dominion over the fish of the sea,
over the birds of the air,
and over every living thing that moves on the earth."

~~ Genesis 1:28

Californians made many beneficial changes to the land in the early 20th century, including changes to San Francisco, shown here before the Golden Gate Bridge spanned the entrance to the bay at the upper left.

## Taking Dominion

THE CALIFORNIA THAT WE LIVE IN TODAY is far different from the land that the California Indians inhabited. Plants from all over the world now grow in California's soil. Waterways have been changed from their original courses. Wetlands and swamps have been reclaimed. Areas that were once deserts now bloom. Today millions of people can live in an area that once supported only thousands.

The Americans who came to California around the turn of the 20th century followed their God-given calling to take dominion over the land and subdue it. Most of these people were either Christians or influenced by Christianity. They worked hard to turn dry ground into a fertile land.

What does it mean to take dominion? God commands Christians in Genesis 1:28 and Psalm 8:6 to take dominion over the earth. He tells us to use His creation to build His kingdom. He wants us to use resources wisely to make the world a better place to live. We are to rule over the Lord's creation carefully, never purposely wasting or destroying. This is called *stewardship*.

In this unit we will learn how the people of California took dominion over their land. We will see how water played such an important part in the growth of the state and how the Californians brought water to the land. We will see how these water systems led to the rise of the agricultural industry so that today California is the fifth largest food producer in the world. Finally, we will see some of the effects of the Industrial Revolution in California and how the people used technology to improve their lives.

Before Californians tamed the waterways, rivers would flood during heavy rainstorms. Farms were ruined, cattle drowned, and often people became homeless.

Chapter 29

# Water for Life

As California continued to grow and prosper, it discovered it had a critical need: water. The thousands of people who flocked to California's cities and towns needed water to live. Without water, farming and industry were not possible. New sources of water had to be found.

The Spanish missionaries built missions near rivers. California's climate is very much like Spain's. The missionaries knew that they had to build irrigation systems, like those of Spain's, to bring water from the rivers to the missions, orchards, and fields. When the Americans first came to California, they were not familiar with irrigation methods. Other parts of the United States do not have dry climates like California's. Instead, they depend on rain to water the land.

Once the Californians learned they needed to irrigate, they had another problem. California's water rights laws were similar to those of countries with abundant water. They were called riparian rights. The Latin word *ripa* means "the bank of a river." It meant that a person who owned land bordering a river had rights to the water, while a person who owned the next plot of land had no water rights at all. Since California has few rivers and streams, it was possible for a few people to own all of the land along the waterways, and consequently, all rights to use the water. The Wright Act of 1887 changed all of this. Under this new law, people could form irrigation districts. This made irrigation possible and allowed much more land to be watered. It also made possible several major projects that changed the landscape of California.

## Taming the Rivers

Many of the men who came to California from other parts of the United States were farmers. When they arrived in their new homeland, they began to look for land to build farms. The Californios owned most of the land along the coast, so they looked inland. When the men had traveled to the gold mines, they had passed through the Central Valley. They noticed how rich and fertile this land was. It had a major problem, however. During the winter rains, the rivers would often overflow, turning the valley into one giant, but shallow, sea of water.

At first the men built farms in the foothills on higher ground that would be safe from floods. This land was quickly settled, and new settlers built farms along the banks of the rivers. For several years during a time of little rainfall, the farmers would be safe. But then a heavy rainfall would come, the water in the river would overflow its banks, and the land would be flooded. Homes and barns would float away. Crops would be ruined. Animals, and sometimes people, would drown.

Farmers thought about how they could protect their land from these dangerous floods. Some began to build huge dirt banks, called levees, along the river that bordered their property. In a flood the river could not rise above these levees, so the farmer's property would be safe. But the farmer down river had an even greater problem. In addition to the flood water, all of the water that was prevented from flooding his neighbor's land came rushing down on his own.

One of the characteristics that Christian communities share is the ability to unite together to work toward a common goal. Most of the American settlers were Christian men and women. They helped each other whenever they could. They united to solve the problem of flooding.

First, the farmers of a certain district got together to build a series of levees. No longer would just one farm be protected from the floods. Each farmer would have a strong, tall wall of dirt along the river to prevent the water from flooding his land. Each farmer was responsible to see that his part of the levee was in good repair, safe from leaks that might be caused by gopher holes or tree roots.

Later these levee districts became more formal. The farmers each paid a tax to the district, which hired engineers to build and maintain concrete levees. As more and more people arrived in the Central Valley, these districts united so that everyone in the Central Valley

Levees are walls built along the edge of a river or stream. At first these were packed dirt, but later they were replaced with concrete.

followed the same rules and a problem in one district, such as a break in the levee, would not affect another. Christians working together made the Central Valley a safe and prosperous place in which to live.

## More Water Solutions

California has always had an uneven rainfall. In some years it is abundant while in others it is very sparse. The levees protected farms in most years but not during heavy rains and floods. The people needed a way to protect their farms when the rivers flooded, especially the mighty Sacramento River.

Engineers studied the problem and recommended a clever solution. The state government bought many acres of land in low areas so that no houses, barns, or other structures could be built there. Engineers built a huge bridge, called a causeway, over this land. They also built gates in the levees so when they are opened, water from the river flows into the causeway, causing no harm.

If you travel along Highway 80 in the Sacramento area during the summer, you may wonder why a long bridge was built over miles of vacant land. But if you travel over this same bridge, or causeway, during the heavy rains of winter, you will pass over a sea of water. This plan has protected California farms for many years.

## Water for the Valley

The rivers were tamed during the winter to protect farms from floods, but the people faced another problem. How could they get water to grow crops during the summer? Many rivers and streams flowed through the valley during the winter, but by summer these were completely dry. The people began to think of ways to save this water so that it could be used to grow crops all year round.

Farmers in the foothills were the first to build dams to store water for the dry times. As more people moved to the area, several farmers built dams on the same river. But by the end of the summer, the farmer who built the first dam would have all of the water, while the farmers who built downstream would have none.

The farmers knew that they would have to work together to solve their problem. Instead of storing water in several small pools, or reservoirs, behind several small dams, they worked together to build one large dam high in the mountains. This dam would hold back the water in a large reservoir so that it would be available all year round to water the farmers' crops. Dams were built by the farmers themselves, using their own equipment and resources.

After the settlers solved the problem of flooding in the Central Valley, more and more people could farm there. At first farmers grew wheat. Wheat was easy to grow because it did not need irrigation. Farmers planted their crops in the fall and let the winter rains water it. Growing wheat year after year, however, was not good for the land. Farmers needed to grow other crops in the summer, but they lacked water.

Because of the Wright Act, people living in the foothills worked with those living in the valley to form very large irrigation districts. They each paid a tax to the district, which allowed them to hire engineers to build even larger dams, reservoirs, and irrigation canals. These irrigation districts were very similar to the levee districts.

Soon dams were built along every major California river. No longer would water madly dash to the ocean every winter and be wasted. Now it would be stored and used by the farmers to raise bountiful crops in the temperate California climate.

Irrigation systems bring water from the river to the farm. In this picture, water comes to the farmer through a channel. When he opens the gate, it flows out to the crops he has planted in his field.

Chapter 30

# Water for the Cities

In 1900, the residents of San Francisco became concerned that their city would run out of water. The mayor of San Francisco asked the federal government for permission to fill the Hetch Hetchy Valley, located in Yosemite National Park, and turn it into a reservoir. Pipelines would be built to bring this water to San Francisco.

*Sacrilege* means blasphemy, treating a sacred object with disrespect.

Very few people had ever seen Hetch Hetchy Valley because it was so difficult to hike to it. John Muir and some of the members of his Sierra Club had visited it and began to fight against the plan. They argued that the valley was too beautiful to fill and should be preserved for the public. In fact, John Muir said that the flooding of the Hetch Hetchy Valley would be as great a sacrilege* as the destruction of a cathedral.

At this time people held two different views about how the earth's resources should be used. The first view, called *preservation*, argued that resources should be preserved in their natural state. They should not be used or changed. The second, called *conservation*, argued that the earth's resources should be used but not wasted. They should be conserved for future generations. This view is closer to the biblical view of *stewardship*: God's gifts of nature are for man's benefit, to be used for God's glory; however, they should not be wasted or destroyed. John Muir believed in preservation. He wanted the Hetch Hetchy Valley to be left in its natural state.

The mayor of San Francisco, James D. Phelan, believed in conservation. He did not believe Hetch Hetchy's beauty would be destroyed. The lake that would replace it would be just as beautiful as a valley, and San Francisco desperately needed the water. While other alternatives were available, Hetch Hetchy would be the least expensive to construct.

Since Hetch Hetchy was part of a national park, Californians needed the permission of the federal government to build the dam. The argument raged for thirteen years. Finally, the project was approved. The 155 miles of aqueduct were completed in 1934, including a twenty-five-mile tunnel under the Coast Range Mountains. Hetch Hetchy continues to supply water to San Francisco today.

The Hetch Hetchy Valley in the early 1900s, before the dam was built and the valley flooded.

The Hetch Hetchy Reservoir in modern times.

# John Muir

JOHN MUIR WAS AN AMAZING INVENTOR. HE BUILT A THERMOMETER that was so sensitive it would record the change in temperature as a person approached. He invented a trick bed that would wake him as the sun's rays, focused through a magnifying glass, burned a thread and released an alarm. His most famous invention was a clock desk which would allo him to study a book for fifteen minutes before the next book in the stack was opened and placed before him.

God had truly given Muir a remarkable talent for mechanical invention. He had also clearly shown Muir the way to Himself. Muir's father had carefully instructed his children in the Christian faith and required them to memorize portions of the New Testament. Muir rejected both the talent for mechanical invention and the gift of Jesus Christ. He felt that by creating labor-saving, mechanical devices, he was robbing men of jobs. He did not consider that these devices would free men to pursue other more enjoyable work.

In 1903, President Teddy Roosevelt (left) joined John Muir (right) on a camping trip in Yosemite Valley.

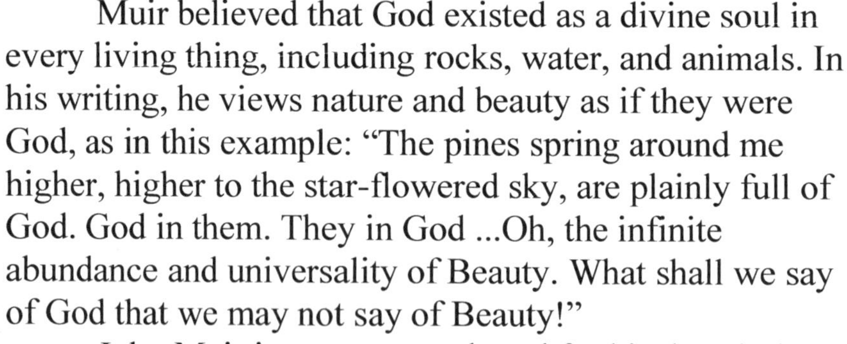

Muir believed that God existed as a divine soul in every living thing, including rocks, water, and animals. In his writing, he views nature and beauty as if they were God, as in this example: "The pines spring around me higher, higher to the star-flowered sky, are plainly full of God. God in them. They in God ...Oh, the infinite abundance and universality of Beauty. What shall we say of God that we may not say of Beauty!"

John Muir is most remembered for his descriptions of his wilderness journeys. He traveled all over the world, but his favorite area was the Sierra Nevada. When Muir was 29, he came to San Francisco and then left immediately for the mountains. He lived in Yosemite for a time and carefully explored the beautiful mountains and valleys. He discovered active glaciers and developed a theory which stated that glaciers helped to carve the mountainous canyons. He founded the Sierra Club to encourage the formation of National Parks, especially Yosemite and Kings Canyon, as well as several national forest reserves. Muir did not think the government of California or private individuals should own this property. The Sierra Club still fights today for the preservation of wilderness areas. Many of its members share Muir's worldview.

# Three Water Projects for Southern California

SOUTHERN CALIFORNIA DID NOT HAVE THE PROBLEMS WITH WINTER floods that the Central Valley had. Although the climate was mild, the soil fertile, and the growing season long, it had almost no water. If a way could be found to bring water to Southern California, the area would produce abundantly. The people of California looked for ways to bring water to the southern part of the state.

## The Los Angeles Aqueduct

By 1900 the work of the Southern California boosters, or promoters, had paid off. During the following five years, the population of Los Angeles more than doubled, from 100,000 to 250,000. With more people, the city needed more water. In 1904 and again in 1905, the city almost ran out of water completely. The city engineer, William Mulholland, quickly investigated ways to bring more water to Los Angeles.

William Mulholland was born in Ireland. He did not have the opportunity to attend a school. When he came to Los Angeles, he worked during the day and studied engineering, on his own, at night. His studies paid off, and soon he was offered the position of City Engineer.

When the first water poured down the Los Angeles Aqueduct, Mulholland was asked to deliver a speech. Always a man of few words, he delivered one of the shortest speeches on record: "There it is. Take it!"

Mulholland proposed to build an aqueduct to bring water from the Owens River in the Sierra Nevada to Los Angeles. The plan was approved, and land began to be quietly purchased in the Owens Valley. The city of Los Angeles needed to own the land in order to have rights to the water, but if word of the project got out, people would ask higher prices for it.

Mulholland planned to build a reservoir to hold water for the Owens Valley residents, but a friend of his owned the land. This friend wanted Los Angeles to pay him $1 million for the land, which was not worth that much. Mulholland refused and broke with the friend. This was an example of Mulholland's integrity. He refused to allow Los Angeles to be taken advantage of. In 1941, years later after Mulholland's death, the reservoir was finally completed.

The Los Angeles Aqueduct was completed within Mulholland's original budget estimate. On November 5, 1913, the first water arrived. Los Angeles and the San Fernando Valley receive water from it to this day. Today the Owens Valley receives some of its water from the Mono Lake Basin.

## The Imperial Valley

When Captain Juan Bautista de Anza came to California from Mexico, he traveled through the hostile Colorado Desert. On his first attempt to get through this dry region, he almost lost his life in the sand dunes and had to return to the Yuma Indian village. More than 100 years later, Californians turned this desert into a garden. The genius behind this project was a self-educated man named George Chaffey.

The Colorado River separates California from Arizona—a raging torrent filled with red silt, or mud. Chaffey looked for a way to bring water from the river to irrigate the Colorado Desert. He knew that this land would be very fertile if it could be watered. Chaffey took less than one year and spent only $100,000 to complete the job. He renamed the region the Imperial Valley to attract people to it. Soon 120,000 acres were being farmed in the former desert. Today this region is one of the finest garden areas in the state.

George Chaffey retired from his work and left the maintenance of the Imperial Canal to others. About a year later, silt began to build up in the intake, the place where water from the Colorado River entered the canal. The engineers that replaced Chaffey decided to open a new intake in the banks of the Colorado River. As they did, the mighty river broke through this new cut and began to rush into the Imperial Valley. The water collected in the lowest part of the valley, at a place called the Salton Sink, and formed the Salton Sea.

Water raged through the opening for two years. Towns were flooded, and for a while it looked as if the whole valley would be under water. A $250,000 dam was built, but it quickly washed away. Finally, the Southern Pacific Railroad began a mammoth effort to close the gap in the river bank. Every day for 52 days, rail cars dropped 6,000 carloads of rock and gravel into the breach. The effort cost $1.6 million, but finally, the break was closed and the Imperial Valley was saved.

## The Hoover Dam

William Mulholland's and George Chaffey's aqueducts satisfied the then-current need for water in Los Angeles and the Imperial Valley, but to let Southern California grow, it needed more water. It began to look to the Colorado River to satisfy all of its needs. This river rages for most of the year, often flooding in the spring. If it could be tamed and the excess water stored behind a dam, it would be available during time of need, and the residents of the Imperial Valley would no longer have to fear a flood that would fill the valley.

The solution was the Hoover Dam. At the time, and for many years afterwards, it was the largest and highest dam in the world. Its construction was an engineering wonder. First, engineers built an air-conditioned city so the people working on the dam had a place to live. Then they dug four tunnels to temporarily redirect the river from the area where the dam was to be built. The dam was constructed out of hundreds of concrete blocks. If one large block had been poured, it would have taken 125 years to dry and would have broken under the stress of the water.

The Hoover Dam, named for the first United States President from California, Herbert Hoover, was completed in 1928.

The world's largest powerhouse was built at the base of the dam to produce hydroelectric power, that is, water-generated electricity. The dam held back the world's largest reservoir, named Lake Mead. The Colorado Aqueduct brought water from the Colorado River to the Imperial Valley and then to Los Angeles. The mighty river was finally tamed. This water supplied Southern California for many years.

## Hydroelectric Power

Building dams on California's rivers did more than provide water to irrigate the farmers' land. It provided something that has made life better for all Californians: electricity.

When the engineers built the dams, they built powerhouses at their bases. Huge pipes channeled water into these powerhouses. The rushing water turned machinery and changed the water power into electricity. After the water went on to irrigate fields, the electricity was sent to farms and cities over heavy wires. Money earned by selling the electricity paid for the construction and operation of the dams.

Electricity provided an inexpensive power source for Californians which greatly increased their standard of living. Streets were lighted, homes were heated, and factories were run with electricity provided from the California dams. This electricity allowed many more advances to be made so that California could continue to grow and prosper.

Chapter 31

# The Rise of Agriculture

California's rich resources benefited people living on its land. Early settlers found wealth in furs as they trapped otter and beaver. The Californios raised cattle for their hides and tallow. People from all over the world looked for their fortunes in the gold mines. But the greatest resource of all was the land itself. Many of the people who settled in California had been farmers. When they made California their home, they naturally turned to farming. They discovered that California was one of the most fertile areas of the country. Their efforts have turned California into one of the biggest agricultural producers in the world.

## Citrus

In 1870, a man named Luther Calvin Tibbetts came to Riverside and found some orange trees from the time when the Spanish missionaries had planted orchards. He moved some to his farm. They were thick-skinned and sour, however, and people did not like them. A little while later he received some different orange trees, navel oranges that a

People living in Eastern states were amazed to hear that oranges grew so close to snow-covered mountains.

missionary sent from Brazil. Tibbetts nurtured these trees and found that they produced a fine, sweet fruit.

As California farmers grew grapefruit, the formerly exotic fruit became more familiar on America's breakfast tables.

Tibbetts had an idea on how to change the sour mission orange trees into sweet-tasting naval orange trees. He grafted, or carefully fastened, buds from the new trees onto the old trees. Soon the new naval buds took over the tree and changed all the mission orange trees into naval orange trees. Later, hundreds of thousands of trees were produced with buds from Tibbetts' trees.

Orange groves multiplied in Southern California. When refrigerated rail cars were invented, the oranges were shipped all over the United States. Children in the East looked forward to a Christmas treat—a California orange in their stocking. Soon the whole country heard the advertising slogan, "Oranges for health– California for wealth." People from different parts of the nation began to enjoy California's Sunkist oranges. At one point, a disease called "cushion scale" threatened to kill all the trees. A man named Albert Koebele went to Australia and brought back some ladybugs to eat the scale. The introduction of Australian ladybugs saved California's citrus industry.

## The Rise of Agricultural Colonies

Many people from all the countries of the world came to California and built agricultural colonies. The Armenians, fleeing from the cruel Turkish takeover of their land, made the Central Valley near Fresno their home. They began producing raisins which they marketed under the name "Sun-Maid."

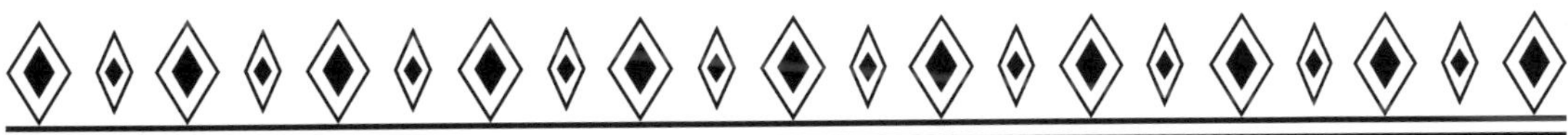

Dairy farmers from Portugal settled in the northwestern part of the state. Italians grew grapes in the north central valley. Fishermen from Yugoslavia settled along the coast. The Mormons settled San Bernardino, the English, El Toro; the Germans, Anaheim; and the Danish started Solvang. Each community tended to keep to itself as it maintained its religious and national customs.

California farmers planted date groves like this one. Cloth coverings protect the dates from the rain.

These agricultural communities prospered as the people united to bring water to their land, invest in expensive farming equipment, and solve their problems as a community.

Fruit dries in California's sun.

## California—The Land of Variety

Most states in the United States produce only a few crops using a few methods of farming. Iowa, for example, has two major crops: wheat and corn. In California's varied climate and long growing season, more than 200 different agricultural products grow. These include field crops (like wheat and corn), fruits, vegetables, and livestock, poultry, and honeybee products. Once Californians brought water to the land, an amazing variety and quantity of agricultural products grew. California's producers were not called farmers; they were called avocado-producers, citrus-growers, and raisin-growers because so many farms specialized in one type of product.

### Farming Technology

As farming grew, industry grew. New farm inventions saved much labor and vastly increased harvests. In California, farmers did much seeding, planting, and harvesting using machinery. Machines were developed to harvest onions and tomatoes. Tree-shakers were invented to harvest almonds.

This increase in industrialization led to another unique part of California agriculture. While in other states families owned most farms, in California they became business ventures. Most families could not afford the expensive equipment they needed, so they organized businesses and cooperatives to share the equipment.

Soon products from all over the world were growing in California's fertile soil. Maize from Japan, alfalfa from Chile, lima beans from the Hopi Indians, flax from India, avocados and tomatoes from Mexico, dates from Algeria, Egypt, and Persia, figs from Smyrna, pears from China, and prunes from France all produced abundantly in California.

Now it shall come to pass, if you diligently obey the voice of the LORD your God, to observe carefully all His commandments which I command you today, that the LORD your God will set you high above all nations of the earth. And all these blessings shall come upon you and overtake you, because you obey the voice of the LORD your God: Blessed shall you be in the city, and blessed shall you be in the country. Blessed shall be the fruit of your body, the produce of your ground and the increase of your herds, the increase of your cattle and the offspring of your flocks. Blessed shall be your basket and your kneading bowl. Blessed shall you be when you come in, and blessed shall you be when you go out.

~~ Deuteronomy 28:1-6

Chapter 32

# The Rise of Industry

At the beginning of the twentieth century, changes were occurring which would make the world a much better place in which to live. The effects of the Industrial Revolution were beginning to be felt even in far-away California. These changes form the basis for life as we live it today. It is hard for us to appreciate the primitive conditions most Americans faced one hundred years ago. They had none of the modern conveniences that we take for granted. They faced great hardships, yet they rarely complained. They believed complaining was a grievous sin against the Lord. Instead, they practiced godly contentment.

Since so many early settlers were Christians, the church was an important part of community life. Nearly everyone worshiped the Lord on Sundays. Sermons were reprinted in the newspapers. Socials and activities held at the church made life more enjoyable as people worked together to help each other in time of need.

After the railroad connected California to the rest of the United States, California began to receive the benefit of advances in technology. Inventions from the East were shipped by rail to California. Soon California had many large factories. Industry began to rise, allowing the people to live better as they took dominion over their land.

Before it was outlawed, hydraulic mining ruined the landscape.

## Advances in Gold Mining

At first when miners flocked to California, gold was easy to find, especially along the streams and riverbeds. Men could take the gold from the water using a pan, rocker, or long tom. Soon, however, the surface gold was mined, and other methods had to be devised to extract gold from the land.

The first method was called hydraulic mining. Water pumped through a small nozzle and sprayed across a large hill or area of land washed dirt into a long trough called a sluice. The sluice contained slats which trapped the gold, while the dirt and water mixture washed back into the stream.

Dredging was also a destructive method of mining that is no longer used.

This method of mining was very destructive. Pressure from the hydraulic hoses destroyed entire hillsides, trees, and vegetation. When rivers overflowed, the silt and debris that was washed into the stream spoiled hundreds of acres of farmland. The silt would also make the rivers and bays so shallow that no ships could travel on them. Finally, the farmers and other California citizens were successful in passing a law which forbade hydraulic mining in California.

The second method of gold mining was dredging. Huge machines would scoop up dirt from the bottom of rivers and pass it through a sluice which captured the gold. But the waste was deposited on the banks of the river and devastated the farm lands when the river overflowed. This method of gold mining was also eventually outlawed.

## Oil—California's Black Gold

Petroleum, or oil, was known to exist in California for many years before it came to be appreciated. Early explorers saw oil on the surface of the water near the Santa Barbara Channel, seeping from cracks in the ocean floor. These were California's first oil spills. The Indians used oil to make their cooking baskets waterproof. The Spaniards used it to make the roofs of their adobes watertight. Oil was not used for industrial purposes, however, because in the 1800s most of the world's oil was supplied by whales.

In 1859, the world's first commercial oil well was drilled in Pennsylvania. The oil was used to make kerosene, which was burned in lamps. Many oil wells were drilled in California, but their product was a

different quality. The kerosene tended to smoke, flicker, and smell. Some oil was used to make asphalt bricks to pave streets, but its use was still limited.

In 1892, a prospector and lawyer named Edward L. Doheny, and his partner Charles A. Canfield, decided to prospect for oil in downtown Los Angeles. They leased a vacant lot and dug a well by hand using only a pick and shovel. When the well was 155 feet deep, they struck oil and were able to hire a rig, a special machine for pumping oil. Doheny's discovery sparked an oil boom in Los Angeles. Soon people were digging oil wells in their front and back yards. Many were dry, but many others produced great amounts of oil.

Next Doheny tried to find a use for all of this oil. He convinced the head of the Santa Fe Railroad to try to use oil instead of coal to run the rail engines. The experiments turned out to be very successful. California had very few coal deposits and had to import most of its coal from the East. Oil was much less expensive to burn. Furthermore, oil burned hotter and cleaner than coal and was much easier to find. Soon oil replaced coal as the preferred fuel for all locomotives.

With the coming of the industrial age, many more uses were being discovered for oil. California continued to be a major supplier for many years, second only to Texas. In the ten years starting in 1920, California's oil production amounted to $2.5 billion. This was more than the value of all of the gold that was ever discovered in California, about $2 billion.

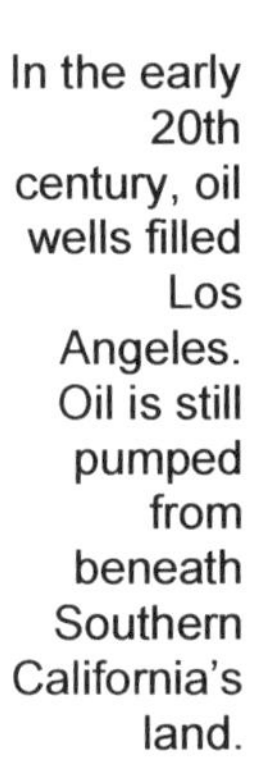
In the early 20th century, oil wells filled Los Angeles. Oil is still pumped from beneath Southern California's land.

## Movies

Thomas A. Edison, the great American inventor, produced hundreds of inventions. He is probably best known for the light bulb, but he also invented the motion picture camera. In the United States, when a person invents a new object, he is allowed to take out a *patent*. A patent allows only the inventor to make and sell his invention. If another person wants to use or sell the invention, he has to pay the inventor a small fee. In this way the inventor is compensated for his many years of work and research. Some men decided to use Edison's movie camera without paying him, a form of stealing. Their flight from the law brought them to California.

These men liked California for many reasons. First, they were close to the border between the United States and Mexico. If the law were to find them, they could quickly flee to Mexico. Second, California offered a delightful climate. Lighting methods were poor, and when making movies, even indoor scenes had to be filmed outside. It seldom rains in Southern California, so movies could be made most of the year. Third, Southern California offered a variety of scenery, including deserts, oceans, rivers, and mountains all within a short trip from Los Angeles.

At first Californians did not appreciate the movie industry. Often movies were made without the benefit of sets. Instead, movie makers would film on the streets, snarling traffic, bothering people, and creating a carnival atmosphere.

Producers built studios when movies began to be made with sound because they had to be filmed entirely indoors. Actors and actresses began to be in demand and earned very high salaries. Slowly the movie industry gained respectability.

Many Christians were very opposed to the movie industry because they felt it was corrupting the morals of society. The movie industry recognized its responsibility and created a *moral code* to regulate itself. Two rules that movies had to obey were that evil could not be made attractive and that evil was always punished. Even so, many times these rules were kept in the letter while being violated in the spirit. Today these rules have been completely abandoned.

## Education

Wherever Christians go, one of their first concerns is for the education of their children. California was no exception. Private schools opened as soon as the Americans were settled in their new land. In 1850, the state constitution made provision for public schools to operate in each district for three months each year. Later, in 1879, this was increased to six months.

John C. Pelton, a Baptist teacher, organized the first free school. Mr. Pelton came to San Francisco around Cape Horn in 1849 with a chest full of school books and a large school bell. He persuaded Rev. Wheeler, pastor of the First Baptist Church, to allow him the free use of the church. All expenses were paid by the church and by Mr. Pelton, the teacher.

Public schools followed, but private schools and homeschools were more numerous. In 1856, San Francisco opened its first public high school. Soon there was a need for colleges, and again Christians took the lead. Most colleges were church-sponsored or run by Christians.

Schools were numerous, and most people were well-educated when California passed a law to require compulsory education at the elementary level. Many people were opposed to this law because they felt that this was not a proper function of the government; rather it belonged to parents.

### Christian Colleges

Most of the colleges started in the late 1800s were formed by Christians. These include:

**University of the Pacific**
*Methodists*

**College of California (forerunner of University of California at Berkeley)**
*Non-denominational*

**University of Southern California**
*Methodists*

**Mills College**
*Non-denominational*

**Occidental College**
*Presbyterians*

**Pomona College**
*Congregationalists*

**Whittier College**
*Quakers*

**Redlands**
*Baptists*

## Temperance Movement

In the early part of this century, Christians became concerned about the effects that intoxicating liquors were having on individuals and society as a whole. They began the temperance movement to make the manufacture, sale, and transportation of alcohol illegal in the United States. Many Californians were involved in this battle.

One of the leaders of the California movement was John Bidwell, who came to California on the first overland wagon train. After Bidwell became a Christian and began farming on his Chico ranch, he planted many acres of grapevines. He used the grapes to produce some very fine wines. One day Bidwell noticed that as his workers were leaving for the day, they had a very unsteady walk. They were drunk on wine that John Bidwell produced. Bidwell was horrified that he was contributing to this sin. At a cost of thousands of dollars, he uprooted all of his grapes and stopped producing wine. Later Bidwell unsuccessfully ran for President of the United States on the temperance ticket.

The temperance movement was especially strong in the southern part of the state. Thousands of people signed a “pledge” and promised not to drink alcoholic beverages. The people of Pasadena indicated their agreement with the temperance movement by a battle song:

*Rise, Pasadena! march and drill.*
*To this your bugle rally—*
*A Church or school on every hill,*
*AND NO SALOON IN THE VALLEY.*

*Stand firm in rank, but do not boast*
*Too soon your victory's tally;*
*You "hold the fort" for all the coast*
*FOR NO SALOON IN THE VALLEY.*

*The siege is on, the bombs aflight!*
*Let no true soldier dally;*
*For truth and right, for HOME we fight,*
*AND NO SALOON IN THE VALLEY.*

The temperance movement was finally successful in amending the U.S. Constitution in 1919 to forbid the sale, transportation, and manufacture of liquor. However, many people refused to obey this new law. Criminal activity increased to provide people with illegal alcohol. The amendment was finally repealed in 1933. The experience had shown that a person's heart cannot be changed by law. He must want to change and ask for the Holy Spirit's help.

## The Automobile

The one invention that has changed California more that any other is the automobile. In earlier times people had to live near the coast or rivers because they used the waterways to ship their goods to other cities, states, and countries. When the railroad was built, people could live near a rail terminal and have access to a major transportation route. Still, people could only live in certain, limited areas.

The automobile made Californians mobile. Before, people would spend five days traveling by wagon to visit their grandparents. Thanks to the automobile, today the drive only takes one hour each way. Travel became more common because it was easier.

The automobile also opened up areas of California that were previously unreachable. Today people live in all areas of the state. Californians can travel anywhere that a road has been constructed. Tall mountains, scorching deserts, valleys, coasts, and forests present no obstacles as long as they contain roads. Today we identify the geography of the state by its streets and highways instead of by its valleys and rivers. Today, most houses have a garage. Before cars, garages were unnecessary. We have gas stations, auto repair shops, driving schools, car dealerships, and manufacturing companies to support the automobile industry. Paved, hardtop roads bisect the state while hundreds of bridges span the waterways. We can thank the automobile for the advent of shopping centers. Before, most people bought their supplies at the general store in town. When the nation became mobile, supermarkets with large parking lots began to appear. The first of these were built in California.

Finally, the automobile had a large impact on California politics. The power of the Southern Pacific Railroad was broken. No longer were people dependent only on the railroad. The trucking industry rose to compete with the trains for freight. Buses began to compete with trains for passengers. The automobile has brought many good changes, and a great deal of freedom, to the people of California.

Today motorists travel on Highway 5 over the Tehachapi and San Gabriel Mountains between Southern California and the San Joaquin Valley. In earlier days, they traveled the Ridge Route. The original Ridge Route contained 627 curves and dangerous drop-offs. The maximum speed limit was originally 15 miles per hour. Still, it united the roadways of Northern and Southern California.

## Taking Dominion

CALIFORNIANS WORKED HARD TO TAKE DOMINION OVER THEIR LAND at the beginning of the twentieth century. Their efforts were rewarded as the land began to produce more abundantly than at any other time during its history. Today, however, these efforts are not always appreciated. Oftentimes we hear of how the early Californians "ruined" the land. They are accused of destroying the California landscape and using up its resources. The people who make these accusations do not approve of the major irrigation projects that brought water to the southern part of the state as well as many other improvements. Instead they say that these projects have ruined the land.

As the early Californians were beginning to take control over their environment, they undoubtedly made mistakes. Hydraulic mining and dredging are two industries which left scars on the landscape. But the early Californians soon realized this and used the law to put a stop to these harmful mining methods. Some early forestry methods were destructive, but today many advances in forestry have taken place so that California's forests are healthier than they were in earlier times. As technology improved and Californians became more experienced, they learned how to improve the management of their resources.

The difference between the view that says Californians are destroying their environment, and the view that says Californians are improving it, is basically a religious one. Much of the so-called environmental, or "green," movement today is infected with the ungodly heresy of animism. Since an animist believes that God inhabits nature, he will resist changing nature or disturbing god. He believes, as the California Indians did, that any change in the landscape is bad. Christians believe God created the world for man's use. We must use these resources wisely, but we must use them.

If Californians continue to be faithful to the Lord and take dominion over their land, the future will be very bright indeed. Experiments have begun with a method to obtain water from the ocean, called desalinization. In this process salt is removed from the water so that it can be used for drinking, irrigation, and industry. Desalinization might provide water for the coastal areas, while inland rivers could be directed to desert and mountainous areas. As energy costs increase, Californians have experimented with ways to produce an inexpensive source of power.

During the many years that the Christian worldview was predominant, Californians made many useful changes in the land. Now, however, the animistic and other worldviews are preventing many changes from taking place. As Christians, we have the responsibility to make changes wisely and carefully as we work to improve the land for the kingdom of the Lord.

Review Questions

# Unit 10 Roundup

## Chapter 29

1. How does California today differ from the land that the California Indians inhabited?

2. What does it mean to "take dominion"?

3. Why are California's water laws based on Spanish law rather than English common law?

4. What problems did California's rivers cause, and how were they tamed?

5. What is a levee, and what problem did it solve?

6. Give some examples of early Californians working together to solve their problems as communities.

## Chapter 30

1. What is the difference between *preservation* and *conservation*?

2. Why do you think John Muir worked so hard to preserve California's natural resources?

3. Who was William Mulholland, and what did he do?

4. What were the three water projects for Southern California? What did each accomplish?

5. What is hydroelectric power?

## Chapter 31

1. How did the orange industry begin?
2. Describe the variety of agriculture that is grown in California.
3. What advances were made in gold mining? Were they good or bad?
4. What is "black gold," and how was it discovered in California?
5. What was the Temperance Movement?
6. What changes did the automobile bring to California?
7. **Thought question:** Do you think the many changes the early Californians made to the land would be allowed today? Why or why not?

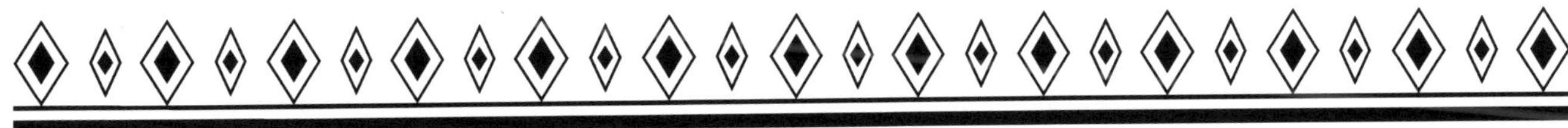

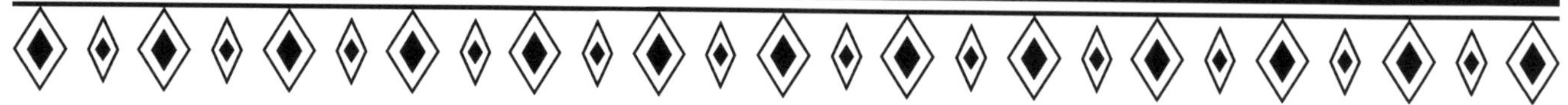

# Epilogue

(And farewell!)

It's time to leave our study of California history and the exciting men and women whom God used to tell His California story. We have seen how the state has grown from a forgotten land at the ends of the earth into a great and might state. We have seen how God has controlled events to bring about His purposes. We have studied the California Indians, the Spaniards, the Mexicans, the Californios, and the Americans God brought to this state. We have seen how He used faithful Christians to tame the frontier, build the state, and take dominion over the land.

What are God's plans for the future of California? We do not know. God rarely reveals the future to men. We do, however, know God's purpose for us, the people who live in California. He wants us to know Him and to enjoy Him forever. He wants us to be faithful to our calling as students, mothers, fathers, and citizens. He wants us to obey His word, the Bible, and to be conformed to the image of His Son, Christ (Romans 12:2).

My prayer for all of you who read this book is that your faith is increased. I pray that the book strengthens your personal relationship with the Lord Jesus Christ. I pray that the faithful work of the Christian men and women who lived in California encourages and inspires you. But most of all, I pray that this book helps to equip you in whatever field God calls you to minister. As we are faithful, God will bless our land (II Chronicles 7:14).

I leave you this charge: Go and be faithful. Let your light shine in the land. Help California to receive God's blessing so that when another book is written about California's history, many years from now, people will admire the faithfulness of Christians—including you—who continued His California story.

Be like Joshua, who said in Joshua 24:15

> "And if it seem evil unto you to serve the Lord, choose you this day
> whom ye will serve; whether the gods which your fathers served
> that were on the other side of the flood,
> or the gods of the Amorites, in whose land ye dwell:
> but as for me and my house,
> we will serve the Lord."

After that, there's just one more thing to say: Amen!

# Bibliography

It is my earnest desire that we reclaim the knowledge of our Christian heritage in California. I hope that future researchers will be able to build upon my work. Therefore, I have included an extensive bibliography here. The most helpful books are marked with an asterisk (*).


*The Bible, King James Version

### The California Indians

*Aginsky, B.W. and E.G., *Deep Valley*, Stein and Day, New York, 1967

*Boscana, Friar Geronimo, "Chinigchinich," in Robinson, Alfred, *Life in California*, Peregrine Press, Santa Barbara, 1970 (originally 1891, first published 1846)

dePrarrie, Paul and Pride, Mary, *Ancient Empires of the New Age*, Crossway Books, Westchester, Illinois, 1989

Evans, William Edward, "The Garra Uprising," *California Historical Society Quarterly*, December 1966

Fages, Pedro, Fage's *Description of California*, Friends of the Bancroft Library, Berkeley

Heizer, Robert (ed.), *Handbook of North American Indians*, Vol. 8 - California, Smithsonian Institution, Washington, 1978

Heizer, R.F. and Whipple, M.A. (ed.), *The California Indians -A Source Book*, University of California Press, Berkeley, 1962

Keyworth, C.L., *California Indians* (First American Series), Facts On File, New York, 1991

Kroeber, A. L., *Handbook of the Indians of California*, Washington Government Printing Office, 1925

Margolin, Malcolm, *The Way We Lived*, Heyday Books, Berkeley, 1981

Merriam, C. Hart, *The Dawn of the World - Weird Tales of the Mewan Indians*, Arthur H. Clark Co., Cleveland, 1910

Phillips, George Harwood, *Indians and Agents, the Origins of the Reservation System in California, 1849-1852*, University of Oklahoma Press, Norman, 1997

_______, *Indians and Intruders in Central California, 1769-1849*, University of Oklahoma Press, Norman, 1993

*Powers, Stephen, *Tribes of California*, University of California Press, 1976 (originally published in 1877)

Underhill, Ruth, *Indians of Southern California*, United States Department of the Interior, 1941

### The Explorers

Bancroft, Hubert Howe, *History of California - Vol. I 1542 - 1800*, Wallace Hebberd, Santa Barbara, 1966

Bandini, Helen Elliott, *History of California*, American Book Company, New York, 1908

Bannon, John Francis (ed.), *Bolton and the Spanish Borderlands*, University of Oaklahoma Press, Norman, Oaklhoma, 1964

*Chapman, Charles E., *A History of California - The Spanish Period*, The Macmillan Company, New York, 1921

dePrarrie, Paul and Pride, Mary, *Ancient Empires of the New Age*, Crossway Books, Westchester, Illinois, 1989

Dimmick, Dorothy, *The Making of American California, A Providential Approach*, 11540 Columbet Ave., Gilroy, CA 95020, 1990

Herzog, B.G. (ed.), *Cortez and the Conquest of Mexico by the Spaniards in 1521, Being the Eye-Witness Narrative of Bernal Diaz del Castillo, Soldier of Fortune & Conquistador with Cortez in Mexico*, Linnett Books, Hamden, 1988

Hittel, Theodore H., *History of California - Vol. I*, Pacific Press Publishing House, 1885

Hunt, Rockwell D., *California the Golden*, Silver, Burdett and Company, New York, 1911

______, *California's Stately Hall of Fame*, College of the Pacific, Stockton, California, 1950

*Morison, Samuel Eliot, *The European Discovery of America - The Southern Voyages A.D. 1492 - 1616*, Oxford University Press, New York, 1974

______, *Admiral of the Ocean Sea*, Little, Brown and Company, Boston, 1942

Prescott, William H., *History of the Conquest of Mexico*, John B. Alden, Publisher, New York, 1886

White, Jon Manship, *Cortes and the Downfall of the Aztec Empire*, St. Martin's Press, New York, 1971

## The Spanish Period

Atherton, Gertrude F. *California, an Intimate History*, Harper & Brothers, New York, 1914

Bancroft, Hubert Howe, *History of California Vol. I 1542 - 1800*, Wallace Hebberd, Santa Barbara, 1966

______, *History of California Vol. II 1801 - 1824*, Wallace Hebberd, Santa Barbara, 1966

*Bandini, Helen Elliott, *History of California*, American Book Company, New York, 1908

*Chapman, Charles E., *A History of California - The Spanish Period*, The Macmillian Company, New York, 1921

Costo, Rupert and Jeannette, *A Legacy of Genocide*, Indian Historian Press, San Francisco, 1987 (NOTE: While most of this book is anecdotal rather than a historical record, the appendix is helpful.)

Dakin, Susanna Bryant, *Rose, or Rose Thorn? Three Women of Spanish California*, Friends of the Bancroft Library, Berkeley, 1963

Englehardt, Charles A., *Mission San Luis Obispo in the Valley of the Bears*, W.T. Genns, Santa Barbara, 1963

Harrison, E.S., *History of Santa Cruz County*, Pacific Press Publishing Co., San Francisco, 1892

Hittel, Theodore H., *History of California - Vol. I*, Pacific Press Publishing House, 1885

Jackson, Helen Hunt, *Glimpses of California and the Missions,* Little, Brown, & Co., Boston, 1916

La Perouse, Jean Francios, *Monterey in 1786*, Heyday Books, Berkeley, 1989 (Originally The Journals of La Perouse, 1786)

Palou, Francisco, *Life of Ven. Padre Junipero Serra*, translated by Rev. J. Adams, P.E. Dougherty & Co. Book & Job Printers, 1884

Roberts, Helen, *Mission Tales, Stories of the Historic California Missions Vol. 1-4*, Pacific Books, Publishers, Palo Alto, 1948

Rowland, Florence Wightman, *Pasquala of Santa Ynez Mission,* Henry Z. Walck, Inc., 1961

Sandos James A., *Converting California,* Yale University Press, New Haven, 2004

Tac, Pablo, *Indian Life and Customs at Mission San Luis Rey,* (Rome, 1835,) The Americas, A Quarterly Review of Inter-American Cultural History, July 1952

*Tibesar, Antoine O.F.M. (ed.), *The Writings of Junípero Serra*, Academy of American Franciscan History, Washington D.C., 1955

Webb, Edith Buckland, *Indian Life at the Old Missions*, Warren F. Lewis, Publisher, Los Angeles, 1952

Weber, Rev. Francis J., *The Pilgrim Church in California*, Cathay Press Limited, Hong Kong, 1973

______ (ed.), *Some California Catholic Reminiscences for the United States Bicentennial*, Published for the California Catholic Conference by the Knights of Columbus, 1976

## The Mexican Period

Brooks, George R. (ed.), *The Southwest Expedition of Jedediah S. Smith, His Personal Account of the Journey to California, 1826-1827*, University of Nebraska Press, Lincoln, 1977

Dakin, Susanna Bryant, *Rose, or Rose Thorn? Three Women of Spanish California*, Friends of the Bancroft Library, Berkeley, 1963

*Dana, Richard Henry, *Two Years Before the Mast and Twenty-Four Years Later*, P.F. Collier & Son Corp., New York, 1969

Garrett, Paul D., *St. Innocent Apostle to America*, St. Vladimir's Seminary Press, Crestwood, New York, 1979

Geary, Gerald J., *Secularization of the California Missions (1810-1846),* The Catholic University of Americas, Washington D.C., 1934

*Hunt, Rockwell D. and Sanchez, Nellie Van de Grift, *A Short History of California*, Thomas Y. Crowell, New York, 1929

Kemble, Edward Cleveland, *A Kemble Reader, Stories of California, 1846 to 1848*, The California Historical Society, San Francisco, CA, 1963

*Loofbourow, Leon L., *In Search of God's Gold*, The Methodist Church, Stockton, 1950

Morgan, Dale L., *Jedediah Smith and the Opening of the West*, University of Nebraska Press, Lincoln, 1953

Quaife, Milo Milton (ed.), *Kit Carson's Autobiography*, University of Nebraska Press, Lincoln, 1966

*Robinson, Alfred, Life in California, Peregrine Press, Santa Barbara, 1970 (Originally 1891, first published 1846)

Robinson, W.W., *Los Angeles from the Days of the Pueblo*, California Historical Society, 1959

Sanchez, Nellie Van de Grift, *Spanish Arcadia*, Powell Publishing Co., San Francisco, 1929

## The American Period

*Bidwell, General John, *Echos of the Past*, from the Century Magazine (Dec. 1890 and Feb. 1891), California Dept. of Parks and Rec., 1987 (reprint)

Cleland, Robert G., *History of California, The American Period*, The Macmillian Company, New York, 1922

*Colton, Walter, *Three Years in California*, Stanford University Press, Stanford, 1949 (Originally 1850)

Davis, William Heath, *Seventy-Five Years in California*, John Howell, San Francisco, 1929

Dimmick, Dorothy, *The Making of American California*, Dorothy Dimmick, Gilroy, 1990

Fremont, John C., *Life Explorations and Public Services*, John Charles Ticknor and Fields, Boston, 1855

______, *Memoirs of My Life Vol. I*, Belford, Clarke and Co., Chicago, 1887

Hunt, Rockwell D. and Sanchez, Nellie Van de Grift, *A Short History of California*, Thomas Y. Crowell, New York, 1929

Hunt, Rockwell D., *John Bidwell, Prince of California Pioneers*, The Caxton Printers, Ltd., Caldwell, Idaho, 1942

Hurwitz, Karen E., *The History of John Marsh and Rancho De Los Meganos*, Morning News-Gazette, Martinez, California, 1972

Hutchinson, W.H., *California - The Golden Shore by the Sundown Sea*, Star Publishing Co., Palo Alto, 1980

Laurgaard, Rachel K., *Patty Reed's Doll, The Story of the Donner Party*, McCurdy Historical Museum, Provo, Utah, 1981

*The Life and Work of General John A. Sutter*, Paper read before the Lancaster County Historical Society, Vol. XVII, No. 10, Lancaster, Pennsylvania, 1913

McGlashan, C.F., *History of the Donner Party, Tragedy of the Sierra,* Stanford University Press, Stanford, 1947

*Munor-Fraser, J.P., *History of Contra Costa County*, W.A. Slocum & Co. Publishers, San Francisco, 1882 (excellent description of the Bear Flag Revolt)

Murphy, Celeste G., *The People of the Pueblo or the Story of Sonoma*, Binfords & Mort, Publishers, Portland, 1937

*Murphy, Virginia Reed, *Across the Plains in the Donner Party*, Outbooks, Golden, Colorado, 1980

*Nadeau, Remi, *Los Angeles, From Mission to Modern City*, Longmans, Green and Co., New York, 1960

*Nevins, Allan, *Frémont Pathmarker of the West*, Longmans, Green and Co., New York, 1955

Paden, Irene D., *Prairie Schooner Detours*, The Macmillan Co., New York, 1949

Schoonover, T.J., *The Life and Times of Gen. John A. Sutter*, D. Johnson & Co., Printers, 1895

*Teggart, Frederick J. (ed.), *Diary of Patrick Breen, One of the Donner Party*, Vistabooks, Dillon, Colorado, 1991

Wilbur, Marguerite Eyer, *Sutter, Rascal and Adventurer*, Liveright Publishing Corp., New York, 1949

*Wiltess, Ernest A., *The Truth About Frémont, An Inquiry*, John Henry Nash, San Francisco, 1936

## The Gold Rush

Browne, J. Ross, *Report of the Debates in the Convention of California, on the Formation of the State Constitution, in September and October, 1849*, John T. Towers, Washington, 1850

*Bari, Valeska (ed.), *The Course of Empire*, Coward-McCann, Inc., New York, 1931

Dillon, Richard H., *Fools Gold, The Decline and Fall of Captain John Sutter of California*, Coward-McCann, Inc., New York, 1967

Dimmick, Dorothy, *The Making of American California,* Dorothy Dimmick, Gilroy, 1990

Engle, Irvin A., *Men Who Dug For Gold and Men Who Preached for God*, United Methodist Church, 1973

Ferguson, Charles D., *California Gold Fields*, Biobooks, Oakland, 1948

Jackson, Joseph Henry (ed.), *Gold Rush Album*, Charles Schribner's Sons, New York, 1949

Manly, William Lewis, *Death Valley in '49*, Wallace Hubbard, Santa Barbara, 1929

McCloskey, Joseph J., *Christmas in the Gold Fields, 1849*, The California Historical Society, San Francisco, 1959

*Royce, Sarah, *A Frontier Lady, Recollections of the Gold Rush and Early California*, University of Nebraska Press, Lincoln, 1977

Taylor, Bayard, *El Dorado*, Lewis Osborne, Palo Alto, 1968

### Beginnings and Endings

Anthony, C. V., *Fifty Years of Methodism*, Methodist Book Concern, San Francisco, 1901

*Bari, Valeska (ed.), *The Course of Empire*, Coward-McCann, Inc., New York, 1931

Bufford, Charles M., *A Hundred Years of Congregationalism in San Francisco*, Prepared for the Centennial Meeting of the First Congregational Church, San Francisco, Held at Portsmouth Plaza, July 31, 1949

Clarke, Dwight L., *William Tecumseh Sherman, Gold Rush Banker*, California Historical Society, San Francisco, 1969

Dasmann, Raymond F., *The Destruction of California*, The Macmillan Co., New York, 1965

Dillon, Richard, *Burnt-Out Fires, California's Modoc Indian War*, Prentice-Hall Inc., 1973

Drury, Clifford Merrill, William Anderson Scott, "No Ordinary Man," The Arthur H. Clark Co., Glendale, 1967

*Ferrier, William Warren, *Pioneer Church Beginnings and Educational Movements in California*, Berkeley, 1927

Fleming, Sandford, *God's Gold, The Story of Baptist Beginnings*, The Judson Press, Chicago, 1949

Hanchett, William, "The Question of Religion and the Taming of California, 1849-1854," California Historical Society Quarterly

Heizer, Robert F. and Elsasser, Albert B., *The Natural World of the California Indians*, University of California Press, Berkeley, 1980

Hurtado, Albert L., *Indian Survival on the California Frontier*, Yale University Press, New Haven, 1988

*Loofbourow, Leon L., *In Search of God's Gold*, The Methodist Church, Stockton, 1950

McKittrick, Myrtle M., Vallejo, *Son of California*, Binfords & Mort, Publishers, Portland, Oregon, 1944

Phillips, George Harwood, *Indians and Agents, the Origins of the Reservation System in California, 1849-1852*, University of Oklahoma Press, Norman, 1997

_______, *Indians and Intruders in Central California, 1769-1849*, University of Oklahoma Press, Norman, 1993

Pitt, Leonard, *The Decline of the Californios*, University of California Press, Berkeley, 1966

*Religious Progress on the Pacific Slope*, The Pilgrim Press, Boston, 1917

Rawls, James J., *Indians of California, The Changing Image*, University of Oklahoma Press, Norman, 1984

Sandos James A., *Converting California,* Yale University Press, New Haven, 2004

*Scherer, James A.B., *The Lion of the Vigilantes - William T. Coleman,* The Bobbs-Merrill Co., Indianapolis, 1939

*Soule, Frank, Gibon, John, and Nisbet, James, *The Annals of San Francisco*, D. Appleton & Company, New York, 1854

*Taylor, William, *California Life Illustrated*, Carlton & Porter, New York, 1858

*______, *Seven Years of Street Preaching in San Francisco*, Carlton & Porter, New York, 1856

Willey, Samuel H., *California's Transition Period*, The Whitaker & Ray Co., San Francisco, 1901

Williams, Rev. Albert, *A Pioneer Pastorate and Times*, Wallace & Hassett, San Francisco, 1879

### The Americanization of California

Bean, Walton, *California, An Interpretive History*, McGraw-Hill Book Company, New York, 1978

*Crazy Judah and the Sacramento Valley Railroad*, Roseville Historical Society, 1989

Hines, J. W., *Pioneer Life on the Pacific Coast*, Eaton & Co., Printers, San Jose, 1911

Galloway, John Debo, *The First Transcontinental Railroad*, Dorset Press, New York, 1989

Gilbert, Benjamin Franklin, "The Confederate Minority in California," California Historical Society Quarterly, Vol. XX, No. 2, June 1941

______, "San Francisco Harbor Defense During the Civil War," California Historical Society Quarterly, Vol. XXXIII, No. 3, September 1954

Hinckley, Helen, *Rails from the West...A Biography of Theodore D. Judah*, Golden West Books, San Marino, (no date)

Kiby, Leo P., "California, the Civil War, and the Indian Problem," *Journal of the West*, Lorrin L. Morrison & Carroll Spear Morrison Publishers, 1967

Kraus, George, *High Road to Promontory*, American West Publishing Company, Palo Alto, 1969

Lewis, Oscar, *The Big Four, The Story of Huntington, Stanford, Hopkins, and Crocker, and of the Building of the Central Pacific*, Alfred A. Knopf, New York, 1941

Loofbourow, Leon L., *Cross in the Sunset*, The Methodist Church, Stockton, 1961

McWilliams, Carey, Southern *California Country, An Island on the Land*, Duell, Sloa & Pearce, New York, 1946

Moore, Dean, *Judah The Dreamer*, Roseville Historical Society, Lincoln, California, 1989 (Reprint of A Practical Plan for Building the Pacific Railroad, by T.D. Judah, Henry Polkinhorn, Printer, Washington D.C., 1857)

*Nadeau, Remi, Los Angeles, *From Mission to Modern City*, Longmans, Green and Co., New York, 1960

Shutes, Milton, "'Fighting Joe' Hooker," California Historical Society Quarterly, Vol. XVI, No. 4, December 1947

*Stone, Irving, *Men to Match My Mountains, The Opening of the Far West 1840-1900*, Doubleday & Co., Garden City, 1956

"A Threatened Invasion of California," California Historical Society Quarterly, Vol. XIII, No. 1, March 1934

### Californians Take Dominion

Bean, Walton, *California, An Interpretive History*, McGraw-Hill Book Company, New York, 1978

Caughey, John Walton, *California*, Prentice-Hall, New York, 1940

Dolan, Edward F., *Famous Builders of California*, Dodd, Mead & Co., New York, 1987

*Ferrier, William Warren, *Ninety Years of Education in California, 1846 - 1936*, Sather Gate Book Shop, Berkeley, 1937

*Hunt, Rockwell D., *California's Stately Hall of Fame*, College of the Pacific, Stockton, California, 1950

______, *California Firsts*, Fearon Publishers, San Francisco, 1957

______, *California in the Making*, Greenwood Press, Westport, Connecticut, 1953

Looney, Floyd, *History of California Southern Baptists*, Southern Baptist General Convention, Fresno, 1954

*McWilliams, Carey, *California: The Great Exception*, Current Books, Inc., A.A. Wyn, Publisher, New York, 1949

Muir, John, *The Yosemite*, Doubleday & Co., Inc., Garden City, New York, 1962

Nordhoff, Charles, *Northern California, Oregon, and the Sandwich Islands*, Ten Speed Press, Berkeley, 1974 (Reprint)

Ray, Dixie Lee, *Trashing the Planet*, cited in Summit Journal, Manitou Springs, Colorado, December 1992

Rolle, Andrew F., California, *A History*, Thomas Y. Crowell Co., New York, 1963

*The Siskiyou Pioneer in Folklore, Fact and Fiction*, The Siskiyou County Historical Society, Vol. 6, No. 1, 1988

Wolfe, Linnie *Marsh, Son of the Wilderness*, The Life of John Muir Alfred A. Knopf, New York, 1945.

W. W. Robinson, *Los Angeles from the Days of the Pueblo*, California Historical Society, San Francisco, 1959

# Picture Credits

Courtesy Bancroft Library: 15, 37, 52, 58, 64, 81-82, 103, 113 (top), 116 (top), 163, 177 (top), 182

Courtesy California Historical Society, Title Insurance and Trust Photo Collection, Department of Special Collection, University of Southern California Library: 56, 118, 122, 161, 165, 183

Courtesy California State Library: 159 (bottom), 134 (top), 136, 139, 140, 146, 174

*The Annals of San Francisco* by Frank Soule: 68, 114, 142, 149, 150, 151, 157, 159

Estremo, Robert A. copyright 2005. Used with permission: 73

Fabricas, published by the Division of Mines: 66, 67, 69 (middle & bottom), 96, 97

GNU Free Documentation License Version 1.2: 27, 94

Library of Congress: 22, 24

*Missions and Missionaries (Vol. II)* by Zephyrin Engehardt: 47, 50, 70

*Tribes of California* by Stephen Powers: 5, 8, 9,

U.S. National Archives: 186

Drawn for the author
- by Craig Bowers: 1, 8, 11, 15
- by Kathryn Frank: 107, 134 (bottom), 195
- by Charlene Mapson: 92 (bottom)
- by Michael Alphin (age 14): 101

Photographs by the author: 12, 45 (bottom), 49, 68 (bottom), 69 (top), 72, 74, 75 (bottom), 76, 82 (top), 98 (top & bottom), 115, 116 (bottom), 128, 130, 143, 173, 177 (bottom), 178 (top), 179 (bottom)

Early postcards owned by the author: 168, 188, 190, 202, 203, 204 (both), 208, 212

Most maps were drawn by Annette Andruss

Other illustrations from the public domain including from Wikipedia Commons: 15, 23, 25, 27, 30, 31 (Yale University Map Collection), 33 top, 33 bottom, 35, 43 top & bottom, 77, 78, 59, 45 (top), 71 (*Exploration du Territoire de l'Orégon, des Californies*, 1844), 75 (top), 78 (Drawing by José Cardero, 1791), 80, 84, 87, 88, 89, 90, 92 (top), 100, 108, 109, 110, 111, 113 (bottom—*History of Contra Costa County*), 117, 119, 127, 131, 135, 142, 152, 155, 156, 160, 164, 167, 179 (top), 180 (all), 181, 191, 193, 197 (both), 198, 199, 201, 206, 207

Extraordinary efforts have been taken to ensure picture usage conforms to copyright law. However, because of the complexity and vagaries of the law and its copious exceptions, if mistakes have been made, please contact the author and they will be corrected in subsequent editions.